Chanting Down the New Jerusalem

THE ANTHROPOLOGY OF CHRISTIANITY

Edited by Joel Robbins

Chanting Down the New Jerusalem

Calypso, Christianity, and Capitalism in the Caribbean

Francio Guadeloupe

UNIVERSITY OF CALIFORNIA PRESS
Berkeley · Los Angeles · London

University of California Press, one of the most
distinguished university presses in the United States,
enriches lives around the world by advancing
scholarship in the humanities, social sciences, and
natural sciences. Its activities are supported by the
UC Press Foundation and by philanthropic
contributions from individuals and institutions.
For more information, visit www.ucpress.edu.

Portions of chapter 4 appeared previously in Francio
Guadeloupe, "Clarke's Two Vitamin Cs for Successful
Living," in *The Caribbean City,* ed. Rivke Jaffe
(Leiden, The Netherlands: KITLV Press, 2008).

University of California Press
Berkeley and Los Angeles, California

University of California Press, Ltd.
London, England

Library of Congress Cataloging-in-Publication Data

Guadeloupe, Francio, 1971–
    Chanting down the new Jerusalem : calypso,
Christianity, and capitalism in the Caribbean / Francio
Guadeloupe.
        p.   cm. — (The anthropology of Christianity ; 4)
    Includes bibliographical references and index.
    ISBN 978-0-520-25488-6 (cloth : alk. paper) — ISBN
978-0-520-25489-3 (pbk. : alk. paper)
    1. Ethnology—Saint Martin (West Indies)
2. Ethnicity—Saint Martin (West Indies)
3. Anthropology of religion—Saint Martin (West
Indies)   4. Religion and culture—Saint Martin (West
Indies)   5. Disc jockeys—Social aspects—Saint
Martin (West Indies)   6. Music—Social aspects—
Saint Martin (West Indies)   7. Saint Martin (West
Indies)—Ethnic relations.   8. Saint Martin (West
Indies)—Race relations.   9. Saint Martin (West
Indies)—Social conditions.—I. Title.
    GN564.S26G83 2009
    305.80097297'6—dc22   2008025295

Manufactured in the United States of America

18   17   16   15   14   13   12   11   10   09
10 9 8 7 6 5 4 3 2 1

Contents

Illustrations

Acknowledgments

It is imperative in these times of rampant cynicism and incredulity regarding the goal of achieving a universality rich with ever-deepening particularities to remain faithful to those whose blood and sweat have afforded us the opportunity to be academics. This book is dedicated to my grandmother Elza and all those other grandmothers and grandfathers in the Caribbean who made these lands liveable after the horrors of the Middle Passage and the *Kala Pani* (the voyage of the dark waters from India to the Caribbean). They understood that by contradicting themselves and making productive use of the contradictions in the capitalist system, they could achieve moments of freedom and human solidarity. In this study I looked to them and their offspring, as well as newcomers to the region, to find ways of rekindling the flame of planetary humanism.

This study concerns itself with the manner in which popular disc jockeys on the binational island of Saint Martin and Sint Maarten (the French and Dutch West Indies) employ Caribbean music and creolized Christianity to put forth all-inclusive politics of belonging. It is about how on a multiethnic and multireligious island, where everyone's livelihood depends on tourism, all social classes seek and are often able to transcend their ethnic and religious differences. This is done paradoxically by employing creolized Christianity as a public religion that does not privilege any of the faiths practiced, not even itself. It is an ethnography that seeks to demonstrate that in a time in which ethnic- and religious-based identity politics are rampant, there are alternatives in the world. There are places where people understand, because of their circumstances, that taking on an identity is about creating for oneself a space to act while taking others into consideration.

All books are joint projects. Though this list is by no means exhaustive, I would like to thank some of the people who helped me conduct this study and transform my findings into book form. To Reed Malcolm, Kalicia Pivorotto, and the rest of the editing and publishing staff at the University of California Press, thanks for lending your strengths and talents to this project. In the same vein I must mention my colleagues at the Royal Institute for Southeast Asian and Caribbean studies (KITLV) and the Centre of International Development Issues Nijmegen (CIDIN, Radboud University Nijmegen), the Netherlands. Your tireless effort and support in helping me prepare this project have not gone unnoticed. Dan Vennix, what would the KITLV and I do without you? I must also acknowledge the extra editing work done by Martijn de Koning.

During the past few years I have benefited from the guidance and insight of my mentors, Birgit Meyer and Peter Geschiere. My heartfelt thanks to both of you for initiating me into the difficult but rewarding world of thinking and depicting the everyday in novel ways. You have both become family. To Gerd Baumann, Rafael Sanchez, Patricia Spyer, Charles Hirschkind, Brian Larkin, Jeremy Stolow, Henk Schulte Noordholt, Peter Pels, and Sudeep Dasgupta, thank you for reading earlier drafts of this manuscript and providing helpful comments. I drew strength from your enthusiasm for my project. To Pedro de Weever, Eileen Moyer, Vincent de Rooij, and Mattijs van der Port, my deep gratitude for reminding me that in writing, one should remain as true as possible to the art of life. Pedro, your photographs interspersed throughout this ethnography tell a story within the general story. To my fellow academic peers, Irfan Ahmad, Anouk de Koning, Basile N'djio, Rivke Jaffe, Martijn Oosterbaan, Marleen de Witte, Yatun Sastramidjaja, Nghiem Lien Huong, Mangalika de Silva, Mirjam Auoragh, Yvonne van der Pijl, Lotte Hoek, Liza de Laat, Ze de Abreu, Carly Machado, Anjana Singh, let us continue to be critical about one another's work and to remember that in anthropology, ethics comes first.

I would also like to acknowledge Gert Oostindie for his incalculable contribution to Dutch Caribbean studies. Together with Bonno Thoden Van Velzen, Rosemarijn Hoefte, Gloria Wekker, Ineke van Wetering, Alex Stipriaan, Anke Klomp, Lammert de Jong, and Chris de Beet, you have created a tradition that all Dutch Caribbeanists must critically recognize. Similarly, I cannot write this book without extending my gratitude to

Maria van Enckevort, Josianne Fleming, Peggy Illis-Bell, Sergio Scatolini, Milton George, and the rest of the staff at the University of Saint Martin. Your support has been invaluable.

I was moved by the courtesy, intelligence, and hospitality of the people of Saint Martin and Sint Maarten. To Fernando Clarke, the Shadow, DJ Cimarron, and all of my other main informants and friends, such as Miss Maria, whom I have had to render anonymous, I appreciate your tolerance and patience in having me in your lives. I have sought to present your points of view as accurately as possible. All mistakes are mine.

My family has had to bear with me, as writing is perhaps the most reclusive practice one can engage in. I thank Chantal and our sons, Arum and Enzo, for being there and for accepting the many times that I was physically and cerebrally off in that other world that became this book. This project is as much yours as it is mine.

Last, to my friend David Chidester, thanks for reminding me that as embattled as we may be, the human being is indestructible. Indestructible because we contradict all racial, ethnic, and religious divides we impose on ourselves.

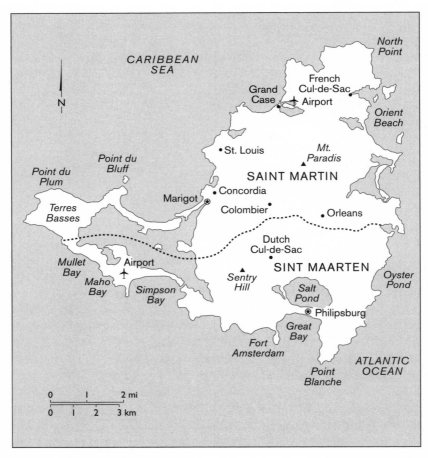

Saint Martin and Sint Maarten

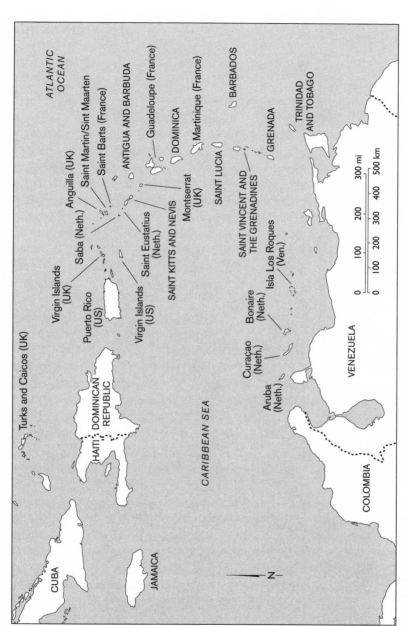

The Caribbean islands

Introduction

A New Jerusalem in the Caribbean Sea

All demands for the recognition of difference presuppose
extensive transcultural knowledge that would have been
impossible to acquire if cultural divisions always constituted
impermeable barriers to understanding.

Paul Gilroy, *Postcolonial Melancholia*

Identity as a problematic category of practice, in which certain people are
viewed as being identical to one another while others are regarded as totally different, is one of the leading themes in the human sciences. In
study after study we are furnished with evidence that identity politics and
the feeling of belonging, an explosive combination of bio-cultural racism
and exclusive claims to territory, are common throughout the world
(Geschiere and Nyamnjoh 2000; Meyer and Geschiere 1999). In response to pressures associated with globalization and the weakening of
the nation-state, ethnic minorities and recently arrived immigrants, de-
mographic categories that oftentimes intersect with religious differences,
are unequivocally portrayed as enemies of the "indigenous people," the
autochthons, to whom the territory supposedly rightfully belongs. Even
within the social sciences one sees that the recognition of class differences, which are relational and non-essentializing differences, are abandoned for the lure of viewing groups as exclusive and wrapped up in
their metaphysical core cultures (Cooper 2005; White 1990).

Ethnic clashes in Rwanda, Bosnia, and Sri Lanka; anti-Caucasian sentiments in Russia; the growth of neo-fascism in northwestern Europe; and
the Bharatiya Janata Party's Hindu fascism are all examples of the violence related to the need to assert one's belonging by claiming exclusive
roots in a territory or the fulfilment of God's will. The evidence is overwhelming. The studies are convincing. This global trend poses a serious

Figure 1. The Franco-Dutch border

Figure 2. The islands

challenge to those who still believe that we need to work toward "humanism made to the measure of the world" (Césaire 1972: 56), or a planetary humanism based on an all-inclusive politics of human belonging (Gilroy 2000, 2006), or a future cosmopolitan humanism (Derrida 2001).

We who still believe in this project must ensure that in our writings we do not unwittingly resort to a Manichaeanism that dehumanizes those of whom we are critical. We must not be racial, gender, ethnic, or religious missionaries. We must practice a systematic disloyalty to those toward whom we feel solidarity. We must deconstruct the naturalizing tendencies to feel a special connection, by virtue of our phenotype, sex, culture, or religious preference, to those whom we are historically connected. An important way of doing so is by constantly reminding ourselves of that old philosophical saying, "You never walk twice down the same river." That is, the self that one recognizes as continuous with an unchanging core constantly changes, as do the places through which one ventures and the people with whom one interacts. Therefore, to some degree, native social scientists are outsiders in their own societies. This is especially the case when they have spent a considerable amount of time outside their country or region of origin and have imbibed the dialect of their professional discipline, with its a priori grounds of knowledge. I was no exception. I learned during my academic study to conceptualize society primarily in class terms. It became my privileged way of seeing, of rendering unfamiliar social processes familiar. There were classes. There was right and wrong.

Before I began my training in development studies and social anthropology, this was not the way in which I conceived of reality. It was only one of the ways in which I understood life in the Caribbean, where I had lived almost half my life. Conceptualizing society in class terms was a principle. It was based on my rejection of rigid hierarchies and on the reality that a privileged few consume more than their fair share of the world's cake. However, in the Caribbean this principle is seemingly kept in check by pragmatism. Pragmatism does not exempt one from understanding that the world is unjust, but it does make one pay attention to the realities of everyday life. It made me realize where I stood, and what I stood to lose if I acted solely on the basis of principle.

I had never paid much attention to the discrepancy between my outlook as taught to me through the social sciences and the one I learned growing up in the Caribbean. But now, heading back to this region of the world to do fieldwork on the politics of belonging, I had to see things the way West Indians see them, and to understand why they see things in that way, without neglecting my anthropological point of view. As I tired myself out by writing down self-reflexive notes on the airplane, practicing the Foucauldian art of not being governed by taken-for-granted epistemes, I was happily disturbed by a voice from the cockpit saying, "This is your captain speaking. Please fasten your seatbelts; we are about to land at the Princess Juliana Airport." These words sounded heavenly after eleven uncomfortable hours in one of Air France's flying birds. There I was, then, on lovely Saint Martin (French) and Sint Maarten (Dutch), where more than eighty nationalities live on an island of just thirty-seven square miles.

In a world of independent postcolonial states, Saint Martin and Sint Maarten (SXM) seems an anachronism. (The acronym SXM is the code used for passenger flights to the island. Today it has become the general abbreviation of Saint Martin and Sint Maarten.) The Dutch side of the island is part of the Dutch Antilles, which together with Aruba and the Netherlands form the Dutch Kingdom. All major decisions pertaining to the Dutch Kingdom are made by the parliament in The Hague. On Dutch SXM, Curaçaon federal administrators supervise the activities of the local civil servants and ensure congruence with the island's direct constitutional partners, Curaçao, Bonaire, Saint Eustatius, and Saba. Dutch SXM as a political entity belongs to three imagined national communities, namely, the wider Dutch nation, the Dutch Antilles, and SXM proper. However, as the Netherlands surrenders more of its autonomy to the European Union, it is widely believed that in the near future Dutch SXM will become a full-fledged member of the EU. A fourth layer of official belonging will thus be added.

The French side of the island already enjoys full membership in the European supra-nation in the making. It is part of the French overseas department of Guadeloupe and as such is an integral part of the French Republic and thus the European Union. On French SXM, Guadeloupean civil servants take care of affairs related to Guadeloupe as a federal entity comprising Guadeloupe proper, Grande-Terre, Saint Barthélemy, Marie Galante, Désirade, Îles de Saintes, and Saint Martin; specific local matters are left to the local administrators and politicians.

Interestingly, notwithstanding the administrative boundary dividing the island, the imagined community of SXM proper comprises both sides of the island. Thus, when the islanders claim belonging to the nation of SXM they are referring to both French and Dutch SXM (Klomp 2000; Rummens 1991). The fact that France's influence in the European Union has ensured that the entire island has been designated a free port, where stringent trade tariffs are not levied and there is little border patrol, has strengthened SXMers' sense of being one nation. The focus of this study is on the politics of belonging on SXM.

The jolly Caribbean music in the lobby of the airport welcomed me to this island where the sun in the sky has nestled itself in the souls of the people. This of course is a cliché. Postcard talk that obfuscates the whips that broke the slaves' backs and the contracts that strangled the indentured laborers (Hoefte 2005; James 1963). Talk that sugarcoats the ethnic and racial tensions for which the anthropological version of the Caribbean is best known (e.g., the facile readings of the nuanced texts of Williams 1991 and Hoetink 1967). As an anthropologist born in the Caribbean, I should know better. But it is exactly because I do know better than to think that Caribbean people are a people traumatized by their past, or a people totally alienated from one another, that I feel I can write that the sun has nestled in the heart of the people of SXM. To me SXM stands symbolic of the social fact that out of the atrocities against human rights that permeate Caribbean history, the peoples of the region have found a modus vivendi that is not perfect but is remarkable in light of the horrors of the past and the divide-and-conquer ideologies still operative today. We may have to stop making too much of the long groan that underlines the Caribbean's past (Walcott 1999: 68).

I resided on the island in the mid-1980s, between my sixteenth and eighteenth birthdays, and I have nothing but fond memories of SXM. In the two years that I lived there, I never once felt like an outsider. I was part of the welcomed stream of immigrants. The fifteen hundred inhabitants who had lived on the island before the 1960s tourism boom—primarily old folks and young children—knew nothing about waiting tables, building hotels, or developing tourist attractions (Kersell 1991: 60). Before the tourism boom, the island was little more than a postal-order economy, running off the money sent from relatives working abroad. As writer-photographer Philip Hiss observed in 1943, "St. Maarten epitomizes the condition of the Netherlands Windward Islands, which live with their memories of the past in a state of suspended animation. Many plantations are deserted, and the more virile elements of the population have emigrated. The people who remained exist largely on money remitted to them by relatives in Curaçao, Aruba, and the United States" (quoted in Badejo 1990: 122). By the 1980s, however, not even the virile "indigenous" elements—the *locals,* as the autochthons refer to themselves—who had returned to cater to the tourists had sufficient capacities to run the island. Without the manpower and financial investments of working-class and upper-class newcomers, SXM's tourist industry would come to a halt. Newcomers were necessary.

The overall awareness of this social fact created a milieu in which differences of ethnic, national, or religious identity did not signify outsider status. These differences were recognized, but not in a manner that led to the idea of irreconcilable differences. This was true among common folk as well as among those in positions of authority. Government officials were predominantly locals, but they did not condone discrimination based on ethnicity, national origin, or religious belief. In campaign speeches popular politicians would talk of unity and belonging. The locals were grateful that the newcomers were helping to build up the island. "Mi casa es su casa" (My house is your house) and "We are one people despite our different cultures" were phrases commonly heard. These words were backed up by deeds that ran counter to the idea of national laws and regulations concerning immigration and citizenship. Rumors abounded that to secure the continued investment of wealthy North American and Asian newcomers, who needed a steady workforce, illegal immigration from the Caribbean basin, Asia, and Latin America was condoned. Residence and work permits were issued without adhering to the official bureaucratic procedures. The lack of regard for institutionalized rules went so far that those who could afford to were able to buy themselves a passport. During my teenage years on the island I personally knew working-class newcomers who had paid to become Dutch citizens. It was often said that the wealthy newcomers showed their appreciation for the leniency of civil servants and politicians by giving them payments under the table, and that their working-class counterparts did the same by voting solely for politicians who in word and deed kept SXM open for newcomers.

From afar these practices might be labeled as corruption and a subversion of democracy. We knew these labels too, but for us it was simply the way things were. The tourist industry needed laborers. The bending of national legislation to accommodate the economy was not spoken ill about, especially not by radio disc jockeys, who were the most popular—indeed the only—media personalities on the island. Like elsewhere in the lesser Caribbean, American cable TV was all we watched. SXMers grew up on HBO, NBC, Showtime, Canal+, and BET. No local programming could compete with the visual effects and storylines of these big-budget TV channels.

Radio disc jockeys would comment on popular TV programs, and every morning the most important articles in the local newspapers would be read aloud by radio disc jockeys. Radio was our window to the world and framed the way we understood what was happening on the island. Instead of stressing an image of a corrupt society needing a radical overhaul, these disc jockeys portrayed SXM as a paradise on earth. The calypso and reggae music that gave tourists a sense of having landed in the Garden of Eden where all was well gave us that feeling too. In our Eden, however, gambling, nightclubbing, and excessive spending were permitted. The musical selections and the sound bites of unity offered by popular disc jockeys corresponded with the smiling faces that were produced for the tourists. And why wouldn't we smile? Abject poverty was nonexistent, as even the poorest earned a decent living.

That the tourists were exploiting our island, that we were being Othered, that as subalterns we were being rendered voiceless, and other such intellectual musings that I was engulfed with when I started studying the social sciences were something to which we paid little attention. Yes there were critical texts addressing these matters, especially "roots reggae" tunes, which critiqued the West and the upper classes in the Global South, but the music always tempered the revolutionary politics it contained. The words said, "Revolution. The poor are God's people. He is on our side," but the music said, "Hold on, child, enjoy life a little." The music, always danceable and community inducing, said, "Life is not so bad. Don't compromise the little you've got for some idealistic heaven to come." Although the texts made us more vigilant, informed us, and opened up our eyes—taught us about class, and about race as a modality of class, which expanded our conception of class from one focused on economics alone— it was the message of the music that usually influenced our concrete actions. This message was also privileged by the disc jockeys and most adults. Put differently, the reality principle, the pragmatism that disc jockeys constantly reminded us of, was that all that little islands like SXM have are sun, sea, sand, and a majority that works hard to be able to provide three meals a day and a sound education for their children. If we fought a class battle on the island, Western tourists would stop coming. And we knew we could not depend on tourism from other parts of the world. The largest countries in the Global South, with all their mineral resources and fertile soils, needed help too, as international capitalists and Western governments were strangling them far more than us. For better or worse, we had to remain one happy island. This was one of the things that bound us to one another despite our differences.

I do not think, however, that this pragmatism meant that we totally acquiesced, that we suffered from a false consciousness. Perhaps Derek

Walcott was right when he stated that for the Caribbean working classes, "the revolution is here. It has always been here. It does not need the decor of African tourism or the hip postures and speech of metropolitan ghettos" (1999: 57). The revolution of the working classes is not based on black nationalism and crude forms of Marxism, but rather their resistance to all forms of social death, slavery, and indenture and their assertion of their somebodiness. This assertion is not made in a situation of their own choosing, as the Caribbean working class resides in countries with elites who are "subordinate" to outside forces. The conceptual and institutional conditions of their subjectivity are the products of a bloody transmodernity, the dialectical relationship begun in colonial times between Europe and "the rest" that has birthed our contemporary world (Dubois 2006; Scott 2004; Dussel 2000). This subjectivity may be why I and many other Caribbean youngsters were brought up with the understanding that one had to alternate between principle and pragmatism. Sometimes, as the Caribbean saying goes, the "lambs" had to lie down with "the lesser wolves." Perhaps this need to compromise principle for pragmatism was the answer to my musings as to why class was one of the ways of constructing reality. This book seeks to answer this query.

In addition to economics, religion was also a binding force. "Everyone belongs because God is the creator of all" was the most widely broadcasted message on both sides of the island. As their voices permeated buses, government offices, stores, hotels, and individual homes, radio disc jockeys dismissed claims of autochthony as un-Christian. "Christian," on the contrary, was a synonym for tolerant behavior that guaranteed everyone membership to SXM society. The use of the word *Christian* did not encourage the display of Christian piety in public. Radio disc jockeys ridiculed and dismissed such behavior as hypocritical. Piety and religious belief were private matters. In public one had to do as Caribbean music commanded, namely, to embrace the worldly and the fallibility of humankind. Most SXM Christians drank, gambled, partied, and did everything else that the Bible forbade. Only young children and old folks went to church regularly. Those in between did not but still considered themselves Christian. The tourists were not looking for piety but for elemental Adams and Eves who knew how to party.

Looking back I realize the power radio disc jockeys had to influence what I and many other SXMers considered reality. I also realize the important role that Christian-derived morals, employed as a meta-idiom of inclusiveness, and Caribbean music played in all this. Although radio messages of equal belonging were Christian inflected, this inflection was so subtle and so well camouflaged with the sweet sounds of calypso that listeners belonging to non-Christian faiths felt that popular disc jockeys were directing their messages to them as well. For instance Catholics, Hindus, Muslims, Buddhists, Baha'is, Vodou practitioners, Baptists, and even self-professed atheists of all social classes were enamored with Mama's Pearl. Pearl was a popular Rasta disc jockey who, while playing reggae music, invoked SXMers to join him in "chanting down" a New Jerusalem. This New Jerusalem was a world where people belonging to different faiths and ethnicities would be able to live a dignified life, a life in which one worshipped God by acknowledging the humanity of all. According to Mama's Pearl, SXM was the place that had come furthest in chanting down this New Jerusalem. The title of this book is borrowed from Pearl.

Understanding that, with the exception of a vocal middle-class minority, most locals were still welcoming to newcomers and hearing that contemporary radio disc jockeys were carrying on the legacy of the long-since-retired Pearl, I came back to the island after more than ten years to research the phenomenon. What were the social processes on SXM that prevented people from a variety of religious, ethnic, and national groups from becoming intolerant to difference? By understanding these social processes, I would be better able to appreciate the appeal radio disc jockeys had when employing Christianity and Caribbean music to put forth an inclusive politics of belonging. The manner in which popular radio disc jockeys constructed an inclusive politics of belonging through a Christian metalanguage and Caribbean music was the prime focus of my study.

This book is divided into six chapters. The first three give a detailed description of the people of SXM. In chapter 1 I demonstrate that the islanders are not interested in constructing a collective history or asserting primacy to a particular history as the basis of belonging. Instead, history functions as a commodity that allows tourism workers to perform the role of historically oppressed people who hold no grudges and openly welcome visitors who benefited from the exploitation of their grandmothers and grandfathers. History is a way in which these "lambs" welcome and simultaneously curtail the power of "the wolves" who come to their shores. In chapter 2 I elucidate the relationship between the locals and newcomers and focus on the small segment of the population that claims autochthony. In addition, I discuss the broader political, economic, and social milieus in which radio disc jockeys operate to promote inclusive belonging. Chapter 3 presents the style of Christianity practiced on SXM, focusing on its role as a metalanguage that transcends religious differences. The three subsequent chapters are dedicated exclusively to the programs and motives behind the politics of two popular radio disc jockeys and one who failed miserably. These chapters describe how disc jockeys address the sporadic xenophobia of a small section of local middle-class people who feel that, as autochthons, they should be privileged above all other SXMers. In the conclusion I present a summary of my findings, illuminating questions left unanswered and suggesting possibilities for further exploration.

So Many Men,
So Many Histories

The History that Matters to the Islanders

So many men, so many histories. Such an axiom is undoubtedly heresy for any serious student of history. Yet on multicultural and multinational SXM this saying is true. Those who think that newcomers can never love a place without a proper grasp of that place's history should visit this island. Those who think that SXM natives (or, locals) are always keen to know and preserve their history would be equally astonished. Newcomers and locals alike claim to love SXM, but their accuracy of (archival) historical knowledge of the island leaves much to be desired. Most of them like it that way. Appealing to a shared history lacks binding power on this island. One does not claim belonging because one knows historical facts. In fact, the opposite is the case: one belongs because one doesn't give a hoot about historical facts. By not caring about history, the island residents render it unimportant. As a result, the line between archival history and pure fiction is constantly being breached. Who gives a damn about Truth? Belonging becomes all about pragmatic truths improvised on historical facts that few people know. Here is a people happily ignorant of history. As Freud long ago taught us, history can contribute to the narcissism of small differences.

Contemporary SXMers do not care that early-twentieth-century SXMers would scarcely recognize the island that has resulted from the 1960s tourist boom. Neither would most of their ancestors have recognized early-twentieth-century SXM; their roots lay elsewhere. Since the tourist boom, 70 to 80 percent of the island's population of sixty thousand,

TABLE I. POPULATION OF SAINT MARTIN AND
SINT MAARTEN BY COUNTRY OF ORIGIN,
EXCLUDING ILLEGAL IMMIGRANTS

Country of Origin	Real Number
Saint Martin	
France (from Saint Martin and mainland France)	18,629
Elsewhere in the European Union	1,658
Haiti	4,508
Dominican Republic	1,432
Saint Lucia	159
Other Americas*	2,220
Elsewhere	506
Total	29,112
Sint Maarten	
Dutch (from Sint Maarten and other parts of the Dutch Kingdom)	15,472
Dominican Republic	3,098
Haiti	2,964
Jamaica	1,516
Guyana	915
United Kingdom	625
United States	564
India	510
Suriname	273
Colombia	178
People's Republic of China	96
Venezuela	73
Elsewhere	4,310
Total	30,594

SOURCES: Institut national de la statistique et des études economiques, Census (Pointe-á-Pitre, Guadeloupe: 1999); Centraal bureau voor de statistiek (CBS), Census (Wilhemstad, Curaçao: 2001).
*Refers to North, Central, and South America and the Caribbean islands.

on both the Dutch and the French sides, consists of first- and second-generation SXMers. Thus, unlike many other Caribbean countries consisting primarily of newcomers from the time of colonialism, people who today refer to themselves as the "natives," SXM is a country of recently arrived newcomers (table 1).

This factor has influenced how SXMers conceive of national history. The collective history of the contemporary population is twenty to thirty years old. Understanding this means understanding that it is not that history itself does not matter, but that a longing to investigate the specificities of SXM history before the tourist boom is quite an unnatural thing for SXMers to have. They are interested in studying the history of other places, such as the Dominican Republic, Saint Kitts, Jamaica, Haiti, and India, but not the pre-1960s history of SXM. Or, more specifically, they are not interested unless they will gain monetary advantages from knowing the history of the island. But there are no such advantages. Tourists who visit the island are not interested in history or heritage. They most definitely do not want to be confronted with an atrocity exhibition. They want fun and sun. History has to be packaged in such a way that it does not disturb their daily rituals of sunbathing, shopping, and dining. Still, if history is all about tailor-made improvisations aimed to please Western visitors, what are the patterns and recurring themes among all these improvisations?

When I first came back to the island, Claudia Schueller, born in the Netherlands to German parents but a resident of the island since 1974 and now the dean of the University of Saint Martin, told me that I should listen to the stories the tour guides told the tourists about the island. They concocted biblically and pan-Caribbean-inspired stories about SXM's slavocratic era and even suggested that Nanny, Tula, and Toussaint had resided on the island. These heroes of Caribbean lore were said to be guided by the Christian God as they led the slaves on the island and in the wider Caribbean to redemption. None of these tour guides seemed ashamed of the fibs they told. None felt the need to set the record straight, to tell an empirically correct story that corresponded somewhat with the archives. It did not take long for me to recognize that Claudia Schueller was right, that my assertion was correct. Even Rastafari were transposed to the time of slavery. I witnessed one the chief cooks at a beach bar tell tourists that some of the island's freedom fighters smoked herb, wore their hair in dreads, and worshipped Jah.

What individual workers did on the streets, the vast majority of the radio disc jockeys, the most popular media personalities on the island, did on the airwaves. For instance, DJ Shadow, the radical Rasta disc jockey that both young and old tuned in to, re-created the island's pan-Caribbean history directly from the soca and conscious reggae hits of such artists as Bob Marley and Alison Hinds. SXM's history of slavery was always at the foreground, with this history becoming a carbon copy of the history of Jamaica or of one of the other islands where slavery was more cruelly practiced. Yet the danceable rhythms and melodies, as well as the way the radio disc jockeys framed the matter, made the terrible history of slavery easier to digest. This was a case of "history lite." The message was that Caribbean blacks had suffered at the hands of the slave

Figure 3. A statue of a slave who never existed: the
closest thing to the experience of slavery on SXM, or
an illustration of fiction becoming fact

drivers, but they had been redeemed by God, just as he had rewarded his
buffalo soldiers who fought back and believed in him. Now the islanders
were all about One Love and held no grudges. White Western tourists
and their money were most welcome. SXM's decision to remain part of
its former colonial masters, France and the Netherlands, was also okay.
God and common sense said so, according to DJ Shadow.

Amused at and sensing recognition of these preliminary findings—for
I too was not well versed in the empirically factual history of the island,
and while I resided there had always been content with imagining it to
suit my fancies and the noble goal of One Love—but feigning concern, I
asked Claudia Schueller if there was any indigenous hero who could re-
place Nanny and who could be disseminated to the tour guides and other
tourist workers. After a long pause her eyes twinkled and she mentioned
Onetitiloke, the one-breasted slave who resisted the dehumanization of
slavery. Then, Schueller's allegiance to the discipline of history, her PhD
subject, made her confess that Onetitiloke is also more than likely an invention. Stories about her have no sound empirical ground. Onetitiloke
is the heroine that the Larosso brothers, the contemporary intellectuals
on the island, created out of traces of the oral histories of slave revolts
to give locals some sense of historical pride. Alfonso Blijden, an archivist
of the Dutch side of the island, corroborated Schueller's confession.

Like the tour guides and the radio disc jockeys, the historically in-clined intellectuals on the island were also fabricators of history: they were imagining the island's past to suit their fancies. In time I would learn that the major project of the Larosso brothers, which was endorsed by Schueller, was to build a sense of nationalism through the publication of books and articles that present an anti-Dutch and anti-French history. Despite the fact that destitution and absolute hunger were not a reality the islanders had to contend with, the fact that SXM had never been a honeypot for these two European powers, and the structural aid of the Hague and Paris, the Larossos insisted that SXMers see the Netherlands and France for what they were: usurpers, vipers, and exploiters of SXM. They wanted the island to become an independent country and to join the other independent nations in the Caribbean in their struggle against Western European and North American imperialism. They were the is-land's freedom fighters. Malcolm X's "By any means necessary," minus the potential for violence or for the loss of their properties and busi-nesses, seemed to be their motto, even if it meant inventing a historic fig-ure to match Nanny.

During my stay on the island, I encountered very few SXMers who were interested in national independence or were avid readers of the Larossos' works. Those whom I met were mostly petty entrepreneurs or schoolteachers. Perhaps those directly engaged in the tourist industry, the vast majority, were too tired after a hard day's work to care about what wrongs the Dutch and French had done umpteen years ago. Per-haps most islanders recognized these works for what they were: more fabrications. In such projects sound empiricism, basing one's historical account on detailed archival research, cross-checked when possible with oral sources, had an insignificant role to play.

The general opinion of SXMers was that the island had no indigenous history and no indigenous culture, except for the Creole Caribbean cul-ture that the contemporary population was forming (Hagenaars 2006). SXM's pre-1960s history was deemed pan-Caribbean, with lots of space for the imagination. History was a game one played for the tourists. It was not a game one played to assert one's belonging or to construct a col-lective identity. Neither was it a way to assert, to the rest of the Carib-bean or the wider world, what SXM meant for the global marketplace. Such processes were nonexistent according to most islanders.

SXM never produced a C.L.R. James or a Fernando Ortiz. Even lesser theorists are missing. Instead, SXM was a place where things hap-pened. It had done nothing to deserve its wealth. It had just been lucky.

Or, as most of the islanders would put it, SXM was blessed. Nestor, a
thickset, bushy-haired Texaco worker who hailed from Providencia, told
me that SXM would be foolish to ever think about gaining political independence:

> Those islands that independent have it so good, that is why they here. You
> name a Caribbean nation, and you find them here. Guyana here, Jamaica
> here, Colombia here. Santo Domingo here, Haiti here. Everybody here.
> Some places have oil and gold and all kinds of minerals, but they people
> still have to leave to come here. What this island have? Sun. Sea. Moun-
> tains. You find that all over the Caribbean, and yet SXM does get more
> tourist than all of them. I tell you is lucky, this place lucky. Is God that
> bless this place. When the tourists stop come, all SXM got to do is pick up
> the phone and call Holland and she there for them. You think we could do
> so with Colombia? You think them British countries coulda do so with En-
> gland? England tell them . . . you there for me, I ain't there for you. Is only
> God know why he bless this place so.

God may be the force behind SXM's rise, but empirically speaking,
from my human-centered view, the cause of this rise is a series of fortu-
nate historical events, with SXM benefiting indirectly from the labors of
others. The French and Dutch governments longed to remain world players after their terrible humiliations, first at the hands of the Germans during the Second World War, followed by the refusal of their prize colonies,
Algeria and Indonesia (respectively), to remain within their fold. Then,
with the clever politicking of Martinique's Aimé Césaire and Curaçao's
M. F. Da Costa Gomez, French SXM became part of the French overseas
department of Guadeloupe, and Dutch SXM, together with the rest of
the Dutch Antilles, became an equal partner in the Dutch Kingdom
(Oostindie and Klinkers 2003). These political changes of the 1950s
eventually led to French and Dutch investments in upgrading the island's
material and political infrastructure.

As it was in politics, so it was in economics. In 1959 Cuba, at that
time the darling of wealthy America, fell into the hands of the rebel
leader Fidel Castro, who nationalized US-owned companies and began
a communist experiment. The American embargo soon followed. Some
of the American hoteliers and financiers sought other paradises in the
Caribbean Sea. SXM, being securely under the control of the French and
Dutch governments, and with little development, was safe, unspoiled,
and ripe for the picking (Glasscock 1985; Hartog 1981). SXM was
deemed by some of these American capitalists the perfect place to invest
and create a smaller version of Cuba. In the 1960s and 1970s, as the
American home-owning middle class expanded and prospered, more

tourists traveled to the island. In the 1980s, the tax cuts of Reaganomics increased the purchasing power of the American upper and upper middle classes even more, and in France, defiscalization laws led to more French investment, indirectly bringing more Western tourists to the island. Today the island receives more than 1.5 million visitors annually, as tourists who come to the island and stay for a period of time or who visit the island for a day or so as part of a larger Caribbean cruise.

All that the SXM political leaders had to do was to capitalize on these opportunities. And capitalize they did. Rumors abounded that with all their hospitality and openness, these leaders enriched themselves. I cannot substantiate any of these rumors, but then again, I did not go looking to find out what was true and what was not. What did become clear through many interviews was that immigrants from the wider Caribbean and investors from other countries such as India, China, and the United States were welcomed to the shores without the necessary papers. Tax breaks were no problem for big businesses, such as hotels, and were granted by the federal government on the advice of the local ones. Speedy naturalization processes were also accommodated. Everything was done to keep the flow of money, tourists, and workers coming to the island.

The only sectors of society that the newcomers had to show absolutely no ambition toward were the political and administrative arenas, as these jobs were reserved for the locals. These locals, or, better put, the offspring of many of these locals, were also coming to harvest the fruits of all the blessings that had been bestowed on SXM. As locals they had the right to run the country. Yet unconditional hospitality to those who were building up the country was also a must. Without them, the locals would have to return to the countries of their diaspora. They would once again be guests in somebody else's country. The "mi casa es su casa" ideology was born.

There could be no talk about integrating newcomers into the local culture, as most locals were also immigrants. Members of the civil service and political machinery of the island became multilingual. Tolerance in all sectors was the new norm, even concerning religion, the seat of collective norms in small-scale communities such as SXM. The locals did not feel threatened by the faiths of the newcomers, since many of their returning kin also brought different Christian faiths to this predominantly Catholic and Methodist island. Christian churches of all kinds were founded along with a few scattered temples—Hindu, Buddhist, Baha'i—and even an Islamic mosque. Amid these different forms of worship, Christianity remained the norm. It was a new public Christianity

though that became the sum of the various Christian faiths, together
with the influences of the other religions, and this new type of faith was
accommodating to the tourist industry. Christianity became a metalanguage, the language of civics. Today it negotiates between the questions
of belonging, for a vocal minority of locals feel that their needs should
come first, and the needs of the tourist industry that is the newcomers'
stronghold.

As interesting as this modern history and the role of public Christianity were—understanding the interface between the mediation of this
public Christianity and the issue of belonging was the reason I was on
the island—it was not something tourists queried SXMers about.
Tourists wanted to know about a long, long time ago, about the time of
slavery. This was after all a black country in the Caribbean. This history
however had to be lightly packaged, as I mentioned before. As such,
there was no reason for SXMers to delve into the past. What would they
gain? For the most part, SXM's past was not their past.

If I were to be true to my first reading of the general mood on the island, I would not bother to write a history chapter, or, better put, an empirically correct historical chapter. Yet the question that every anthropologist working in the Caribbean has to face is this: what about the
slavocratic history of this place and its people? It is an academic question, but it is also more than that. Mintz and Price (1976) and, before
them, C. L. R. James (1938) made the answering of this question a prerequisite for any anthropologist claiming to write anything academic
about this region of the world. Moreover, being the academic-activists
that they were, they made us aware that paying homage to the slavocratic history in anthropological studies of the region is important to
everyone. It is a question related to that all-powerful of Caribbean par-
adigms, namely, that Caribbean culture ought to be understood as a culture of resistance (Scott 2004). It is within this framework that one
should place one's empirical findings. The systemic creation of slaves and
indentured servants on the plantations failed to dehumanize the primarily though not exclusively black and brown downtrodden of the region.
The Caribbean stands as a symbol of the unconquerable human spirit.
From Marti to James to Mintz to Brathwaite to Chagan to Nettleford,
these theorists have been responsible for disseminating this idea of the
Caribbean, which has become the hallmark of the region. It is the way
we like to imagine ourselves and like others to imagine us in academic
settings. Nettleford worded it best when he wrote, "The mind is always
creatively active to guarantee survival and beyond. Many a Caribbean

intellectual, like the Caribbean artist, has got to be a latter-day maroon, ambushing society under the camouflage of intellectual investigation, analysis and artistic invention" (Nettleford 2001: 182).

Lest I be misunderstood, there is much truth in this idea of Caribbean culture as a culture of resistance. There is no need to deconstruct this reading of the region. I cherish it as much as I do the "One Love" history-lite version and believe that it should be told to the descendants of the enslaved and indentured and to those whose nations committed the atrocities (Price 1998; Oostindie 1999). It is a valuable way to counter the racist notions of black and brown inferiority that still unfortunately prevail. But it is only one of the ways, and I began to understand that it needs to be complicated and complemented with another way of reading the past to do justice to SXM and the history that matters to the people on the island.

In addition to acknowledging that Caribbean culture is a culture of resistance, we also need to begin to explicitly acknowledge that much of that celebrated culture of resistance was born and took place within co-optation. In other words, co-optation changed the institutional and conceptual conditions upon which the Caribbean downtrodden created and performed their acts of resistance (Dubois 2006; Guadeloupe 2006; Scott 2004; Ford 2004). These acts of resistance include constructing oneself as a proud person of color and a Christian, running trade unions, and touring the alternative world music circuit in Europe, with a stiff upper lip when necessary, to be heard and acknowledged. Other acts of resistance include the cases, as few as these may be, of a cosmopolitan race-less identity that some Caribbean intellectuals assert (e.g., Gilroy 2006; Phillips 2002; Conde 2001; Glissant 2000; Walcott 1999; Harris 1970; James 1969).

However, the brute force of colonialism was not solely negative. It also enabled certain modes of being, with all the maroon varieties therein. Another way of saying this is that if the plantation is one the bellies of the world, as Glissant so poetically phrased it, and if tourism is built upon the palimpsest of the plantation system, as so many Caribbeanists assert, then we need to recognize that resistance took place within the conceptual framework of the system, not without.[1] Statements such as "That slavery as an institution survived must have been due to the capacity of the Africans to submit themselves physically to enslavement without at the same time committing themselves spiritually and psychologically to bondage" will not do.[2] These Africans chose, yes, but not under institutional or conceptual conditions of their own choosing.

Furthermore, these conditions also changed the Caribbean people. It made them different persons, different subjects. They were not transcendental egos—no one is—but rather social egos formed by the institutional and conceptual conditions they simultaneously had to tackle. In other words their culture of resistance was born within co-optation. Hence, even the acclaimed Caribbean maroon villages can be read as de facto weak antithetical protectorates of the plantation system that connected the Caribbean to the wider world, whose nation-states were growing more interdependent with the advent of Europe's ascendancy as a world power.

These conceptual and institutional conditions remain active and continue to influence what kinds of subjectivities Caribbean people, and more concretely SXMers, can exhibit to guarantee survival. The One Love ideology guarantees this while allowing Caribbean people to assert that their ancestors were agents during the long winter of slavery. A history written from this perspective is one that takes the stories of the people seriously while complementing and cross-cutting these with archival sources.

SXM history effectively starts with colonization and the struggle of European powers to conquer one another and the rest of world. SXM before the ascendancy of Europe is of little historical significance. The pre-Columbus presence on the island left no traces except the curiosa of archaeologists, which adorn the two museums on the island, and the trivia that the more cultivated of the islanders refer to their island by the Amerindian word *Suaouliga:* land of salt. It is widely believed that after the thirteenth century the Amerindians migrated to other islands.[3] Thus, when the Spaniards claimed the island in 1493, it belonged to no one. Considering it an insignificant rock, one of the *islas más inútiles,* of little worth to the mercantile form of capitalism that they practiced, they made little effort to colonize the island (Paula 1993; Glasscock 1985; Hartog 1981). It would take more than one hundred years before Europeans decided to settle it. In 1627 the French landed and were quickly followed by the Dutch, who claimed the island as their own. The ensuing history of the island can be read as an infantile game of European countries outdoing one another for this thirty-seven-square-mile piece of rock: then the Spanish took over, then the British, then the French, then the Dutch, and so forth. Read another way, the game involved major stakes. Many of the seventeenth- and eighteenth-century struggles among European powers were fought out in the Caribbean.

To effectively defeat their Spanish overlords, the upstart Dutch traveled to the New World. The Dutch West India Company (WIC)—one of the precursors of transnational companies—had been granted a trade monopoly by the Staten General in 1621. They decided to strike the enemy where it hurt most: their treasure chest, which was the New World. The latter part of what became known as the Eighty Years' War (1568–1648) between the Spanish and the Dutch took place in the Caribbean. Notwithstanding the superficial religious motivation of the Dutch, it was commerce and greed that dictated their actions (Oostindie 2005: 3–4). The WIC sought to circumvent the salt prices established by King Phillip IV of Spain after it had defeated Portugal, the main supplier for the Dutch, in 1580. In a bid to secure salt for WIC's growing herring industry in northeastern Brazil, the Dutch settled SXM. The Spaniards eventually put a stop to this Dutch adventure, conquering the island in 1633, but they continued to consider it one of the *islas más inútiles*. After the Eighty Years' War ended, SXM lost its geopolitical value and the island was once again deserted.

The departure of the Spanish caused the return of the French and the Dutch, who divided the island between themselves in 1648. The story of the division of the island has two versions: the tongue-in-cheek folklore that all the islanders know, involving alcohol and the possibility of making fun of the white metropolitan Dutch and French, and the more empirically factual account that speaks more to the geopolitics of the time. One of the most charming tongue-in-cheek accounts was told to me by six-year-old Veronica, who wore her hair in pom-poms that made her resemble Minnie Mouse. Veronica was sweet yet feisty and quick with her mouth. She was the spitting image of her mother, if one disregards that Veronica was bony and her mother, Yaya, heavy-set. Yaya, who was of Curaçaon extraction, would turn out to be one of my main interlocutors and friends.

Veronica was a master storyteller who had learned the trade from listening to her mother and her mother's friends. Her hands and head moved in circles, imitating the movement of the female artists on the American music channel BET, as she told her story. Veronica began by explaining to me that French and Dutch soldiers had discovered the island simultaneously. Columbus and the Spaniards did not feature in her tale or in most people's versions. The soldiers had to determine which group would be awarded the largest portion of the island, so they decided to playa game. A French and a Dutch soldier were positioned back-to-back, and each began to walk around the island in opposite directions; each country kept the amount of island its soldier covered while walking. The French soldier kept a steady pace and did not stop to rest. When he was thirsty, he sipped his wine and kept on walking. Veronica would emulate this imaginary soldier walking quickly up and down Yaya's small living room. Holding an imaginary glass between her fingers, she also imitated what she considered the proper way to drink wine.

It was no secret that Veronica had a liking for the French soldier; her body language revealed that much. She was all smiles and thrills as she played that part. Not surprisingly the Dutch soldier was the loser in her tale. He was lame, lazy, and above all had no style. He walked uptight, according to her, like the American tourists on Front Street—one of the main shopping lanes on Dutch SXM. He also liked "the bottle," alcohol, too much. His favorite drink was rum, she said, likening him to the working-class men whose hangout spots were the many rum shops on the island. So fond was this Dutch soldier of rum that he drank it without soda water or ice. His excessive consumption of rum eventually took its toll, and the Dutch soldier had to lie down and rest. When he came to, resumed his task, and finally arrived at the camp, his French counterpart had long since beaten him there. That was how the French got a larger part of the island. And that was also why her mother never dated men from the Dutch side. No style.

Veronica's father was a Saint Martinoise, a Frenchie, as she put it, which meant that she too was a Frenchie. The fact that she identified herself as a Frenchie but was always glad to practice her Dutch on me, and at those moments was Dutch Antillean, was a mode of performing multiple national identities to bridge gaps in interactions and to create temporary unity. That SXMers had multiple identities was a recurring social fact on the island with which I will deal more extensively in chapter 2. Here it is worth noting that, like their laissez-faire attitude toward knowing the factual history of the island, SXMers endorsed an ethic of contextual national identity. It was more a matter of who one was relating to rather than of asserting one's roots.

This story of the division of the island, as told by Veronica, came in many versions. Sometimes the white metropolitan French were chastised for being too decided, and therefore dangerous to the "relax and enjoy yourself" ideology of the island. Then the Dutch soldier would be the hero, as he embodied the Dutch government's policy of very little interference with the daily running of the island. That was the version I heard from politically inclined middle-class French SXMers of local extraction, who sided with the Larosso gang and for whom political independence could not be granted soon enough. Hearing such talk, Yaya would explode. The metropolitan French were good; it was the local French who were the problem. She meant that her ex-boyfriend was always late with his financial support for their daughter. At other times Yaya would impishly state how much she loved the local French men because they knew how to gyrate. Both white metropolitans and Dutch SXMers did not measure up to local French men, for they were crude and did not know how to treat and talk to a woman.

The tongue-in-cheek story of the island's division was common knowledge. It was the story SXMers told one another and visitors. Although quite amusing, this folktale is a simplification of how the division came into effect. According to the archives, soon after its decision to leave the island, the Spanish government sent a detachment from nearby Puerto Rico to effect the departure. On the ship were four Frenchmen and five Dutchmen, all of whom were prisoners of war. After arriving on SXM the prisoners fled to the hills and hid until the Spanish left. Thereafter they decided to pool their resources and inform their governments that they could share the island in a similar fashion to Saint Kitts, which was French and English. Despite a certain amount of mistrust between France and the Netherlands, the two countries agreed to share the island, and the treaty of Mount Concordia was signed. In the words of Jean Glasscock, who wrote a history of the island, "The treaty provided that the French would occupy the northern part of the island, that facing Anguilla, and the Dutch the regions of the Fort and the lands around it on the south side. Inhabitants on both sides were to have equal rights to hunting, fishing, salt ponds, dye-woods, rivers, pools, mines or minerals, ports and moorings, and other commodities of the island" (Glasscock 1985: 11). Although often breached—symbolized by the fact that the island changed hands sixteen times before 1816—the treaty is still in effect today. Both powers share the island's international airport and harbor, which happen to be located on the Dutch side of the island, where the tourist boom first took off.

In modern times the treaty has brought the island stability and prosperity, as the French and the Dutch have given the island structural aid, but in the past it occasioned SXM to be involved in one of the worst crimes of human history: the enslavement of more than twelve million black Africans. Greed and the need to be the most powerful player in Europe and increasingly on the world stage overruled any sense of civic decency (Oostindie 1995). What cotton was to the enslaved Africans in the southern states of the United States, sugarcane was to the Caribbean. And in this regard sugarcane production outdid cotton: "The human toll of slavery, both physical and cultural, was intimately tied to exigencies of production, notably the work regimen. Working conditions generally imposed lower life expectancy, higher death rates, and much lower birth rates among Caribbean and Brazilian slaves than among their U.S. counterparts. From that viewpoint, sugarcane was the slaves' most sadistic tormentor" (Trouillot 1995: 18).

Because of the deep impact sugarcane production had on the lives of slaves, when SXMers spoke about slavery, and for the most part this was only when tourists asked about it, they spoke about sugarcane. The image they depicted of what took place on the island was usually what they grew up hearing or reading about in their former home countries. Even the local black SXMers, whose slave ancestors mostly worked the salt pans rather than the cane fields, spoke about cane. I learned that they had to make up some of this history, because their grandparents did not speak about slavery to them. One local, Miss Maria, a slender former schoolteacher in her mid-sixties with snow-white hair and brown skin, was adamant about the matter. Slavery was not something people spoke about when she was growing up. "Who want to talk about that? Boy, why you don't behave yourself?" For black locals, slavery was an episode worth forgetting. All that their grandparents had conveyed to them were the ideas that they should never think anyone better than themselves and that they should never let anyone take advantage of them, especially white people.

What the grandparents of locals did speak about was struggling in places like the Dominican Republic where they cut cane as guest workers. After slavery was abolished on both sides of the island, in 1848 on the French side and in 1863 on the Dutch side, SXM was a forgotten island, as *inútil* as in the time of the Spaniards. To survive and provide for their families, the able-bodied had to roam the Caribbean and the wider Americas. These stories of roaming and struggling always contained the message that unconditional hospitality to strangers was a must, for it was strangers who opened their houses to these workers. And it was strangers who had helped build up the island. Unconditional hospitality to strangers was one of God's commandments, Miss Maria believed, which is why she always prepared more food than necessary at mealtimes. "You never know when someone will come begging you for a plate of food."

One disc jockey, DJ Cimarron, tried to capitalize on this God-given commandment in his activism on behalf of the illegal workers on the island. He believed the children of illegal workers should be granted the same rights as the legal population's children. They should be allowed to attend school and to receive a scholarship if they qualified. DJ Cimarron was a modern-day Jeremiah: no one wanted to hear his message. Even Miss Maria could not condone such radical politics. Unconditional hospitality was God's commandment, yes, but she reasoned that God would not want the legal population to sacrifice their livelihoods for illegal workers who were already tolerated and who made a fair living on the island. Granting scholarships to their children was nonsensical. She reasoned that if these children wanted to go to school, they could do so on the French side of the island. The French were lenient on this matter, and the schools got more money from Paris. Miss Maria was pragmatic, while Cimarron was principled. Pragmatism was judged to be the better option. In chapter 5 I will deal extensively DJ Cimarron's quest and his radio program.

The commandment of unconditional hospitality resembled the One Love ideology, though the former spoke about the post-abolition rather than the pre-abolition period. What they shared was the appeal of a magical resolution to the lingering scars left by the history of slavery. It thus allowed all black SXMers to speak about sugarcane slavery with a heavy dose of poetic license that did not tear down their pride or give white tourists a guilty conscience. Even those whose ancestors did directly experience the horrors of sugarcane slavery were less than truthful with the facts. Let me furnish an illustration. Haitian-born SXMers have all but monopolized retail sales of touristy arts and crafts on the island. One of my most memorable experiences was observing an interaction in Marigot, the capital of French SXM, between a tall, pink-skinned American visitor somewhere in his late thirties and a Haitian vendor. The visitor was accompanied by two women, one of whom I assume was his wife. He was a walking Lonely Planet guidebook. I imagined that he had read up on the Caribbean before taking his cruise and wanted to show off his tourist-guide knowledge. He asked the vendor, who managed to subdue the Creole and French in her tongue and speak "American," if arts and crafts were part of her African heritage and whether she had made any of the pieces on display. He already knew that the answer was yes, for he had read that Caribbean people were good with their hands. Hence, before the vendor could begin to formulate an answer, he spoke about how much he admired the strength and artistic creativity of black women in the Caribbean.

The vendor, a very smart-looking caramel-colored woman whose beauty and slender figure were somewhat offset by her potbelly, seemed to know with what kind of expert she was dealing. Here was one of the men for whom SXM was just part of what in his country's media is referred to as "the islands," the imaginary Caribbean of sun and fun, where a few bad events happened in the distant past. She told him that though she was an artist in her own right, her pieces were not on display. Her job as a saleswoman and a homemaker occupied too much of her time. But, she quickly stated, the pieces she sold were part of her culture. She was from Haiti, the land of Toussaint. The man's eyes lit up, and the rest of his body said, "Yes, please tell me more." The vendor did not fail to register the request and the opening to make a sale. What followed was a story about Haitians heroically fighting for their freedom on the sugarcane plantations, about the historical situation of SXM being a mirror of Saint Domingue, about the One Love resolution of all conflicts, and about her love of arts and crafts that was handed down to her from her mother, who learned the trade from her grandmother, who inherited it from *her* mother, who was from Africa. In all this she was displaying her batik dresses to the women as well as enticing them to try on the necklaces and bracelets she had on display. Although the man was all ears, his female companions were more interested in the goods and how they looked. The saleswoman skillfully balanced her time between their wants and the man's need for a history-lite lesson. She was a historian and a salesperson all in one. Her efforts paid off, as his companions bought several of her touristy pieces and did not ask again about her self-made ones.

Though this folk historian's stories of the Haitian revolution, slavocratic SXM, and her family's history were interwoven, they were logically incompatible. On the one hand there was the dehumanizing tale of being beaten into accepting infrahumanity and the struggle to overcome this situation through the One Love ideology taught by God, and on the other hand there was this folksy narrative in which there existed an idyllic Haiti whereby "Africanisms" were easily bequeathed. It is this second Haiti, this Caribbean, that made the most impact on tourists. This was the SXM of their tourist brochures. While observing the spectacle, I mused that whereas Afrocentric historians have to twist and turn to argue that African cultural expressions have been retained in the face of the terrifying power of the plantation system, this vendor inherited her knowledge of arts and crafts straight from Africa. She did not have to struggle to obtain this inheritance. Her grandmothers did not have to hide to pass on the knowledge. It was all lovingly handed down to her in a Haiti that was part of and yet juxtaposed to the Haiti of the bloody rebellions. These two Haitis were dialectically resolved in the One Love Haiti, so unlike the Haiti where African descendants continue to struggle.

The idyllic Haiti of the vendor was of course a fabrication, but so too was her claim that slavocratic SXM was the spitting image of the Haiti that Toussaint and the other black Jacobins sought to liberate. The differences were major. SXM was not a country of incessant slave rebellions. Far from it. SXM was an island where enslaved Africans enjoyed a relatively high amount of freedom, despite their enslavement and the ensuing social death, as Orlando Patterson so fittingly termed it (Patterson 1994; Paula 1993; Hartog 1981). These were Creole slaves who knew how to negotiate with their masters, who lacked the will and means to implement the de facto and de jure power they had over their slaves.

Whereas in Haiti many of the enslaved came from Africa, and we know today that they played a pivotal role in the Haitian revolution, on SXM there is no archival proof or credible oral sources that can claim that SXM's slaves came directly from Africa. Enslaved Africans, who had been living in the surrounding countries, arrived on the island with their slave masters after they had been allotted pieces of land. In 1763 "France accepted anyone to live on the island: English, pirates, Dutch, French" (quoted in Glasscock 1985: 23). This was mirrored by a similar Dutch initiative issued a few years earlier. These initiatives were necessary, for SXM was empty. Even so, in the second half of the eighteenth century, only one-third of the island was inhabited (Paula 1993: 35). SXM was an island of creolized blacks and whites where revolts were sporadic.

Another telling difference is that unlike on Haiti, which was a quintessential plantation society with all of its associated hardships, on both French and Dutch SXM, the hard labor of sugarcane production played a minor role. The horrendous images of human defilement—of blacks surviving the hell of the Middle Passage only to enter the sugar or cotton plantations, where laboring meant precipitating one's demise,—does not apply to slavocratic SXM. In fact reports dating back to 1795 show that only thirty-five of the ninety-two plantations on the entire island were sugarcane based.

The sugar production yield on SXM was hardly enough to compete with the yield on other Caribbean islands, which were the major producers of the crop. Remedying this by importing more slaves was not possible because the slave trade was officially abolished in 1814, and planters on SXM lacked the finances to acquire the substantial number of slaves needed on the illegal market. Climatic factors also played a role, as the hurricane of 1819 devastated the crop yields and left only four boilers in working condition. Planters were not given a chance to recover, as in 1830 there was a drought that left the island's plantations in shambles. One also has to mention the rise in the 1830s of sugar beet growing in Europe and the cultivation of sugarcane in such far-off places such as Java, both of which signaled the demise of the Caribbean as Europe's primary source for sugar.

SXM was part of the evolving world market that today we take for granted. What connects the SXM of the slavery system to the SXM of the tourist boom is that the island remains a minor player on the global stage, susceptible to the whims of larger powers. I would also learn from popular disc jockeys, such as the immensely popular DJ Fernando Clarke, whose philosophies of belonging were based on a humorous and inflated mimicry of the common sense on the island, that SXMers were acutely aware that when the United States sneezes, SXM catches a severe cold. Clarke knew better than to encourage his listeners to get involved in the fights of the big players of the world, no matter how unjust he found their antics. SXM would suffer, and thus the people would suffer. This was definitely not part of God's plan, as far as Clarke was concerned. In this pragmatic stance he resembled the Rastafarian DJ Shadow, notwithstanding Clarke's preference for playing Calypso.

The other important factor, as I mentioned before, is the climate. Human history changes far more rapidly than environmental processes do. The threat of hurricanes and the unpredictability of global capital are the recurring *ketos megas,* the metaphorical big fishes of Jewish lore, that constantly threaten to destroy the precarious economy of the island. These were the two things that SXMers feared most. Months later Miss Maria, Yaya, and others would caution me not to speak too loudly about hurricanes, lest I precipitate God's fury.

The realization that the power of nature and that changing global economic and political conditions could negatively affect the island at any time lacked any historical grounding. No one I encountered on the island spoke about the 1819 hurricane or about the perils of sugar production there. It was too far back for them to remember and too much effort to look up in a history book. As I stated at the beginning of this chapter, the empirically factual history had long since left the island, and few mourned its loss. SXMers were also not catering to tourists who were interested in archival facts. They were interested in a good tale of the horror of slavery that did not upset their stomachs and could quickly be digested. The history-lite rendition of slavery went together with the history-lite rendition of hurricanes.

Figure 4. Re-creation of the time of slavery at the Emilio Wilson estate: it's all about singing and having fun in spotless white clothing, not about the enactments of hardships.

I witnessed a conversation between a handsome waiter and two female tourists that concretized this reality. The waiter, judging from his accent a Kittitian-SXMer who couldn't have been on the island very long, was in his late twenties and obviously took care of himself. He seemed to have come out of the primal seas of Africa—the Africa of the Parisian catwalks, that is. He had a strong back and a chiseled face, which his short-cropped hair accentuated. He knew he looked good, and he knew how to work tourists. His clients were two dark-skinned, chubby Americans in their late forties who were looking for a good time. They asked him if he worked out, to which he replied that this was all natural, Mama Africa. Exactly what they wanted to hear. Aware that he had them eating out his hands, he continued by telling them that their ancestors had come over in the same boat as his; the only difference was that his had been put in a place where hard work was a killer. His great-great-grandfather chopped cane all day, and that's what gave him his great physique: genetics. But despite the sufferation that he inherited from slavery times, like Marley he was chanting down Babylon. God was on his side. The women loved it. He was the typical rude boy talking the history-lite talk that they liked.

In the flirtations that continued (they referred to him as "pure choco-late"), the subject of hurricanes came up. They began talking about how terrified they would be, and heaven forbid they ever experience a typhoon. The waiter saw his chance to show off and began talking about the hur-ricane of 1995 that had completely devastated the island. He mentioned that there was no electricity, running water, or cable TV, at which the Americans gasped. They could not imagine such a life. No TV, no clubs. He assured them that if a hurricane were to pass over the island, they need not worry, for his arms were broad enough to shelter them both. This simply made their day. When asked how often hurricanes pass over the island, he replied, "Every ten years or so." He lied, of course, but his audience was not interested in the truth. They were interested in him.

Most tourists liked to be lied to. That hurricanes are rare but unpre-dictable was not what they wanted to hear. Neither would it have satis-fied them to tell them that historical records show that plantations were not big business on SXM; that, with only a few exceptions, many planters barely eked out a living for themselves; that, as a result of the climate, the market, and the wars of the European overlords, planters saw their wealth dwindle; that, as a result of misfortune and inept management, slaves dangled on an existential limb between a life of continuous hunger and death by starvation. That type of story line is not a story line that would have worked. Neither black nor white Americans who visited the island wanted to hear that history. They wanted an easily digestible form of history that fit the familiar. SXM history had to resemble the domi-nant image of the resistance music of Marley, which spoke about strug-gle culminating in the One Love ideology.[4] And it was this SXM with which the islanders furnished the tourists.

This fabrication of SXM's pre-1960s slavocratic history was for the tourists, not for the SXMers themselves. Their peculiar histories re-mained. Both Haiti's and India's independence days were intensely cele-brated on the island. On these days, the Haitians and Indians dressed up and remembered their ancestors and their struggles. On SXM day, when the islanders commemorate the treaty of Concordia, all the islanders come out to celebrate their multiculturality and have a good time. There is always the obligatory ten-minute sketch of the hardships of slavery culminating in the One Love ideology, whereby everyone claims to care about the hardships of those who lived that nightmare. But few care to truly know what they experienced.

Irjanyani, an Indian merchant whom I spoke to during an SXM day cel-ebration that was held at the renovated Emilio Wilson slave plantation, put it this way: "Slavery was bad; you know, the British were harsh with us too." That was as far as he got. What he really meant was, "Slavery was bad; you know, the British were harsh with us too, but the island has been good to me and my family. What would you like to drink, my friend?" Yaya was even coyer. Engaging a militant local, she said, "They really was animals, but thank God we survive." When he left, she murmured that he was a real ass. She was a Yu Korsow, a Curaçaon. Yaya did not visit the Emilio Wilson plantation to learn about her roots; she had come to see what it looked like, as she was planning to rent the grounds for Veronica's seventh birthday party. It was telling. The two renovated plantations on the island had swings and seesaws for the children, and one of them, the Lottery Farm, even served gourmet meals to tourists.

Both Irjanyani and Yaya created a shared past with the descendants of the locals—Irjanyani, as part of Europe's colonial history, and Yaya, as a descendant of the enslaved Africans—and thereafter went back to their ethnic particularities. This was simply a question of contextual identity, or relation identity, as Glissant (2000) would put it. Understanding the skillful use of both national and transnational identities to forge temporary shared identities, and why it was deemed effective, is the focus of the following chapter.

CHAPTER 2

Performing Identities on Saint Martin and Sint Maarten

"All of them are important to me; they have a reason. Now stop minding my business." In her characteristically temperamental style, Miss Maria, an ex-schoolteacher in her late sixties, replied to my observation that although she considered herself a local, she also displayed national allegiance to Anguilla and Curaçao. There was no contradiction, according to her, since she was born in Anguilla and had lived practically all her life in Curaçao. Furthermore, as a local she claimed both Saint Martin and Sint Maarten as her own, the national boundary notwithstanding. Besides her Anguillan, Curaçaon, and SXM sense of national belonging, Miss Maria had several other national and transnational allegiances. As an Anguillan, part of the British Overseas Territories (BOTs), she identified with the United Kingdom.[1] Since she also carried a Dutch passport, she likewise identified herself as being a member of the Dutch nation. Finally, Miss Maria also identified with the West Indies and the black diaspora in the West.

Depending on the person with whom she was interacting, Miss Maria would perform one of her national or transnational identities, canceling out others. Most SXMers did the same. The fact that 70 to 80 percent of the population were recently arrived immigrants from the four corners of the globe whose livelihood depended exclusively on tourism created a social environment in which all the inhabitants of the island had to continuously perform a series of national and transnational identities to create common worlds. These performances depended on the places SXMers

Figure 5. The "manna" arrives: every SXMer's livelihood depends on tourism.

had lived, the socially ascribed roots of their ancestors, and the passports they wielded. In short, what Glissant (2000) has termed a *relation identity* was a prerequisite for an open politics of identity.

This continuous performance of switching from one national or transnational identity to another was encouraged by radio disc jockeys, the most admired media personalities on the island. They constantly reminded their listeners that everyone had migrated to and stayed on SXM to earn a living. Therefore, all relationships, including the (trans)national identities SXMers mobilized during their daily encounters, were based ultimately on acquiring more money and power, the *money tie system* as it was locally termed. This was true of locals as well as newcomers, those with and without the appropriate passports or permits. Employing a Christian meta-idiom to get their message across, popular radio disc jockeys claimed that everyone on the island was a sinner and fell short of the glory of God. SXMers also had access to more than fifty Western TV channels and several regional and international weeklies and dailies, which strengthened their awareness that naturalizing any one national or transnational identity could create societal tensions and threaten the tourist industry.

Most SXMers knew they needed an encompassing and open identity under which the different nations on the island could unite and that could curtail the sporadic xenophobia of the locals. They privileged international and nonterritorial cultural categories of identification, the most widespread of which was the performance of being Christian. The popular radio disc jockeys employed Christianity as a metalanguage that conveyed tolerance and egalitarianism. Through this they actively sought to keep their social performances of national and transnational identities open to all. Christianity employed as a metalanguage was the social glue of this multiethnic society.

During my stay on the island, I took up residence in the Dutch Quarter (Lower Princess Quarter). The Dutch Quarter, a residential district bordering the French side of the island, is located in one of the inland valleys, a location that made good sense as a site for my home, since SXM is a mountainous tropical island that is annually threatened by hurricanes. Building one's home in a valley offers some protection from hurricanes, and it is less costly to put down a good foundation on flat land. The French and Dutch administrative capitals, Marigot and Phillipsburg, respectively, the hotels and marinas, and the businesses and mansions of the upper classes are located in the coastal areas. Every morning the majority of the working population drives to the coasts to earn a living. They cater to the 1.5 million primarily white, well-to-do Western tourists who visit the island annually. And they work for the government, law firms, construction companies, and so forth, industries that are indirectly related to tourism.

The bulk of the inhabitants of the Dutch Quarter were working-class West Indians, some of whom were illegal. Whether one was illegal or legal, one could find a job on SXM, since there was work in abundance. In the Dutch Quarter I came across newcomers from mainland Caribbean countries such as Venezuela and Guyana to those from the tiny islands such as Petit Martinique and Providencia. I also interacted with middle- and upper-middle-class locals who owned plots of land and rented out apartments. For example, Miss Maria lived in a five-bedroom house and collected rent for the two two-bedroom apartments that she built on her parcel of land. She also received a government pension and supposedly some remuneration for the afterschool foundation, which she ran with a middle-aged social worker named Rebecca. Roughly speaking Miss Maria had a monthly income of about two thousand US dollars, while many working-class newcomers made about twelve hundred US dollars working two jobs five days a week. From this salary they had to pay their

Figure 6. Columbus rediscovers the Caribbean: Western tourist ships line up in the SXM harbor

expenses and remit money to loved ones in their home countries. Despite class differences and vicious stereotyping of each other from time to time, locals and newcomers got along quite well in the Dutch Quarter.

These locals and working-class newcomers were directly or indirectly connected through work and other ties to the upper classes of SXM society. Most members of the upper classes—the *money people,* as they were locally termed—were wealthy newcomers from the United States, Western Europe, or emerging powers such as India and China. They invested in the island or brokered the monies of their overseas counterparts. The North American and Western European newcomers owned the larger contracting companies, hotels, yachts, restaurants, and marinas. In economic terms they were the most powerful SXMers. The Chinese for their part had almost complete dominance of the supermarkets and midrange restaurants. Everyone on the island knew that the large-scale import and sale of foods was primarily a Chinese affair. The niche of Indian and Pakistani merchants was the clothing, appliance, and jewelry stores. On SXM one came face to face with the global order: Western capitalists dominated the economy followed closely by their Asian counterparts.

The locals controlled both the civil service and the realm of formal politics and therefore interacted with these wealthy newcomers on matters pertaining to permits, taxes, and upgrading the infrastructures. They were aware of their political power, as a comment to me by the former Dutch commissioner of tourism, Julian Rollocks, reveals: "Them Americans have the money, but we have the power of the pen, and we must never forget that. No matter how much friend we be, we must never forget that." Through this awareness many locals have bettered themselves financially. Rumors involving bribery and corruption of influential locals abounded on the island. After the wealthy Westerners and Asians, they were the entrepreneurial class on the island. They owned motels, apartments, car rental agencies, restaurants, smaller contracting firms, virtually all the bus and taxi licenses, and most of the real estate on the island. Locals were not the most economically powerful group on SXM, but they were powerful enough.

The working-class inhabitants of the Dutch Quarter also possessed power, but it was of a different kind. They were the gardeners, housekeepers, casino dealers, security guards, and store attendants employed by the wealthy hoteliers and merchants. Without them, the tourist industry would come to a halt, and they knew this. This is how a group of young West Indian men who referred to themselves as the More Fire Crew put it: "Without we Caribbean people, there is no SXM. We build here."

There was also the issue that newcomers, most of whom were working class, made up more than 50 percent of the eligible voting population on both sides of the island. For example, of the 15,325 eligible voters in the 1999 Dutch SXM election, 5,652 were naturalized citizens and 1,080 were Dutch metropolitans. Of the remaining 8,593 voters registered as born Dutch West Indians, only 3,789 were born on the island. According to civil servants at the census office, the largest group of these SXMers born on the island had at least one parent who was a newcomer. They base this on the fact that interethnic love relationships are the rule rather than the exception, and that many of the second-generation newcomers have voting rights. I could not obtain the exact figures, however, because the census did not register mixed ethnicity as a category. Civil servants also claimed that many of the voters registered as having been born on another Dutch West Indian island could also be considered immigrants. There were, for example, a considerable number of Dominicans who came to SXM via another Dutch West Indian island. Thus although the total aggregate vote of newcomers—naturalized citizens, Dutch metropolitans, born SXMers, and born Dutch West Indians—was obfuscated by the categories of the census, civil servants believed that they far outnumbered the locals.

The situation on the French side of the island was similar. Although I could not gain access to the actual statistics for different ethnic groups who made up the voting population on French SXM, I was told by the civil servant in charge that on this side of the island, it was also the new-comers who decided who would be voted into office. The major differ-ence between the French and the Dutch system was that French metro-politans automatically qualified as voters. Since the social securities and amenities were the same on SXM as in France, one found many upper- and middle-class French metropolitans who had made SXM their per-manent home. One also encountered many working-class metropolitans who collected unemployment benefits in France and worked for a few years on SXM illegally. Taken together with immigrants from other French West Indian islands and working-class West Indian immigrants who had obtained French rights, especially those of Haitian extraction, newcomers indeed decided French SXM's politics.

There was the awareness that all the social classes on SXM were de-pendent on one another. Everyone had power, though like the island's wealth, this power was not distributed equally. The economic and ac-companying class-based stratification on SXM was plain to see. Never-theless, while I categorized SXMers in class terms, they preferred to em-ploy inter- and intra-class categories. Cultural lifestyle was more important than class on SXM. This was true both on the streets and the radio. The most widespread cultural lifestyles, coined as *rummies, fortune seekers, in-tellectuals,* and *Rastafari,* defined how the most popular radio disc jock-eys encouraged the island inhabitants to tune in to in their programs. These cultural lifestyles should not be interpreted as fully absorbing identities. They are privileged, though not exclusive, social performances.

Although they represented two separate social performances, rum-mies and fortune seekers were usually mentioned in one breath. Rum-mies were primarily, but not exclusively, working-class newcomers. I fre-quently encountered upper-middle-class SXMers who were, after work, as raucous as their working-class buddies. Rummies spent most of their leisure time in pubs and rum shops, telling one another vulgar stories and relating the latest gossip. A rummie, short for rum drinker, enjoyed con-suming lots of alcohol and professing to care little for highbrow etiquette and to value above all hanging out with friends and enjoying the simple things in life. He or she was known to be a *sin vergüenza,* someone with-out shame, as they say on the island.

Those who performed the fortune-seeker lifestyle differed in an im-portant regard: they had few qualms about letting others know that their desire was to get rich as soon as possible. When not engaging in ex-changing tips and tricks on how to make quick money, even on the backs of others, fortune seekers usually talked about how close they came to winning the elusive "grand prize": getting rich quickly. While playing the slot machines or sipping whiskey, they daydreamed about what they would do if they ever became millionaires. Here too one encountered persons from various class backgrounds. The music that rummies and fortune seekers most enjoyed was Caribbean dance music, and DJ Fernando Clarke's calypso show was a favorite among them. Clarke, a bank manager and part-time Calypso disc jockey, performed the rummie and fortune-seeker lifestyles on the radio like few others, and I frequently discussed various issues with him during my stay on the island.

If fortune seekers believed that through trickery and luck they would be able to shoot up the socioeconomic ladder, then those who performed the intellectual lifestyle proposed that their brainpower was sufficient. Intellectuals were bookish people who believed that the country needed their guidance. In their opinion they were born to be philosopher-kings, high-ranking civil servants, or the government's main advisers. For many intellectuals with little economic clout, networking at debating clubs with the wealthy about international events was a way to start climbing the social and economic ladder. During call-in radio talk shows, intellectuals would talk for hours, displaying their savvy about world matters. They were men and women of principle, so it seemed. However DJ Cimarron, whose ambition in life was to be recognized as an intellectual and who sought to cater to this group with his program, helped me gain an understanding of the pragmatism behind their principles.

The last category was that of the Rastafari. As in most parts of the world those who performed the Rastafari lifestyle on SXM were rhetorically anti-Babylon, their term for global capitalism. Class discrimination, racism, and ethnic strife throughout the world were blamed on the meddling of Western capitalists and what they considered their pawns in the Global South. But like the three other categories I discussed, Rastafari was not reducible to class. While most Rastafari were of the working class, there were also many upper-middle- and upper-class youths who listened to DJ Shadow, an upper-class Rasta disc jockey who enjoyed the respect of most working-class Rastas. For them the Shadow was beyond class.

Throughout this study I will continually refer to the mismatch between the cultural categories the SXMers employ and the class categories I use. This mismatch is constructive, because it reminds me once more of the truism that the perspective one privileges determines to a large extent what one considers socially factual. And this perspective in turn colors social life. Class may be rigid in my mind, but this was not true for most

SXMers. I was able to speak to several business owners and politicians through the inhabitants of the Dutch Quarter, for these inhabitants visited the upper classes at their homes and interacted free of highbrow etiquette. This was part of a wider pattern, for in their day-to-day dealings SXMers glossed over their differences in symbolic, social, cultural, and financial capital as much as possible (Bourdieu 1997). For instance, in the presence of some of his employees, Jeff, the North American owner of several restaurants, opined, "There is no difference between us. On this island we are all the same."

This opinion referred neither to income nor to nationality. Jeff carried a coveted American passport, and his personnel were for the most part citizens of poor West Indian countries. Calvin Boasman, the director of the labor office, was the first to explain to me what this rhetoric referred to. He told me that on SXM people imagined an invisible chain binding them. This chain was primarily based on the fact that everyone's livelihood was dependent on tourism. No one was willing to risk igniting any form of communal tension, for they knew this could potentially spell disaster for the island's tourism industry. Tourism, and indirectly the entire services industry that depended on it, was the only industry on SXM. Manufacturing, mineral extraction, and agro-industry were nonexistent. Every bottle of water, can of beer, carton of juice, kilo of steak, bale of wheat, television set, and automobile had to be flown or shipped in.

For the islanders the global flow of goods was plain to see. The islanders themselves were also a product of capitalist flows, as most had migrated to the island after the tourist boom took off in the 1960s. Most of the people I spoke to reasoned that everyone was on SXM because of what they called the *money tie system,* the notion that all relationships are somewhere along the line based on a quest for more money and power. This was true of the Colombian maid, the local politician, and the Chinese merchant, as well as the North American hotelier. This continuing quest for more money and power is what made SXMers, in Jeff's words, "all the same." The money tie system was the island's constantly enacted hegemonic performative space, which set the conceptual conditions for SXMers to exhibit the appropriate social performances to get ahead.

While some Caribbeanists such as Mimi Sheller (2003) identify tourism as the newest form of capitalist exploitation in the region, this view is not shared by most working-class SXMers. When I confronted Yaya, a single mother who worked as a casino dealer, with this thesis, she said: "Them people them head ain't no good. Tell them I say it is because of the tourists we can feed we children. We *want* the Americans to come down here. I don't know what wrong with them people. They have it good—that is why they can talk that nonsense." Gaston, a Haitian gardener, was even clearer on this point. He asked me rhetorically if I knew how he lived in Haiti. He said that I might consider the few hundred dollars he earned small change or his little apartment he rented with another Haitian not much, but that was because I did not know what being poor in Haiti means. Because of tourism, he could earn a living cleaning yards and doing other odd jobs. When he traveled back to Haiti he was respected as a man who had come a long way in life. In Haiti, the average annual income amounts to five hundred dollars: he earned in a month what most Haitians cannot even dream of earning in a year. Within co-optation he was surviving and even resisting the dehumanization wrought by the capitalist order.

The difference between Yaya's and Gaston's understanding and that of scholars speaking primarily about Cuba, the Dominican Republic, and Jamaica may have to do with the fact that on SXM, abject poverty was nonexistent and sex tourism was not well developed. The working population earned enough not to have to perform the pejorative social identities of Rent-a-Dreads, sweet Indian girls, or Mulatta and Negra *preciosas*, which are all terms for working-class men and women who perform sexual favors for tourists. Tourists and well-to-do SXMers interested in sexual contacts visited clubs where women from Asia, Eastern Europe, and Latin America worked on three-month contracts as "exotic dancers."[2] The few islands where tourism has led to the improvement of the material well-being of the general population should get as much recognition as those where tourist resorts coexist with squalid local living conditions. The effects of tourism are dependent on a range of societal factors, and therefore it is important to tone down such meta-narratives as Sheller's that obscure how tourist workers in the wealthier Lesser Antilles, islands still tied to the EU or the United States, understand their realities. On SXM the most pertinent issue related to tourism was the question of illegal workers.

I chose to live in the Dutch Quarter because SXM is an expensive island. The main currencies on the island are the euro, the American dollar, and the Dutch Antillean guilder.[3] In this setting, where the official minimum wage is set at 610 dollars on the Dutch side and 1090 euros on the French, "underprivileged" had a connotation somewhat different from what one imagines when one thinks of the working classes in the Global South. Most of the working-class newcomers on Dutch SXM had two jobs so that they could earn twice as much as the minimum wage.

One did not encounter beggars or homeless people on the street, because if people were unemployed and had no other form of income, they left the island. On the Dutch side that meant returning to their "home" countries or, if they had the right passport, migrating to the Netherlands, where the unemployment benefit of 620 euros for a single man or woman was reasonable. On the French side, where the social benefits for citizens were the same as in France, unemployment was not a reason to emigrate.

The unspoken rule in the Dutch Quarter and the wider society seemed to be that if people did not fit into the money tie system and hence could not financially support themselves, they were found socially unfit to reside on the island. All the classes observed this rule. I often heard from Miss Maria and other SXMers that the only way the island's local police force would deport an illegal was if he or she did not have a job and was a public nuisance. It was rumored that some police officers even went so far as to warn befriended illegal immigrants whenever the authorities of Guadeloupe or Curaçao were planning a raid. Alex, an illegal immigrant from Haiti who had been living in the Dutch Quarter for more that twenty years, corroborated this. It was rumored that, like many successful illegal immigrants, Alex saved diligently and had built a few homes in Haiti as an old-age pension. He told me he did not have to process his papers because he earned a living cleaning the yards of many police officers, and one of them was his main domino partner: "I no worry 'bout that. The police is my friend."

Other influential players in society also condoned and even encouraged the presence of illegal immigrants on the island. Roland Tobias, the Anguillan-born head of public relations of the Windward Island Bank and a popular radio disc jockey, told me that his bank and others had often intervened when undocumented SXMers were being deported. Many of them, especially Haitians, known as the hardest working and most stingy people on SXM, had sizable bank accounts, displayed thrift, and were contributing to the island's economy. Through their savings the banks on the island could lend money to larger overseas banking conglomerates, which enabled these conglomerates to balance their books after a day of heavy investments.

According to Roland Duncan, a successful Aruban-born local businessman, lawyer, and Dutch Antillean minister of constitutional affairs who usually espoused his views on the radio, deporting hardworking illegal immigrants was a waste of the taxpayers' money. He claimed that all sensible civil servants and businessmen on the island knew that in leaner times, no one had to instruct the undocumented workers to leave the island. They knew that it was impossible to be unemployed for a lengthy time on SXM: "This island doesn't have any gardens or mountains where they can go and grow their provision or keep some chickens. This is not Jamaica, my friend. So what most illegals do is head back to their country when things bad, and when they know the tourist season swinging again they will just book a flight or come back in on a boat."

He also mentioned that people would be sent back to their home islands after a hurricane. Such was the case with illegal immigrants from Haiti and the Dominican Republic in the wake of the 1995 hurricane that left SXM in shambles. Being deported because one lacks a job or has been victimized by nature is quite harsh, but it is no more inhumane than the welfare arrangements propagated by Western governments. Europe and the United States close their borders to stop the starving and needy in the Global South from immigrating to earn a decent living. (Messer 1993; Kristeva 1991; Cohen 1989).

Illegal immigrants have easy access to SXM because the entire island is a free port for goods, and therefore customs operations at the various bays are minimal. Also, some customs officers at the airport do not even check passports. I experienced firsthand how officers half-checked passports on major flights and on late flights coming from Saba or Anguilla or simply waved passengers through the gates. Illegals lived on the island with such ease that a newcomer such as Danielle, a young woman from Petit Martinique who worked at a petrol station, was able to pick up relatives at the airport with no trouble whenever they came to visit. Because of this leniency, no one knew how many undocumented newcomers there were. The government did not conduct research on that matter.

Like Danielle, many illegal immigrants left their husbands, wives, or children in their home countries and sent remittances. They lived as frugally as possible, usually sharing the rent with other illegal immigrants. Recently, however, some illegal immigrants have begun to bear their children on the island. In the 1970s and 1980s, women would go back to their "home" country to deliver, but this was changing as they became more aware that under French law they could not be refused medical treatment. The constant upgrading of the hospital on French SXM has contributed to this trend. Many reckoned it safer to give birth in such a modern facility. On the Dutch side illegal immigrants also bear their children on the island, usually with the help of midwives. It was rumored that in this way, certified midwives earned extra money.

Most of these children are then sent to relatives in the home countries. Danielle's son was actually born on SXM, but her parents in Petit Martinique were raising him. She and her boyfriend hadn't the time to raise him properly, and it had been a financial burden staying home the first few weeks after pregnancy. She also said that it was cheaper to raise him in her home country.

A few illegal immigrants preferred to have their children remain with them on SXM, despite all the expenses and other difficulties that came with this choice. Often these were people who had problems with family members back home. Popular politicians turned a blind eye to the matter, even when they knew that these children were enrolled in some of the schools the public funded. According to Roland Duncan, this was because all politicians knew that coming down hard on the issue of the illegal children and threatening to implement stricter custom controls were sure ways of being voted out of office. The officially registered West Indian newcomers—many of whom came from the same countries as the illegal newcomers—had electoral might, and most business owners would lobby against these policies. The latter employed these illegal immigrants as a cheap labor force. They did not have to pay any social security taxes for them and could fire them easily when things were a bit tight. Regardless of the mandates of the French Republic and the Dutch Kingdom, SXM politicians had to take the local situation into account. Hence, the money tie system was given preference above French and Dutch laws.

Many West Indian immigrants told me that even if what some immigrants were doing might be illegal, it would be unethical for government officials to punish the children for their parents' deeds. These immigrants had a fondness for local public figures who employed Christianity as metalanguage to promote this idea. One such figure was Virgillio Brooks, the representative of the Dutch Antillean Civil Servants Union and head of the local branch of Consumer International. Brooks also reasoned that, in the interest of the tourist industry, it made good sense to provide basic education for the children of illegal immigrants.

Nevertheless, like most SXMers with citizenship rights or other residence permits, Brooks did not believe in awarding the children of illegal immigrants full rights, and without full rights, these children could not apply for a scholarship to study abroad. Such a move was politically and economically unfeasible: "Then is just as well as we abolish citizenship. We can't do that. We can't afford to do that. Who is going pay us for doing that? Holland? Not Holland 'cause them makambas so cheap and won't even allow any illegals up there. [*Makambas* is a Papiamento term for a Dutch metropolitan.] I know. I does travel. At least we are doing what we can." This general sentiment was encountered on most popular radio shows as well. The idea of full rights for children of illegal immigrants was not even a topic of discussion. DJ Cimarron tried to go against the grain and propose equal rights for these children but was unsuccessful.

Because of the government's handling of the issue of children of illegal immigrants and the disappearance of most of the excess labor in leaner times, SXM remained that paradise where tourists could relax unencumbered by sights of abject poverty. Tourists were delighted that the island was so clean and orderly and that they could go wherever they wanted without the constant fear of being robbed. The SXMers seemed to get along so well. But there were tensions in the air.

Every paradise has its dark side. On SXM tensions developed when some locals reasoned that they should be the privileged nationals. Here too autochthony discourses tempered equality discourses. There seems to be a correlation between the growing importance attached to autochthony discourses and the expansion of global capitalism. The global flows of goods, finances, and laborers enhance socioeconomic anxieties and induce indigenous populations to present their autochthony as their bill of rights against foreigners and minorities (Geschiere and Njamjoh 2000; Meyer and Geschiere 1999).[4] On SXM authochthony is also strikingly gendered. Some local women were infuriated because many of their husbands were having affairs with working-class newcomers who were, they thought, only after their men's wealth. They felt that these women were immoral, as one woman told me: "Most of them women don't respect marriage. They ain't care if a man married or not."

Newcomers contested this assessment. They claimed that local women also had extramarital affairs and that everyone was aware of this. When I invited some local married women to respond to this accusation, they confessed it was true and told me about several local men who had had their hearts broken by unfaithful wives. One of these men had taken to heavy drinking after he had caught his wife in the act. This is how a local woman described the matter, playing in to stereotypical representations of British Caribbean men as studs: "He couldn't take it; I tell you he couldn't take. He see it coming in and coming out, and man with a rhythm and speed he know he couldn't compete with. Is the bottle he run to. What else he could do? 'We' men can't hang with them boys from the English islands. SXM men want to dish out horn, but when they get horn they can't take it."

I also spoke to two local women who confided that they engaged in such activities. They rented rooms where they would meet with what they called their "sweet boys." Both told me they were not about to leave their husbands but were having fun, just as they knew their men also had fun with working-class women. These women nevertheless claimed that because of the skewed societal morale, the transgressions of married women were more condemned than those of men. They felt that things were changing, however, since members of the younger female generation were more open to the idea of having sex with other men if their partners could not satisfy them in bed. They believed that because women now earn enough to be financially independent (although they still earn less than men), SXM was becoming a society in which most women who could afford it could have their "sweet boys," just as married men have "deputies."

It would seem, then, that what Caribbeanists such as Christine G. T. Ho (1999) and Raymond T. Smith (1996) have termed the *dual-union system*—men marrying within their class and then choosing a steady mistress from a lower socioeconomic bracket—was "democratizing," as middle- and upper-class women on the island had begun doing the same. Gender, although certainly not reducible to class, was becoming the venue in which socioeconomic positioning was playing out. Although men of all classes sought to maintain their patriarchal privileges, one of the unintentional consequences of the money tie system was that it led to new economic and conceptual conditions that allowed all women to contest patriarchy.

Women in female-headed households, most of which were West Indian newcomers, also displayed assertiveness as far as their sexual activities were concerned. Many told me that as the main wage earners and caretakers, their sexual acts were their personal affairs. Yaya was quite adamant about the matter. Her ex-lover, a local from the French side, was upset that she had a new boyfriend. He started showing up more often to see his daughter and even started coming by every Saturday to clean her yard. Supposedly he did not want his daughter playing among the weeds. On the third consecutive Saturday that he was playing gardener, Yaya invited her new boyfriend over. Her ex-lover got angry and started to curse, shouting that he was being disrespected, to which Yaya replied, pulling out her machete, that she was her own woman. Many of the male residents chose her side and told him that he was wrong. He left shouting that she could forget about alimony. This did not impress Yaya; she told me that she could still force him to pay it by French law.

The idea of women having a right to be as sexually active and promiscuous as men was forwarded by popular radio disc jockeys such as DJ Fernando Clarke. He employed it to claim that the xenophobia of local women against newcomers was problematic. Using the money tie system to obfuscate the dynamics of gender, class, and ethnicity regarding this issue, Clarke placed SXMers' supposed proneness to promiscuity under the rubric of humankind's sinful nature. He reasoned that this Christian motif should be the basis for an all-inclusive national politics of belonging. I will discuss his radio program in chapter 3.

The gendered nature of SXM society was real, depending on one's perspective, but it was not a privileged societal representation and therefore not an issue most women reflected on consciously. Maria Kruythoff, one of the few feminist activists on the island, lamented this state of affairs, verbalizing her frustrations: "Women on this island don't have it so bad like in other places, but they ain't have it easy either. I hate to say it, but we have a long way to go before we have any genuine female solidarity on this island. The rush for the dollar making that impossible." Kruythoff's argument about the importance of the money tie system was reiterated several times by other SXMers. Most SXMers I spoke to felt that local women's complaints about newcomers were based on their fear of losing their own privileged status. They agreed with the manner in which popular radio disc jockeys such as Fernando Clarke framed the matter of promiscuity as involving all adults, regardless of national, class, or gender distinctions. Gender did matter, but making it matter regardless of the importance attributed to it on SXM would make this a different study.[5] My choice was to follow the gender dynamics on SXM self-reflexively and sensitively, without abstracting and critiquing the lived dynamics.

There was a consensus among all classes that no one should upset the business of tourism, regardless of his or her status as local or newcomer, and there was little tolerance for anyone claiming to occupy the moral high ground. The tourists, they would say, should never be exposed to communal tensions. This belief also complicated my ability to gain the SXMers' trust, as I was reckoned to be a first world visitor coming to eavesdrop on a third world people. Western media also played an important role in constructing the supposedly irreconcilable differences between the West and the Global South.

Though it is a symbolic construct that veils a world of diversity, one of the imagined transnational identities to which many Dutch Quarter residents adhered was that of belonging to the third world.[6] It was one of their cultural resources, to use Stuart Hall's (1991) term, through which they imagined a transnational identity that suited their historical realities. In the Caribbean, identification with such an abstract category as *third world* is considered more authentic when one takes into account that the "origins" of people from the Caribbean are not localizable in the region itself. They are a transplanted people.

Even many wealthy SXMers claimed to belong to the third world, or the peripheries of the first world, in an effort to differentiate themselves from their Western counterparts. For instance, Han Hamaker, a Dutch metropolitan businessman and owner of SBN radio who had lived most of life in the United States, presented himself as a Limburger, a person from the Dutch province of Limburg. In his opinion Limburgers were always discriminated against by people living in north and south Holland. He felt that Dutch metropolitan technical assistants who stayed on the island for a year or two exhibited the same type of *Hollandse arrogantie,* Holland arrogance, that had appalled him in his youth. Their experiences of discrimination brought Limburgers closer to locals than to other Dutch autochthons.

While Hamaker and other wealthy newcomers got away with mobilizing these kinds of first world peripheral identities, I was considered a visitor from the first world, even though I had ties to the region. The term some used was *negropolitaine,* a black metropolitan. In the beginning one of the Dutch Quarter residents called Nestor, a man from Providencia who worked at the Texaco oil terminal, boldly said to me, "So they send you here to make monkey of we. Just remember to tell them that we does speak English just like them and we can read and write, thank you. Oh yeah, and tell them we is Christians too." The last phrase was significant, as being Christian seemed to allude to the historic struggle of Caribbean people to be recognized as equal to Westerners. Since in colonial times being a Christian meant being able to enjoy equal rights and being regarded as a full-fledged human being, in the Caribbean the working classes struggled to possess this identity and make it applicable to all (Hall 1999, 1995; Walcott 1998). Though there are records of black men seeking to use this identity to achieve a patriarchal equality to their white counterparts, we also need to take into account that black women contested and deconstructed these moves.[7]

Nestor's other point, that I considered SXMers exotic, that I wanted to make monkeys out of them, was not new. It was not the first time I had heard this, as Lasana Sekou, a businessman and a popular poet, had cynically interrogated me, asking whether I was an Evans-Pritchard painted black. (Evans-Pritchard is one of the most famous British anthropologists.) Sekou had been to a black Ivy League college in the United States and was well read, so I knew where he got his information from, but Nestor was another story. This was a man whom I never saw

Figure 7. Pastiche upon pastiche: the islanders playing Europe's Africa with a bit of Fred Flintstone to enhance the authenticity

read newspapers, let alone academic books. When I questioned Nestor about why he thought I would want to make monkeys of them, he replied that people on SXM had televisions. He was alluding to those who understood that I was a social anthropologist, which placed me in the category of Westerners who narrated ethnographic accounts on the Discovery and National Geographic channel about "tribes" living in Africa, Asia, and the Amazon rain forest. There was also the usual depiction of third world peoples on other, more informative channels, such as CNN America, as the victims of war and natural disasters. In the more positive accounts they were presented as excellent athletes or emotionally engaged musicians.

Traditionally Western media representations and racist depictions of black bodies, viewed as sub- or supra-human, have gone hand in hand. Blacks were reduced to stereotyped images of their bodies and to how these body selves were featured in the earliest televisual representations (Gilroy 2000; Hall 1997; Rony 1996; Wynter 1992). Although contemporary Western media are not as explicitly racist as before, "race" and, for that matter, gender remain important structuring principles. Most SXMers knew this, and I often overheard them comment at the beginning of a thriller that the dark-skinned male or female actors would be the first to be murdered. Pow, a construction worker from Dominica, phrased it this way: "If is Wesley Snipes or Denzel, well then you know they going survive. They is the star. But when you see somebody name Laquisha or Jamal—you know, one of them funny names those Americans does give they children—you done know they is the first one to get murdered. Ain't no surprise star. All man know that."

Those who read Western newspapers are also confronted with the racist depiction of blacks and the negative reporting on the peoples living in the Global South. They have ready access to these since, to satisfy the tourists who want up-to-date news about their countries, the major international newspapers and journals are readily available on the island. Many of the housekeepers brought home these newspapers, which were read together with *Today* and the *Herald,* the two locally produced regional dailies.

SXMers could read and see how Western-produced print and visual media imagined the third world. They were not the intended recipients of these newspapers and TV programs, the audience that Western editors had in mind or actively sought to keep attentive. From this position what they often saw and read disgusted them, and this disgust would be uttered on SXM's nine radio stations. The wealthy Asian, North American, and European newcomers, who bought most of the advertisement slots, financed these radio stations. Without their investments, professional radio stations with their staffs of disc jockeys were unthinkable on SXM. Predictably, the management of the radio stations did not condone critiques of these upper classes.

Since the major focus of my study is how radio disc jockeys broker the tension between the needs of the tourist industry and the issue of belonging, uncovering the ins and outs of SXM's radio landscape was an important part of my research. Only in the light of this landscape would I be able to understand the answers disc jockeys furnished as to what constitutes true "SXMness" and why they reconcile the tensions between locals and newcomers the way they do. I soon came to realize that all the radio stations are privately owned, and unlike in most other countries, there has never been a state-owned radio station on the island. This is because the appearance and growth of radio coincided with the development of the tourist industry, in which entrepreneurs and politicians who were proponents of free market ideology played a leading role. Several owners of radio stations told me that local newspapers or TV would not be economically viable: SXM's reading population was too small, and there was no competing with North American TV. Therefore, radio was the only viable local media on the island whereby global and local events were synchronized through the crafty programs of the radio disc jockeys, giving SXMers a sense of grasping the complexities of our world.

Radio disc jockeys would make sure their critiques of Western domination and racism, as presented in the media of these countries, were divorced from critiques of Western tourists visiting the island. This is how DJ Fernando Clarke blanketed his critique in a Christian idiom when he discussed the refusal of the US government to accept Haitian boat refugees: "The Cold War done so they accepting people all the way from Russia, but lil Haiti still on the black list. I wonder why? Anyway people, God don't sleep. Is the system what bad, not the tourists. They can come down here anytime to spend they money. We ain't going refuse it. The Lord say is better to be a cheerful receiver than a hungry criticizer." Even if in their hearts radio disc jockeys and other SXMers conflated their resentment of Western imperialism with the tourists who visited their island, I never caught them expressing this view in the media. Tourists were never made to feel as though they were under suspicion for the manner in which the media in their home countries Othered blacks and third world peoples in general. Neither were they confronted with the fact that their governments and big businesses wreaked havoc in the lives of billions.

My case was different, however, since I wasn't a tourist, and perhaps this was why Nestor and others were so candid with me. I came for information, not for relaxation. In addition they probably sensed that they were not deemed ethnographically interesting to the Western media. There were hardly any *National Geographic* accounts of the Lesser Antilles. They were not "third world enough," since their indigenous tongues were European languages and their native dress ranged from Karl Kani to Naf Naf. With a third to half of the Caribbean population originating in Western countries, their fantasies about the United States and Western Europe were closer to the realities there.

I felt compelled to prove that this "negropolitaine" or "Rastafarian journalist" did not forget that Caribbean people lived in the same time as those in the West. I did not have to do too much work in that area, for one of the known facts of the Caribbean is that every inhabitant of this region has to be reflective of their national and transnational identities. They all know that their roots lie elsewhere and their cultural arsenal is a creolization of borrowings from abroad (Glissant 2000; Mintz 1996; Miller 1994; Hall 1999, 1995, 1991; Mintz and Price 1976). Primarily this gave those whose ancestors arrived in the region during colonialism a sense of a transnational West Indian identity. It was nevertheless also an identity that was partly constructed through media representations.

Time, and the courtesy and respect I showed them, led Nestor and other SXMers to believe that I was not there to make "monkeys" out of them. It also helped that my mother and father resided on the island. Locals took a liking to me, and I entered their houses freely. Open hostilities were minimal, and they often referred to themselves as the "West Indian masses," highlighting their transnational commonality as Caribbean people struggling to make a living. Despite their struggles they would often reiterate that they were a happy and nonremorseful people, a One Love people. This was again another imagined transnational identity they constructed out of their cultural resources, namely, a selective interpretation of the hardships of slavery, indentured servitude, and the post-abolition period.

SXMers had no illusions that their small country would ever become a new superpower, as their indigenous elites were an extension of those in Western countries or lacked the potential to surpass elites there. Pow put it this way: "Partner, the Watheys or the Flemmings might be something on SXM, but they is little boys compared to Donald Trump or even say a Puff Daddy." Partly as a result of this awareness and the stories of regional working-class solidarity, an ethic of hospitality seemed to have been bred among them. Experience had taught them and their ancestors that sooner or later another island would overshadow theirs. Sooner or later they would have to move. They often said that SXM was on top today, but tomorrow it would be somewhere else. They were a transnational people who had kinship links that superseded the administrative boundaries that divided the West Indies into French, Dutch, English, and Spanish territories. With this transnational identity, accompanied by heroic narratives of being the ones who survived slavery and indentured servitude, came the ideal performance of being a hardworking and hospitable people who were all for equity and equality.

This transnational identity, which most working-class SXMers performed during working hours, overlapped nicely with the image most of the visiting tourists had of the Lesser Antilles. Two white-collar, middle-aged American women put it this way: "These islanders are so different from us; there is not an aggressive bone in their bodies." This was the reason why, when scouting for a place to go on vacation, they chose what most Americans simply refer to as "the islands," the touristy Lesser Antilles. No noteworthy differences among the islands are recognized, except, as these two women told me, that on SXM all the modern conveniences were more readily at hand than in other parts of the Caribbean.

These tourists' stereotypical talk is understandable when one bears in mind that even though Western media promote themselves as covering the world, SXM and many other countries of the Lesser Antilles are not considered newsworthy. What happens there is not considered part of international events because it does not impact significantly on Western commercial or national interests. Derrida phrased this issue magnificently when he stated: "Among the filters that 'inform' actuality—and in spite of the accelerated but all the more equivocal internationalization—there is this privileging of the national, the regional, the local, or indeed the 'West,' that still overdetermines all other hierarchies. . . . This privileging renders secondary a whole mass of events: all those that are judged to be far from the (supposed public) interest and the interests of the nation, the national language, the code or national style. On the news, 'actuality' is spontaneously ethnocentric" (2002: 87).

This ethnocentrism even manifests itself in the obscuring of what is considered the "foreign" within Western nation-states (Derrida 2002). This is the case even in France and the Netherlands, to which SXM is constitutionally tied, as the island is hardly ever mentioned in the mass media. Therefore, most Western tourists' images of SXM before visiting it are the media images and those of brochures of the lesser West Indies produced by the island's tourist bureaus. These images are almost identical to those produced by the tourist bureaus of other Caribbean islands. These images portray partying yet hardworking islanders, elemental Adams and Eves who welcome Westerners to their unspoiled paradises. White sandy beaches, lush vegetation, smiling faces, picturesque houses, and beautiful hotels, casinos, boutiques, and restaurants, accompanied by island rhythms, are the main ingredients of these commercials and brochures. These are what all West Indian tourist organizations present to Westerners.

The majority of the tourists that one encounters in the SXM tourist ads are white Westerners, because, as I mentioned before, they compose the bulk of the tourists who visit SXM annually. Officials I spoke to at the French and Dutch SXM tourist bureaus were also aware of the growing niche market of African American tourists—the fastest-growing market among the minorities in the United States—but reasoned that SXM could not compete with places such as Jamaica and Brazil. SXM does not have slave trails, maroon villages, or African-inspired festivals that could attract these heritage tourists. Therefore, its tourist bureaus decided to try to attract the more affluent of the African American traveling public. SXM caters to those African Americans who, like their Euro-American counterparts, want to be pampered with the finest that Europe and the Caribbean have to offer and are content to look for their roots elsewhere. The money tie system determines SXM's attitude toward Westerners, regardless of the color of their skin.

What is striking in the tourist ads is that even the landscape of the island is presented as a welcoming host inviting Western tourists to spend their dollars and euros. For instance in *Saint Martin Tourism,* one of the glossy tourist magazines distributed on and off the island, the landscape speaks, saying: "My name is Saint Martin, an island like no other. The extraordinary variety of my beaches will fulfil all your desires. . . . The Atlantic Ocean to the East, the Caribbean Sea to the West, perfect temperatures all year round, cooled by the gentle breeze of the trade winds, the thirty-six beaches of Saint Martin are so many jewels that will offer you some of the best times in your life!" The text seems to suggest that the landscape presents itself to tourists free of charge, but the visuals that accompany the words tell a different tale. Huge yellow and red parasols placed side-by-side are prominently featured and overshadow the palm trees on the white sandy beach. These parasols, along with the vacationing feeling, bring to mind the red and yellow MasterCard logo. The message? Come to relax *and* spend.

What becomes clear when one analyzes the ads produced by the island's tourist bureaus is that SXM is sold as a paradise island that is a bit French, a bit Dutch, and a whole lot Caribbean. In addition, the fact that more than eighty nationalities live on the island is presented as proof that it is paradise on earth.

Thus, as I observed during my research, the "authentic" SXM culture as presented in the ads of the island's tourist bureaus, which were primarily run by locals, was actually pan-Caribbean culture with snippets of culture from the rest of the world. Tourists, however, interacted primarily with newcomers, so this group was actually the source of tourists' positive ideas concerning SXM. The working-class newcomers who danced in the calypso revues and sold them "authentic" art produced in Haiti and Jamaica primarily signified SXM culture and the SXMers for visiting tourists.

"Authenticity" on SXM mattered little to most tourists. For instance, I often witnessed Canadian and American tourists of Eastern European descent visiting a restaurant called Olgies Perogies to eat traditional Ukrainian pierogies made by a jolly Jamaican chef named Centipede.

They were delighted that Centipede and Olga, the Canadian-Ukrainian owners, served them food made from the recipe of a Ukrainian grandmother while swinging to calypso or reggae music.

Because all SXMers could tune in to more than fifty Western TV channels, including the major US networks, BBC World, BVN, Deutsche Welle, and Canal+, and had access to Western print media, they knew how their tourist bureaus represented them. For instance, every Sunday afternoon, BET, a large US network and one of the more popular cable stations on the island, was replete with advertisements of Caribbean tourist paradises. Thus, as I mentioned before, Western representations of the world were accessible to those who worked in air-conditioned offices as well as those who spent their days gardening in the hot sun. The working classes could see what audiences in Western countries saw. This was the edge SXM had over, say, Jamaica and Dominica, places where tourists are confined to resorts and where only a few people have access to Western-produced TV and print media.

SXMers know the social performance that Western tourists expect of them, and, aware of their dependence on tourism, they embody the smiling faces on the brochures and TV ads. It would be a mistake to interpret this performance as faked, for many SXMers have come to see it as part of who they are. I stress *part* of who they are, for there are other media images that feed into their transnational self-identification. These images are ones with which Western tourists are less familiar.

In addition to the tourist friendly narratives of SXM presented by cable TV ads and glossy tourist magazines, there are also narratives of past and present struggles against Western imperialism, and these are expressed in Caribbean music. I witnessed tourists dancing to Ellie Matt's "Something Must Be Wrong" and Sparrow's "Capitalism Gone Mad" without being aware that these songs contain a damning indictment of Western geopolitics. For them, they were tunes similar to Belafonte's "Banana Boat Song," just enticing and catchy rhythms to dance to. They were oblivious to the fact that the lyrics of "Banana Boat Song" are about the exploitation of hardworking Caribbean peasants

Most tourists' listening practices were informed by the way calypso and other Caribbean music is usually promoted in their countries. It is feel-good, summer music, produced by the adorable or hedonistic West Indians. For most SXMers, listening to these musical forms also induced aesthetic and psychic pleasure, but it did more than that. It was, as many told me, their "second avenue of education," one more attuned to their experiences than the education they received in the classrooms. Musical compositions have been the main mode through which Caribbean people have documented their experiences. This is especially true of the working classes, most of whom are black: "Mark how, displaced from a logocentric world—where the direct mastery of writing, and hence, both of the criticism of writing (logocentric criticism) and the deconstruction of writing—the people of the black diaspora have, in opposition to all that, found the deep form, the deep structure of their cultural life in music" (Hall 1998: 27).

Though the music tempered the revolutionary deep structural content, dictating that pragmatism should rule above principle, the content was registered. It was a matter of knowing that the world is not an equal place, and socioeconomically West Indians are not equal to Westerners. Knowing, however, did not entail rashly doing something about it. For within that knowing, there was also the acknowledgment of West Indian complicity with the current global order. No one was outside the system, but the West benefited from this system more than others.

This understanding about the unjust world order, which includes everyone, is still being promoted by popular radio disc jockeys. DJ Shadow phrased it this way during one of his radio programs: "We music is we history books. Listen and learn." Shadow's and other SXMers' comments showed their awareness of depictions of West Indian working classes as survivors of the human carnages of slavery and contemporary forms of subordination in the various Caribbean music styles, including Rikki Jai's and David Rudder's calypso, Bob Marley's and Sizzla's conscious reggae, Juan Luis Guerra's and Chichi Peralta's merengue, Celia Cruz's and Ruben Blades's salsa, and Rara Machine's and Boukman's explosive kompa. While on other Caribbean islands the various musical forms are nationalized—soca being Trinidadian and kompa, Haitian, for example, with all the chauvinism that this entails—on SXM, despite recognition for national specificity, these genres belonged to all Caribbean people. The average SXMer danced the zouk as well as he did the dancehall and merengue, regardless of her or his extraction. A good dancer on the island was someone whose hips and feet could accommodate various rhythms. It was part of being able to perform multiple national and transnational identities.

What needs to be highlighted as a commonality among many Caribbean music forms is that the strong motif of social justice is usually cloaked in creolized Christian terms. This wrapping, or sugarcoating, to paraphrase Hall again, is "itself the subject of what is going on" (Hall 1998). It symbolizes the way the working classes in the Caribbean have

identified themselves as God's chosen people (Hall 1999; Cooper 2004).
Nestor corroborated this point:

> Partner that is we, we is a bacchanal people; a jolly people always hos-
> pitable. Like Rudder say, God is a Trini. [David Rudder is popular calypso
> singer, and "God is a Trini" refers to the representation of God as a deity
> who loves to party.] We is God's people. The Caribbean man ain't got no
> time for malice. The only time you will see us get angry is when we see in-
> justice. We can't see other people ill-treating other people. Is then the devil
> in we does come out. Even talking to you about it I can feel myself getting
> fucked up. I think that slavery thing have lot to do with. You treat a man
> like a dog here, and you will see how many people will jump up to fight
> with you. And when they done with you they going to beat that other man
> for not standing up for himself.

Nestor, like others on the island, believes that God's chosen people are
a bacchanal people and are partly to blame for their current situation.
Moreover, it is quite interesting how God and the devil are creolized to
the point that the former is presented as a partying deity and the latter is
personified by a tendency within human beings. This reveals the extent
to which Christianity has been creolized, adapted to the specificities of
the island and the wider region.

There are two general ways in which creolized Christian motifs are
worked out in Caribbean popular music. In Caribbean music that is dedicated to a more politically straightforward and explicit denunciation of
Western and regional forms of domination, the oppressed classes in the
West Indies are prefigured as the Old Testament chosen people who per-
severe and one day will overcome their subordination. They are the
modern-day transnational Jews of the Old Testament. Though complicity is admitted in these compositions, it is usually downplayed. Though
they sin, these "Jews" are God's chosen people. They may not have any
control of the flows of global capitalism, but their God, who is the creator of this universe, will never forsake them or their offspring. Herein
the more traditional biblical understanding of good and bad as opposing poles, with the meek inheriting the earth, is highlighted.

This God also acts as a guarantor who keeps the forces of nature,
specifically the annual threat of a hurricane, in check. I heard from various SXMers that the shadow side of God for most Christians on the island was the uncontrollable flow of global capitalism—on which island
or region of the world would the capitalists bestow benevolence next?—
and the potential of a typhoon to transform the luxury hotels into a heap
of rubble. Most SXMers ridiculed the idea that the devil could control a

typhoon, telling me that they had the Weather Channel and had learned in primary school how a storm system develops. God was the only one they feared, and most argued that he was against any form of hierarchy among humans. In songs dedicated to hurricane disasters, the message is "we shall overcome."

On the other hand, in songs that address the complexities of everyday interactions, "real life," the context and implications of one's actions are deemed *the* important criteria in judging good and evil. Complicity is highlighted. Good and evil are presented as opposing tendencies within humankind, and no one can occupy high moral ground. In this alternative identity construction, Caribbean people are a branch of the human family who in Christian terms are born into sin. Besides this exclusive biblical reading, this identity also ties in to the manner in which life is understood according to ideas propagated in Kali Mai, Obeah, Vodou, Santeria, Shango, and many other related spiritual philosophies found in the region. Because of the extensive creolization of Christianity in the region, these spiritual philosophies figure prominently in the daily practices of even the most devout Christians. A clear-cut boundary between religions in the Caribbean is a fiction many profess but few live (Van der Pijl 2003; Chevannes 1994, 1995; Brown 1991).

While this more complicated understanding of human potentialities and universal identity are often cited by SXMers in their everyday interactions and in evaluating their society, it is the more Manichaean view, placing Caribbean people as God's chosen ones, that comes to the fore when they discuss Western imperialism and the impossibilities of understanding nature. I had the opportunity to witness this firsthand while watching TV with some Dutch Quarter residents. I also was able to identify a third important transnational identity SXMers employed, namely, that of being members of the black diaspora.

For many people who have been subordinated by Western imperialism, mediated messages of oppression come very close to the recorded experiences that they or their forebearers have suffered (Rony 1996). Dark-skinned Caribbean people, as Maryse Conde (2000), has argued, are especially sensitive when faced with images or other representations that remind them of the time when their ancestors were made to feel inferior to light-skinned Westerners. It usually provokes an enormous anger, as they would rather not be reminded of this past.

During an encounter with some Dutch Quarter residents at the home of Yaya, I understood what Conde meant. Together we were following a Christian TV broadcast on one of the American cable channels. Yaya had called us in to observe the arrogance of a North American Seventh-day Adventist missionary on crusade in the mountainous regions of Cameroon. Hundreds of Cameroonians had gathered to hear him preach.

What disturbed Yaya and the others most was the passivity with which the Cameroonians accepted the missionary's ridicule of their customs. During his sermon he stuck a dollar bill in each ear and told the congregation that since he didn't wear his wealth on his body, they did not have to do so either, alluding to the fact that among many of these people adorning their bodies with jewelry was contrary to Seventh-day Adventists' teachings. In addition he admonished them that as good Christians, they should not engage simultaneously in the practice of "African traditional religions," for these were cults of Satan. He prophesied that until the day that they and all other Africans dedicated their lives to Christ and lived accordingly, Africa would remain a plagued continent.

Yaya and the others were so infuriated by his sermon that they seemed to be oblivious to the fact that the camerapeople, sound technicians, editors, and even the TV itself were mediating what they saw. This "mediatic real," or simulated reality, to use Baudrillard's term (1983), was real for them. In their opinion it fed into the idea of blacks needing to be civilized by Westerners. In a world where race remains a guiding fiction, blacks in the Caribbean are affected by both the negative and the positive representations of Africans, African Americans, and Afro-Europeans. As a result, a transnational identity among blacks is continuously fostered. Yaya and the others understood that these media images spurned effects as real as the realities mediated outside the purview of TV. These realities are not completely captured by the mediatic, but they are not completely free of it either. The many racialized realities we live in inflect on one another. Racist depictions in the media inform how people of different skin tones and phenotypes treat one another in their daily interactions.

Yaya and the others were so infuriated that they cursed both the Africans and the North American pastor. Rita, a thickset Guyanese in her middle years whose ancestors had been indentured laborers from the Indian subcontinent, got involved and said that poor Indians were also too compliant with those of a higher caste as well as wealthy white Westerners: "Them people there too *gatchu* [stupid]. I glad my people leave there. When you see how they grinning for PBS and the children running behind the white man for a sweety, I does feel ashamed."

Miss Maria, the oldest woman in the company, acknowledged Rita's comments. She played the transnational card, saying that as West Indians, despite the hardships of slavery and colonization, Asian- and Afro-Creoles had been blessed. She also reminded them that many of the East Indian workers on the island displayed that same slavish mentality. Rita agreed, saying that that was why she didn't take a job in a store owned by Indian merchants: "They can't stand that the caste system don't work with we anymore."

Miss Maria nodded, then ended the tit for tat with Rita, turned her gaze to the TV, and spoke to the Cameroonians and the missionary as though they were in front of her: "That is why all you is where all you is today. All you making it hard for we. Me not me, such a skinny and ugly man like you could never fool me. I keeping my Science [SXM's counterpart to Haiti's Vodou] next to my Bible. I ain't letting go of my culture for nobody. Nowhere in the Bible Jesus tell people to forget their culture. That man is a Pharisee."

The others nodded in agreement, alerting me to the fact that Miss Maria was not the only one who practiced both Science and Christianity. The manner in which Christianity became creolized, and as such was employed as a metalanguage to promote an inclusive politics of belonging, is an issue that will be dealt with extensively in this study.

Science, unlike Vodou, remains an explicitly spiritual philosophy, with its main practitioners not showing any desire to have it recognized as a specific religion divorced from Christianity. The way in which Science is intertwined with Christianity's role as a metalanguage in the public sphere, influencing how popular radio disc jockeys seek to resolve the issue of belonging, will be a recurring topic in this book.

Science provides SXMers with an alternative concept of personhood. Miss Maria informed me of an important category of spirits that practitioners of Science revere: those who had been human. Many of these spiritual beings are understood as additional selves that surround the socialized Self, "the I." Thus, there is a concept of multiple identities. One is surrounded by deceased Others who are parts of one's persona, but one cannot integrate them into the socialized Self. The dead might regain a kind of life through a living person, but they are too powerful to be controlled and assimilated. Therefore, it is deemed important to keep these identities to oneself or to share this knowledge only with intimate friends or close family members, since someone with bad intentions could abuse this information.

From observations and the few talks I had—Miss Maria and other SXMers were not keen to reveal their additional selves to me—I gathered that the specific types of additional spirits a person has breach the boundaries of one's kinship ties and gender, ethnic, and socioeconomic status. The social identities that one cannot lay claim to in the dominant societal representations are brought in through the backdoor by this spiritual philosophy. For instance, if one is black, one also has a white spirit as an additional self. These spirits seem to function as reminders that, despite one's skin color, sex, or social status, one is a product of all the men and women who lived in the region. Science is a popular philosophy, reminding SXMers of the transnational links binding them. It is the manifestation of an alternative history that resists class reductionism, racial exclusivity, and Manichaeanism. In addition through Science, each SXMer can construct an identity as a fractured individual, with all the accompanying psychological modifications, one in which every person is a transnation unto him- or herself. This belief strengthens his or her performance of relational identities.

Many black working-class women I encountered who were explicitly into Science said that they had dead family members as additional selves as well as deceased European men. Yaya confided to me that she had a white spirit who had been a wealthy man in his lifetime and who was jealous of whichever man she dated. Although she saw her daughter's father as a two-timer, she also blamed the failing of the relationship partly on herself, as her white spirit caused her to be extremely materialistic and selfish. Since it is believed that these spirits remain with you until you die, Yaya took the advice of Miss Maria on how to placate this spirit. From time to time she dined in luxury to give this spirit a sense of how he had lived during his lifetime.

Miss Maria's comments about not giving up her Science while performing Christianity spurred several reactions. Yaya, for instance, commented that through working with American tourists, she knew that many Westerners were also fond of dabbling in the occult: "You think we bad, you ain't know them. They got all kind of lucky charm to win the jackpot. When you start up a conversation with a tourist about those things, man they can't stop talk. That is the only difference between we and them. They like to talk about it. We know that ain't any- and everything you must talk about. That man there talking shit. You full a shit. You doing your thing too."

Uncle Henry, a wealthy, respected, retired local entrepreneur who owned several apartments and plots of land in the Dutch Quarter, had his own opinions. Uncle Henry was a high-ranking member of the Freemasons, which most SXMers considered a form of Science. He was known for his claims that if locals were not hospitable to newcomers,

they would summon the wrath of their deceased parents, who had survived only because of the hospitality of strangers in the strange lands they
had migrated to. This idea, borrowed from Science, made him immensely popular among working-class newcomers, who knew he always
did what he could to help them out. In chapter 5 I discuss DJ Cimarron,
who sought to build an inclusive politics of belonging based on this idea.

Uncle Henry commented that Yaya spoke the truth about Westerners
having their own occult beliefs, for there was nothing more esoteric than
the secret orders in which Western preachers were initiated. He qualified
this by saying that he was talking about the preachers of more established churches, such as those from the Seventh-day Adventist and
Catholic churches, and not to those who headed what he referred to as
"shoemaker shops," small Baptist and Pentecostal churches whose
nonordained pastors read the Bible too literally for him.

Uncle Henry retold an experience of a run-in with a Dutch metropolitan Catholic priest when he was living in Aruba. A friend of his had
passed away, and he wanted to attend the funeral dressed in certain regalia of the Lodge. He was not allowed to enter, as the Catholic priest,
the personification of the long tradition of Catholic-Freemason strife,
forbade him from entering in his regalia.[8] What angered him most were
the rude manners of the priest. Without uttering a word, he simply signaled with his hands for Uncle Henry to remove the regalia. Despite
wanting to pay his last respects to his friend, he refused to comply and
left. Weeks later he encountered the priest again at his job as one of the
heads of security at Lago, the name of the island's oil refinery back then.
The priest had forgotten the pass that gave him access to the complex.
Normally the security guards would let the priest pass, for they had respect for a man of the cloth, but on this day Uncle Henry took charge.
He told the priest that even though he was sympathetic, understood that
he had forgotten the pass, and recognized him as a priest, the rules dictated that he could not let him in. It would set a bad example for the
workers. Then without uttering a word he reproduced the same nonver-
bal gesture that the priest had displayed during the funeral of his friend.
At that moment the priest recognized him, turned around, and went to
collect his pass.

Most were delighted with the beguiling manner in which Uncle Henry
told his story, which added more luster to his status as a knowledgeable
and benevolent gentleman who was all for egalitarianism, a man who had
stood up to the priest, an embodiment of Western power. Yaya then took
the lead, saying that what Western missionaries should do is to convert

their own respective societies: "Them people only care about themselves. You mean to tell me you can have all that money and know that children in your own country hungry and you don't give a damn? Leave that man go and preach to them. And they say they is Christians." She then alluded to *Feed America's Hungry Children,* a popular TV program of the Feed the Children Fund that aired a few times a week on BET. In this program the Other America, as Kathleen Stewart (1996) termed it, the America of the endemic poverty that is the daily reality of most blacks and poorer whites, is presented "en plein publique." This program, and others that displayed the manner in which the disenfranchised of the Other America lived, was enormously popular among SXMers. A widespread rumor on the island was that some SXMers had sent donations to the program. It seemed to give them satisfaction, knowing that all was not well in what is considered to be the most powerful country in the Western hemisphere.

Though they sympathized with the poor—I often saw Yaya teary eyed as she watched the program—these shows also gave SXMers awareness. They made working-class SXMers aware that they had nothing to expect from the wealthy North Americans, who seemed oblivious to the pleas of their disenfranchised fellow citizens, white and black, for human dignity. In his seminal study, *The Fire Next Time,* James Baldwin eloquently observed this indifference to which most SXMers were exposed via cable TV: "This is the crime of which I accuse my country and my countrymen, and for which neither I nor time nor history will ever forgive them, that they have destroyed and are destroying hundreds of thousands of lives and do not know it and do not want to know it" (Baldwin 1977: 15).

Noticing my silence, Yaya asked me what I thought about the falseness of Westerners. Playing devil's advocate but with the necessary tact, I told her that while I agreed with her for the most part, I also felt that SXMers who lived relatively prosperous lives could not equivocally point fingers at wealthy Americans without interrogating their own position in the global order of capitalism. Though poverty is a relative term, the poorest SXMers were not as poor as their counterparts in the United States and many third world countries. In addition, since SXMers were not in the position of the impoverished Cameroonians represented on TV, they should be less harsh with their judgments about them.

Blacks in the Caribbean and the wider Americas make it a habit to look down on Africans. This looking down is often based on using Africa to understand the racism that has affected their own predecessors and affects them now. Africa is imagined as a motherland, while the contemporary realities are scorned as the products of degenerate peoples. From this skewed perspective, the true Africans should think and behave as the dark-skinned people in the Americas do. The starting point is thus often that of a misguided racial kinship instead of a solidarity premised on empathy or camaraderie. Caryl Phillips observes: "All is not well in Africa, but the continent is no more guilty than Europe or Asia in the atrocity department. What Africa needs is critical self-analysis, and intellectually rigorous minds and impassioned voices to dissect the past and suggest a future. What Africa does not need is a continual flow of disaffected African-Americans, wounded by race, acting out their fantasies of belonging and alienation with a presumed authenticity which is underscored by the figment of the pigment" (Phillips 2002: 93).[9]

Yaya and the others granted me that maybe their judgment was a bit harsh concerning Africans, but they reminded me that they worked hard to earn a decent living. Life was not bad for them, but it certainly was not paradise. They were not in the position of these Cameroonians, but they were also certainly not in the category of the Western tourists that visited the island. Furthermore, hinting at my position, Uncle Henry added that they were also not journalists who got paid to come to an island to investigate how poor people lived.

At that moment Trevor, a young man from Jamaica who worked as a carpenter and who had also been silent all this time, cut in. He partly sided with me but claimed that I overlooked selfishness as an essential part of human nature that capitalism privileges. Here is the gist of his long observation:

> You know something Ras, you right and you wrong. You right that we should not point fingers too easy at the Itiopians [Africans] and the Americans 'cause all man is sinners and this here is Babylon land too. A thing that all over. The money tie system all over. The only thing that is different between SXM and Africa is that here is John Pope land [part of Western Europe], so things better for the hand-to-mouth people here. But you wrong when you think that Babylon causes man to behave that way. Yes, Babylon make it worse 'cause Babylon is pure wickedness, but man will always be selfish. That is the way man plan. I am looking out for me, and you are looking out for you. I can't come to you to ask you for money 'cause you only going to say yes if you have enough for yourself. Everybody is checking for himself. So I got to fortify myself. Consciousness [conscious reggae] is what keep I man [here it means "my"] heaven clear [heaven is a Rasta term for the mind], and Science as Miss Maria says is what helps me to know how to move and get ahead. I man nah renounce that culture because I know that man there in foreign [lands] also do them things. When man a talk to the tourists they does tell man about their mysticism. They have their mysticism, and I man have his. Science, Obeah, and them things is I

man culture. It is not because of hard work or their wickedness that them
Babylonians [wealthy Westerners] living nice. You can't compare I and I to
the Babylonians. Nah, Ras, that is where you wrong. All of we selfish like
the Bible a say, sinners, seen ["seen": understanding something that leads to
a change of heart]. But why some man born in luxury and another man in
the gutter [is] a thing that is mystic. Only Jah knows. Only Jah knows why
some islands get mash up by hurricanes and others just feel a gentle breeze.
Ras, as long as the money tie system around, I going to do everything to get
ahead. We the West Indian massive got to live.

Jokingly calling Trevor Bob Marley, Yaya said she had worked all
night, so she had to take a rest. "You preaching man. You preach to him,
Bob Marley, but not too long 'cause I work until three o'clock this morning, so I got to take a rest before I go pick up Veronica." It was an indirect request for us to leave. Everyone got up and started talking about
all the things that they had to do.

As I was leaving, Miss Maria asked me if I could give her a lift to town
around two o'clock in the afternoon. It was by driving her around that
I realized that next to the wider transnational and universal identities
that SXMers employed, they also pragmatically performed multiple exclusive nationalisms. They presented themselves as members of various
nationally imagined communities.

At two o'clock sharp I honked the horn of my rented jeep at Miss
Maria's house. She looked through the window and took her time as I
sat there waiting in the jeep. It was the month of April, and the midday
sun was scorching. During April, the average annual temperature of
SXM was eighty degrees, so one did not sit comfortably in an American
Pathfinder without air conditioning. Luckily my rented jeep came
equipped with this modern convenience.

It took about ten minutes before Miss Maria finally came out of her
house. She uttered her pleasure that there was air conditioning in the
jeep, but also remarked that I should at least try to conceal my irritation
that she had taken her time getting ready. As only an older woman who
feels that she has earned the right to instruct the younger generation
could, Miss Maria told me I had much to learn. I had to learn how to
conduct myself according to who was in front of me. She used biblical
terminology to make her point: "Ain't any- and everybody you must
show your face to. That could get you into trouble. Why you think the
Pharisees choose Judas? He had greed all over he face. You might think,
What that old lady know? But you must remember I live longer than you
and I know my Bible." Miss Maria was alluding to her awareness that

social interactions involve a performance. This was especially the case on a tourist island such as SXM, where one had to produce a continuous Colgate smile for the tourists and build common worlds with fellow SXMers who hailed from various parts of the globe.

During our drive to Philipsburg, the capital of Dutch SXM, Miss Maria informed me that she had several errands to run and "hoped" that I would be gentlemanly enough not to allow an elderly woman such as herself to walk up and down in the hot sun. I replied that I had a few spare hours and was willing to help her out. That afternoon we traveled from place to place, and I felt like Morgan Freeman's character Hoke in the Hollywood blockbuster *Driving Miss Daisy*. Instead of doing her a favor, I was Miss Maria's personal chauffeur, and she was the one putting up with me.

Nevertheless, it was a learning experience, for I was quite taken by the way Miss Maria wove various exclusive senses of belonging together. She was a member of many nationally imagined communities and skillfully accentuated or downplayed these as necessary. She was a seasoned performer. Though she played her cards of national belonging according to the situation, for the most part, in the neighborhood of the Dutch Quarter, she performed her "Curaçaoness" next to her "West Indianness." She did this in a few ways. First, she used the radio to make others aware of her connections to Curaçao. She always tuned in to the broadcasts pertaining to news and events in Curaçao. When the broadcasts were in Papiamento, a language primarily spoken by the Dutch Leeward Islanders, she would turn up her radio a bit louder to make it clear to the passersby that she understood this language.[10] In addition, when she called in during the weekly calypso program of one of her favorite disc jockeys, DJ Fernando Clarke, she would usually throw in a sentence or two in Papiamento. Miss Maria also played music of Curaçaon artists and read Papiamento newspapers, such as *Ultimo Noticia*.

Another way in which Miss Maria performed her Curaçaoness was through her bodily representation. Regardless of where she was going, Miss Maria always dressed to impress, revealing that even at her age, she still knew how to take care of herself. Her predilection for fashionable clothing was considered a stereotypical attribute of Curaçaons. Because of the strong influences of Latin America on their culture, Curaçaons considered themselves, and sought to make others consider them, the best dressed and most cultured of all the Dutch Antilleans. They felt that the others displayed the stiffness and aesthetic poverty ascribed to the metropolitan Dutch and the British in general.

What was interesting was that I realized that SXMers with ties to Guadeloupe proper also performed their nationality, but in different ways. They read *Journal Caraibe du Jour*, often listened to zouk music, and regardless of their age were usually dressed in the latest French haute couture. For them local French SXMers were heavily influenced aesthetically by the bland North American fashion that predominated on the neighboring English islands. Both Curaçaons and Guadeloupeans presented themselves as the Caribbean versions of the more high-cultured and spiritually inclined Latin Europeans.

Miss Maria's performance of Curaçaoness was also quite beneficial to her in the wider society, because, politically speaking, it was Curaçao that ruled Dutch SXM. Most federal civil servants were Curaçaons, and Curaçao, being demographically and territorially the largest island, held fourteen of the twenty-two seats in the Dutch Antillean parliament. Performing Curaçaoness meant Miss Maria could claim belonging to those who ruled the Dutch Antilles. In a neighborhood where there were lots of illegal migrants anxious to obtain a work or residence permit, Miss Maria could always play the card of being in contact with some influential civil servant. This was the same for those hailing from Guadeloupe proper on the French side of the island.

On the day that I drove her around, she stopped at the office of one of the federal civil servants. I realized that through her performance of Curaçaoness, Miss Maria could appeal to a common sense of belonging to the Curaçaon nation to secure funds for an after-school foundation she co-directed with Rebecca, an Aruban-born social worker and a Buddhist who formerly practiced Catholicism. That they had different religious views mattered little to Miss Maria: "Boy, that don't mean nothing. Is for the children we doing it, and furthermore the worse thing you can do is argue about religion. Rebecca doing her thing; I doing mine. If she feel that chanting to that big belly man will do her any good, that is fine with me. Is one God anyway." The pragmatism with which Miss Maria dealt with religious differences was something I encountered among many Christians on the island. Christianity on SXM involved an extreme tolerance, even an obfuscation, of differences in faith. It was the island's public religion that superseded religious differences.

When she came out of the federal civil servant's office, she was speaking Papiamento and alluding to their common task of teaching SXMers how to govern themselves. "Nos tin ku sinanan kon ta goberna un pais [We have to teach them how to run a country]." She also enhanced her status in the eyes of the civil servant by claiming that I was a researcher from the Netherlands who could vouch for the good Christian upbringing she was furnishing the immigrant youths in the Dutch Quarter.

On that same trip, her performance of Curaçaoness was abruptly abandoned when she encountered local civil servants and politicians. At those times she was as local as local can be. She could do this because she had Anguillan ancestors who had intermarried with locals. There was no allusion made to her inclusion in the Curaçaon nation on those occasions, for she knew that regardless of politics, one of the things most local politicians and civil servants agreed on was that Curaçaon domination was unacceptable. This was because when SXM was a backwater and many of the parents of the locals had migrated to Curaçao to work in the Shell oil refinery, they were discriminated against and treated as second-class Dutch Antilleans.

Coming from SXM via Anguilla, Miss Maria was an "older head" who had personal scars from the negative treatment she had received in Curaçao. When she performed her SXMness in front of local politicians or reconstructed her experiences, she aggrandized the thrift and discipline of her parents and other West Indian newcomers in Curaçao and claimed that the autochthon Curaçaons were usually people whose ambitions were incongruent with their talents. Here she was also playing in to a well-known Dutch stereotype concerning Curaçaons, alerting me to her awareness of prejudices in the Netherlands. In addition, she highlighted that in their xenophobic behavior, Curaçaons forgot that they belonged to the West Indian transnation:

> My mother and father was hardworking. No matter what pay they were offered, they were willing to work. Now my countrymen, the Yu Korsow [child of Curaçao], that is another story. They too lazy ["they" means autochthons]. No qualifications, but they want the best job. They want to be foremen while they don't know how to work the machines. And when the Ingles [Curaçaons of English extraction] get it, man, they getting on bad telling them to leave they [the autochthons'] country. They bawling out, "Ta Yu Korsow mi ta [I am a child of Curaçao]," forgetting that we is all West Indians. We is one people. Fools. They is my people, 'cause I grow up there and my children born there, but my son, they still got to learn a thing or two. Whenever they can't dress up as they please, they does turn to finger smithing [thieving]. I know in Holland they giving Antilleans a bad name. Whenever you see an ambitious Curaçaolean woman, ask her who her people is, and you will hear, "They is West Indian [meaning British Caribbean]."

To connect with the non-Dutch West Indians in the Dutch Quarter, Miss Maria evoked her social identity as an Anguillan, making her part of the British legacy in the Caribbean. This is how she could create a sense of camaraderie with Rita and Trevor, born in Guyana and Jamaica, respectively. At those times she glorified the virtues of thrift and intellectualism among British West Indians.

Nevertheless, as with her other identities, Miss Maria was also quite dismissive at times about the British Caribbeans. For instance, at times she criticized the stuck-up nature of the working-class West Indians hailing from the former British colonies. She was especially cross about Rupert, a waiter born on the island of Dominica, with whom she had disagreed about the focus of the Kids Care foundation; Rupert believed the foundation should focus more on cricket lessons for children, instead of basketball, because cricket was a much more noble game.

> That Rupert too bold. He is not willing to put his money where his mouth is but he criticizing. He don't have no money but he talking. He always, "About the youths in Dominica this" and "When I was growing up in Dominica that." Is like SXM youths is no good. I had to set him straight. I tell him that if Columbus return today, the only island he would recognize would be Dominica. Everybody do something to the island. Build it up. Is only Dominica that remain the same. All they do there is learn to speak like the queen of England and play cricket. Not a cent in the pocket, but they want to correct everybody English and talk about how great cricket is. I don't know why he don't catch a plane back to Dominica. All of them English people like that. They must know that if it wasn't for we Antilleans, they would be starving with all they properness.

Miss Maria's actions were typical of the way SXMers negotiate their many national affiliations on the island. However, not everyone could perform every nationality at his or her whim. Although national traditions are invented, there are still traditions of invention and rules as to who can perform what (Hall 1995). These inventions have to be congruent with one's socially ascribed "roots." DJ Shadow, whom I discuss in chapter 4, denounced the whole idea of nationalism, because it cannot be performed at random. His experiences had shown him that nationalism contains the seeds of irreconcilable differences, as not everybody can perform the national identities he or she wants to. A telling example of how SXMers curtail one another from randomly performing national identities is the way Miss Maria engaged Rupert for daring to ignore these traditions of invention. Being befriended by many fringe nationalistic politicians, Rupert was one day defending the idea that the locals, as the natives of the island, should be specially privileged by law. He said that this was so all over the world, and it was only natural for these politicians to want the same in their country. This, he continued, did not mean that they would treat the newcomers as lesser citizens or abuse their power, for he knew them to be upstanding people who believed in Caribbean unity. They were for multiculturalism and curtailing the power that The Hague wielded over SXM. In his talk, he made the mistake of saying "we" when referring to the locals from time to time. Miss Maria, who had been alert to his slipups, intervened with her characteristic lucidity, saying, "Excuse me, Rupert. I forget your grandmother born here." Everyone present began laughing, and afterward I heard Uncle Henry remark that Rupert represented the unsuccessful way these politicians sought to conceal their hypocrisy and lust for power.

Like Uncle Henry, most SXMers I spoke to indicted these fringe politicians for wanting to ignite ethnic tensions on the island and for being worse than those who held power. The latter were also distrusted and accused of being corrupt and exploiting the working classes. This is the way Nestor explained politics on SXM to me:

> A little boy come from school, ask his father, "What is politics?" His father say, "Boy, you're too young to know. But let me explain it to you this way. Politics is like our household. I is your father; I am the prime minister. You is the country. Your mother is the cabinet, and your brother, the people. Oh yeah, and the maid, the working class." The boy say, "Daddy, I don't understand." Then the father said, "I know you wouldn't understand." That night his little brother shit all over him. So the boy went to the maid room to let her clean him. He saw his father screwing the maid. He went to his mother, but she wouldn't wake up. So, disillusioned, he went back to his bed full of shit. The next morning he told his father, "Daddy, now I understand politics." So the father said, "Tell me what you understand, son." The boy said, "Daddy, while the people shitting on the country, and the prime minister screwing the working class, the cabinet lays fast asleep, so the country has nowhere to turn to." That, Francio, is politics on this island.

Nevertheless, corrupt politicians who didn't espouse the ideas that SXM should be independent from France or the Netherlands and that locals should have more rights than nonlocals were the most popular. They also displayed a down-to-earth attitude, despite their wealth and power, that most SXMers appreciated. One bus driver put it this way:

> We know that all of them on the take, so we' ain't expecting miracles. Albert is the best among all of them [Albert Flemming is the mayor of French SXM]. If you hear him speak, man, you'd think he's Jesus Christ, but when you know what going on you realize that he remain a man from the Sand [Sandy Ground: a working-class district on French SXM], and you know Sandy Ground people have a tendency to bend the rules. But Albert all right, man. What I like about him is that he'll sit at the waterside and drink two rum with the boys. And he don't make distinctions between who's local

and who is not. He knows that SXM people had to go to Santo Doming
back in the days. Every shirt that man wear I can afford. That ain't so with
those who come back with their big degrees. When I hear them talking that
we need more freedom from the French man, I does think to myself, "You
ain't like me for true; you don't want me to wear that expensive shirt you
wearing." Independence ain't no good for the small man.

But the question was, Who were these local fringe politicians? Were they
an exception to the rule that one must perform multiple identities? And
what did being a local mean on this island?

Officially speaking, the category of *local,* denoting SXMers who have
ancestral ties that go back at least three generations, does not exist. According to the French and Dutch census definitions, *locals* are persons
born on SXM. This means that the children of newcomers from such far-
flung places as Hong Kong are just as local as someone whose mother
and grandmother were born on the island. This is the official state of
things. And most SXMers want it to remain this way, as revealed by their
vote to remain part of the French Republic and the Dutch Kingdom
(Oostindie and Klinkers 2003; Oostindie and Verton 1998).[11]

Even if one puts aside the official definition of *local,* there is also the
issue that the origins of those who call themselves locals are more like a
Caribbean mangrove tree than the neat and orderly arrangements found
in the Generalife garden. Clear-cut lineage, based on procreation solely
within one's ethnic group, is an identity few locals can seriously claim.
Their family histories typically resemble what George Lamming (2001)
has aptly termed a "family of islands." All the locals I encountered had
grandparents, aunts, uncles, nieces, nephews, or spouses who had been
born elsewhere. No one had roots that were not traceable back to other
countries. Creolization is the rule rather than the exception. On the most
superficial level, this is symbolized by the surnames locals carry, which
are found throughout the Caribbean: Arrindell, Richardson, Regales,
Flemming, de Weever, and Brown.

This creolization goes even further, penetrating the supposedly purest
of realms: religion. Popular religious leaders such as Father Charles and the
Pentecostal preacher Norma Reyes told me that local families were not
only multiethnic but also ecumenical. Catholics, Methodists, Pentecostals,
Muslims, and the occasional Buddhist and agnostic had to relate to one another during family reunions. They did this by visiting one another's
churches and by encompassing opposite views under a creolized Christian
cloak. These families were by no means exceptions, as this Christian tolerance prevailed on SXM. This is an issue I deal with in chapter 3.

Nevertheless, creolization does not erase the existence of SXMers who can claim that they are autochthons. How could there not be those who wish to self-identify as autochthons in a world of nation-states and UN agencies promoting the rights of indigenous peoples? The dominant logic among most locals is to occupy a position of localness in a temporary and pragmatic fashion. It makes little sense to do so all the time in a country where the performance of multiple national and transnational identities is what guarantees one a better living. For instance, it probably would have been counterbeneficial for Miss Maria to stress her identity as a local in her dealings with federal civil servants from Curaçao. Pragmatism is the name of the game among most locals.

There are certain locals who emphasize their autochthony: the fringe nationalistic politicians. To be truthful their numbers are small, but they exist. One can divide these politicians into two camps: the *independistas* and the *reformistas*. The *independistas*, or independence fighters, are headed by the Larossos, a pair of brothers born and partly raised on Aruba who seek complete independence from France and the Netherlands. The Larossos are middle-class entrepreneurs whose main businesses are real estate and publishing. They have enjoyed the finest schooling in the United States. In their talks they constantly emphasize slavery and the UN Charter, which states that every colony should become independent. The charter also states that the formerly colonized can choose a form of federalism or full incorporation into the West, annulling the necessity of formal independence, but this is conveniently not mentioned. For them it is a matter of principle that SXMers sever political ties with those who enslaved them and who still treat them as dependents to be exploited. Reclaiming the heritage of local SXMers—the way slaves cooked and danced, for example—is enormously important. They believe that all SXMers should understand their history within a theoretical framework of anti-imperialism, and this is a point they constantly stress. They also emphasize that the "core culture" of SXM is based on respect, tolerance, decency, and an untiring work ethic and that both locals and newcomers have to acknowledge this.

During the early months of my stay on the island, I visited a few of the Larossos' lectures and cultural presentations. I thought they would attract hundreds of locals. I thought disgruntled local women who accused working-class newcomers of seducing their men would be present, endorsing the Larossos' claims about the "core culture" of SXM. I thought I would witness the mass hysteria of exclusive nationalism. I was wrong. The Larossos' presentations are attended by a handful of like-minded individuals who are in fact their close friends. There were never more than fifty people, and most were middle-class black locals like themselves.

The Larossos' problem is that their historicizing appeals only to people who can trace their ancestry back to those who were enslaved by the Dutch or the French. And many of those who can are not too interested in that history. Moreover, the roots of most SXMers lie elsewhere. There is also the embarrassing fact that many prominent white locals descend from the plantation elite. The Larosso brothers seek to circumvent this problem by emphasizing pan-Caribbeanness; they never explicitly blame the white locals for slavery. Their quarrel is with the West, because during colonial times, all Caribbean peoples, whether Afro-, Asian-, or Euro-Caribbean, were considered less than those who resided in the Western metropoles.

When the Larossos stress this pan-Caribbeanness, they run the risk of ostracizing those who recently came to SXM or whose parents migrated from Europe, the United States, or Asia. The Larossos have an impossible task. They can never get it right, for people like Rita take issue with the uppity behavior that some Asian merchants (and other wealthy newcomers) display toward her and other Asian Guyanese. Yet to get these wealthy newcomers on their side, the Larosso brothers nevertheless include them among SXMers for whom there will always be a place after the country gains its independence. They are constantly slipping and sliding to include all SXMers against France, the Netherlands, and the rest of the West. At the same time they continue stressing that the "core culture" of SXM is that of the locals. And while they are never explicit about it, they believe that the locals should hold the most prominent place in their scheme of things. The Larossos' politics can be described as a failed populism.

The second group of fringe nationalistic politicians, the *reformistas,* has gathered around the Baines brothers, who are also Arubans by birth. Like the Larosso brothers, they too are middle-class entrepreneurs. However, the Baines studied in the Netherlands, where they were active in the black power movement. They are far less inclusive than the *independistas.* They are unequivocal in their views that the locals should always come first. They believe that laws are needed that privilege the "true" sons and daughters of the soil, even though they themselves were born on a different soil. And this they feel can be done within the Dutch Kingdom and the French Republic, even though they accuse The Hague and Paris of racism. SXMers should always keep one eye open while dealing with white French and Dutch metropolitans. The issue of SXM's integration with Europe is not something they stress. The Hague and Paris are still the bosses, as far as they are concerned.

Of the two groups, those gathered around the Baines brothers have been less successful. Speaking to me about the Baines's black power rhetoric, Violet, my landlady from Aruba, noted that the sweetest part of the joke is that the youngest and most vocal of the two is married to a white Dutch metropolitan. Thus, while he claims whites are not be trusted, he goes home and sleeps with one. She went on to state that the older brother struts into town with his Jamaican and Guyanese girlfriends while spouting his "locals must come first" speeches during public meetings. By unveiling the gender-based incongruencies of the Baines's politics, Violet disrupted their black and ethnic nationalism.

I understood that my landlady was voicing a common criticism. During a public gathering on environmental matters, Baines senior took the opportunity to espouse his hyper-nationalism. He claimed that many working-class West Indian newcomers are uncouth and are destroying the ecology of the island. The real threat, according to him, is the influence these West Indian newcomers are having on local youngsters. His Jamaican girlfriend, who was ten to twenty years younger than he was, sat doing her nails without the least bit of irritation. After the session she took him in her arms, and they left as though nothing had happened. When I asked the woman who sat next to me what she thought about this, she said that everybody on the island knew that Baines "loves to run his mouth." She continued that his girlfriend could care less what he said, because what mattered to her was that at the end of the month he would give her money to send to her child in Jamaica. More tellingly, the men at the gathering were less impressed with Baines's words than with the question of whether an old man like him could satisfy such a young woman.

I heard from other SXMers that the Baines brothers also forget about their nationalistic principles when it comes to making money. They have no qualms about privileging newcomers above fellow locals if more money can be made that way. Many recalled that after Hurricane Luis of 1995, homeless locals had to wait while the Baineses repaired the houses of wealthy newcomers who paid them more. Their quest for laws that favor locals is read as a ploy through which they hope to become as powerful as the wealthy newcomers. They want more government contracts for their construction company.

In contrast to the monetary motivation of the Baines brothers, power and status motivate the Larosso brothers' political quest, according to most people I spoke to. They want to go down in history as being the people who led SXM to independence. Uncle Henry told me this is the only way they can come close to their deceased father's shadow, as José Larosso Senior was an astute businessman and politician. In the hands of his sons, the Larosso holdings have not grown. Miss Maria was even more cynical as she told me that what the Larossos forget to mention in their glorification of the locals' core values is infidelity. She claimed that their father, who was a handsome man, had several mistresses. Rumors abound that these two apples have not fallen far from the tree: they forget about the core value of decency when they visit the many brothels on the island.

Localness is a position that no local can occupy all the time, not even the staunchest nationalists. The reality of the money tie system cannot be denied. Everyone knows this, even though many commended the Larossos and the Baineses after one of their public talks. Without mentioning their names, DJ Shadow has exacerbated people's distrust in them and their quest for more autonomy from France and the Netherlands. The popularity of DJ Shadow and others, such as Fernando Clarke, has stemmed from the disc jockeys' employment of a Christian discourse to obfuscate class, ethnic, gender, and even creedal differences. What the Larossos term the core culture of the locals, successful radio disc jockeys dub a manifestation of Christian values. By doing this they cease to be ethnically specific and instead become universal. This is the message that most SXMers I spoke to wanted to hear. As Trevor aptly phrased it: "Americans, Indians, Haitians, Dominicans, Chinese, all nations here. It is the nations that build up SXM. This is what make SXM what it is. But a lot of people does forget that, and that is why everybody looking out for themselves. The Christian leaders should be talking about that, Overs. Catholic, Rasta, Methodist, Seventh-Day, or whatever, them should unite. Them all is Christian anyways, Overs."

For Trevor, as for many other SXMers, Christianity is a metalanguage to talk about and simultaneously promote an inclusive politics of belonging and moral behavior. If every society has religion—a transcendental and integrative sense of itself, as Derek Walcott (1999) has asserted, a point originally made by Émile Durkheim (1984, 1954)—then, as in the rest of the Caribbean, SXM's public religion seems to be Christianity. Christianity, as a religious tradition, has undergone a peculiar adaptation on little SXM.

CHAPTER 3

Christianity as a Metalanguage of Inclusiveness

I knew that Violet was angry with Mervin by the way she spoke to him. Her eyes were filled with rage. He had had the audacity to disturb her afternoon quiet by using a portable amplifier and microphone to give an open-air service within a few meters of her yard. Violet, my landlady and a certified nurse, yelled at Mervin, a Saint Lucian missionary who had arrived on the island a few weeks ago, for breaking the law, as he was making noise without a permit on her family's land. What was even more heinous, according to her, was that Mervin's actions were symbolic of his feelings that she and her working-class neighbors needed salvation, that they were not Christian enough. She felt insulted and told him that had they been in Belle Air or the Low Lands where the elites lived, he would not have been so intrepid.

Mervin never showed up again, for Violet was not the only one he had angered. I heard from others in the neighborhood that they too had told him off. They worked hard all week in the tourist industry, and the last thing they wanted to hear on their day off was someone lecturing them about not being good Christians. Unwittingly, Mervin was doing the same thing the Western and Caribbean elites of old had done when legitimizing the subordination of poor people by claiming that they were not good Christians and therefore not fit for equal citizenship. In Violet and her neighbors' opinion, being a Christian meant being for equity, equality, and, in its most concrete form, tolerance. A Christian could not refuse anyone membership to SXM society.

Moreover, these people sent their children to church, and the elderly always said a prayer for them, so who was Mervin to judge them? The Lord understood that after retirement they would return to active church life and be more steadfast in their faith than they were now. As children they learned the rituals, as adults they immersed themselves in "the worldly," and as older people they lived in a pious manner. This understanding of what it meant to be a Christian, and how the different generations should perform Christianity, was widespread and accepted on the island.

What this short vignette alludes to is that the needs of the tourist industry and the perennial struggle against the hierarchical conceptions of society prevalent in the West Indies work in tandem to curtail world-renouncing forms of Christian piety. Most SXMers employ Christianity as an idiom, a metalanguage promoting an inclusive belonging that transcends an individual's specific denomination. This inclusive politics of belonging is also the template they employ to construct a transcendent sense of "society" and an overall system of morality based on tolerance.

The idea of belonging to the territory of SXM cannot be taken as a social fact that has existed since time immemorial. Everyone's "roots" lie elsewhere. Some SXMers trace their roots back to their parents' birthplaces in Asia, Africa, or Europe, while others know that during colonial times, their ancestors were forced to cross the Atlantic or did so by choice.

Most societies have a religion—a transcendental sense of themselves—and on SXM, Christianity occupies this place. Christianity is the public religion, the metalanguage, but one that is kept at a distance from issues of conversion or inner belief, which are considered private matters. Thus, although religious belief is considered a matter for the private sphere, the public sphere is explicitly infused with a Christian meta-idiom whose primary function is to promote tolerance and an inclusive sense of belonging while condoning the money tie system. Because of the leeway that SXMers give themselves in interpreting the Bible to fit their realities, even the figures of the devil and God are being reconfigured. The devil is becoming more human, while many of the social practices attributed to him are slowly being ascribed to God. For many it is impossible that God should be against vices such as gambling and hedonism, since the majority of his flock on the island encourage tourists to engage in such activities.

Many different religions are practiced on SXM. I have met Christians, Baha'is, Hindus, Muslims, Jews, Sikhs, Buddhists, and Vodou practitioners, to name but a few. On the island one can find a mosque, a synagogue, Hindu temples, Vodou shrines, and other places of worship where non-Christians can gather. Nevertheless, churches constitute the greatest number of houses of worship, and Christians account for almost two-thirds of the population. SXM's churches are not gigantic cathedrals or modern masterpieces employing radio or television to convert sinners. Such operations are not viable on an island of seventy thousand. Most Christians I interviewed said they would not be interested in media that catered exclusively to the Gospels. As one informant put it, "That is boring. We Caribbean people like variety. I love Jesus, but, Lord, I can't hear them call his name the whole day."

The prevalence of this attitude was made even more evident by the fact that a few months prior to my arrival on the island in 2003, a group of churches had started Radio Maranatha, a gospel radio station, but they had to close shop since businesses on the island declined to buy advertisements.[1] The major sponsors of radio stations are nominal Christians or Muslim, Buddhist, or Hindu merchants. They have no problem with sponsoring Christian-oriented radio stations, but a Christian radio station dedicated to promoting the Gospels went too far for them. They want to invest only in nominal Christian activities or those that promote ecumenism. They cannot be accused of being unfair, for neither do they campaign for Hindu or Muslim programs on the radio. They are content with a Christian-inflected but not wholly Christian local media.

Regular churchgoers also refused to add extra money to the collection plate to support Radio Maranatha. Some told me that if they wanted to listen to gospel music, they could tune in to one of the gospel radio stations from neighboring islands, which were qualitatively much better. Many nonchurchgoers, however, suggested that regular congregants could not stand listening to gospel all day long. I noted that regular churchgoers usually kept their radios tuned to non-gospel radio stations in their homes. SXMers preferred Christian-oriented radio that was not entirely infused with gospel and sermons on righteous living. Yet Christianity remained important; it served as a stamp of approval to legitimize the social actions of public figures, even those not linked to churches. All the DJs who gained popularity demonstrated their reverence for God and brotherly or sisterly love, but they played primarily conscious reggae, calypso, hip-hop, and whatever else was hot and happening on the Caribbean and North American charts. The only time one heard gospel on the radio was weekday mornings from 6:00 to 7:00 A.M. and on Sunday until the early afternoon.

TABLE 2. RELIGIOUS AFFILIATION
ON DUTCH SXM
In percentages

Roman Catholic	40
Methodist	12
Evangelical	12
Seventh-day Adventist	6
Baptist	6
Anglican	4
Other	13
No affiliation	7
Total	100

SOURCE: Central Bureau voor de Statistiek, Census (Wilhemstad, Curaçao: 2001).

NOTE: Three qualifications need to be made. First, the category *Evangelical* serves as a container for all that does not fit into the other Christian categories. Under the rubric of *Evangelical* one encounters various forms of worship, many of which are syncretic. For instance, on the island I visited Pentecostal churches where Baptist style was practiced, as well as neo-Pentecostal churches where spirit possession was not practiced. The category also includes revival churches brought to the island by Jamaican migrants, Jehovah's Witnesses, and Mormons. The second qualification is that on Web sites advertising the island, one will find mentioned the importance of Catholicism and Methodism, but also Vodou and Hinduism, which are not explicitly measured in the census. See, for example, www.st-martin.org/us/discovery/art_and_culture.php. The third qualification, which has nothing to do with these census figures per se, is that based upon conversations with civil servants on French SXM, I presuppose that the percentage of Catholics on that side of the island is higher. This has to do with the population of metropolitan and Haitian SXMers, who are usually Catholic. The census of French SXM does not record religious practices.

In correlation with their radio preferences, SXM Christians usually downplayed denominational differences. According to the census, 40 percent of Christians were Catholics and 12 percent were Methodists, but most simply referred to themselves as Christians. The remaining 48 percent consisted of practitioners of other denominations or other faiths and those without affiliation.

An inclusive Christian politics of belonging that did not require an exclusive allegiance to a particular denomination was often articulated among nonchurchgoing Christians. This was also the case among active churchgoers. To give an example, Ben, a Vincentian construction worker and staunch Catholic, argued that regardless of doctrinal differences, all Christians were one. He described the different types of Christians as disguised Catholics:

> You have all kinds of churches here on the island—Baptist, Anglican, Church of God—but it is all the same. I say, any church that worships on Sunday, regardless to what they say and what they think, they are basically Roman Catholic churches. The Roman Catholic Church is the original church. It is the first one who brought it about in the first place. So if you choose to do the same thing as them, that means you are just a side branch of the original

church. I never meet any other church besides them. Different people find different things, but all of them using the Bible that the Catholic Church edit. We are all Christians 'cause it is from the Roman Catholic Church that all churches learn that a believer in Christ is to be called a Christian.

Ben's inclusive talk does indicate a hierarchy, since he believes that Roman Catholicism is primary, encompassing all other Christian denominations and yet converging with them. The creation of hierarchy is a well-known phenomenon among persons who promote ideologies of equity and equality based on ecumenical arguments. Gerd Baumann writes: "The belief in convergence with the 'Other' and the claim to encompassment of the 'Other' appear thus as two sides of the same coin. What one dynamic grants, the other claims back. Thus is tolerance of, and more than that civic equality with the 'Other' reconciled with an overarching, selectively encompassing 'own' claim to truth. Both of these dynamics, beliefs in convergence and claims to encompassment, can coexist in the same social arena and indeed the same informants' minds" (Baumann 1996: 186). Nevertheless, one of Ben's intentions, while employing convergence and encompassment strategies simultaneously, was to promote an inclusive politics of belonging for Christians. If all Christians were Catholics, then there should be no discrimination among them.

However, convergence and encompassment do not necessarily go hand in hand. For instance, Ida, a Curaçaon-born Pentecostal preacher who also worked in the Department of Culture, endorsed Ben's remarks while sophisticatedly stripping them of their encompassing strategy by introducing spirituality, suggesting that one could differentiate between spiritually connected Christians and those who were not. Spiritually connected Christians could be found in all churches, Catholic or otherwise:

When you hear people like that gentleman say those things, you must remember that what he is saying has a lot of truth to it. Our foundation was Catholic and Methodist. It is only later that the others sprang up. So the foundation of SXMers is Catholic or Methodist. In searching they took in others. I always say we should not criticize the Catholic Church all the way, 'cause they did good things. The nuns did good things. They built churches and schools. It is from them that we are where we are today. But if you look at a lot of things the Catholic Church does, and I am one that will not condemn them because I respect all churches, a lot of the things are not identical to what the Bible says. But with time, they gave it certain flair and made it nice and acceptable, for people to want it. We would say then you compromise spirituality. So we Pentecostals brought it back. What is important is to remember that religion is man-made, in my opinion. It is structural and institutionalized. Christianity is about spirituality. Someone can be Catholic but very much in connection. You have Catholics who read the Bible for themselves. And there are Pentecostals who don't read their Bible and it is gathering dust. It is about the relationship of individuals with Christ. So while I might be Pentecostal, I believe we can't be separated by religious institutions. We have to come together as the bride of Christ.

Another similarity between Ida and Ben was their refusal to criticize other religions. While non-Christians were not categorically excluded from their inclusive politics of belonging, that politics was marked by Christian rhetoric. When asked about Hindus, Ben's reply was: "I can't deal with no religion where I can't eat meat. No, I joking. You cannot condemn what you don't understand, right? Only when you know it can you really say something, right? That is only ethical. But from the little that I can see they worshipping the same God as the Catholics." Similarly Ida commented: "If you haven't studied something, you can't form a judgment. Right now I attending some Buddhist sessions to know what it is about. By studying another religion, you can better understand your own and see how they meet."

Ida and Ben refused to use Christianity as an idiom of exclusion. For them, Christianity was defined by its inclusiveness, by its tolerance for religious difference. Most of the SXMers I knew, who rarely attended church, were equally eloquent and pragmatic in explaining why they accepted other religions as alternative pathways toward God. They were firm in their belief that good living was possible only if one practiced the ideology of "live and let live." This stance was usually legitimized by their claims of being good Christians who adhered to the imperative "Do unto others as you would have them do unto you." For instance, Terry Gumbs, a social worker from Aruba and the head of one the island's largest community centers, believed that criticizing her fellow SXMers who professed other beliefs would be un-Christian:

> God does not want me or anybody to be unhappy, so why should I stand in the way of anyone who believe he or she can find happiness praying to Buddha or whoever. I have my way that I know is good, but if you feel like doing it another way, that's your business. So it is not that I completely accept the other religions and say that they are good; it is more that I accept that my friends, colleagues, or neighbors choose these. Once they don't bother me, I don't really bother them. Listen here. Christianity for me is in one sentence, "Do unto others as you would have them do unto you." So [it is] helping your neighbor, giving good advice, being honest. These things. It is also having an intimate relationship with God, Jah, Buddha, or however one chooses to call the Supreme Being. A true Christian will not criticize his neighbor's religion.

If a true Christian did not criticize his or her neighbors' religion but accepted it as another avenue toward God, then calling oneself a Christian on SXM was an appropriate way to talk about and promote an inclusive politics of belonging that went beyond denominationalism. The more I observed and interacted with the island's population, the more I saw that presenting oneself as a Christian required people to go beyond the boundaries of denominational exclusiveness. Performing the role of a Christian on SXM did not mean that one belonged to any exclusive church. Christianity was employed as a metalanguage to talk about and promote inclusive belonging, regardless of one's participation in church life or other religious organizations.

Most SXM Christians had loose ties to churches. They were Christian Creoles in word and deed, religious *bricoleurs*. They engaged with one another's denominations and borrowed extensively from non-Christian religions. Ben, who was a devout Catholic, also attended the Seventh-day Adventist Church and had no qualms about visiting Obeah sessions. He tied this to a personal politics of inclusive belonging:

> Of course I visit an Obeah doctor, plenty of times. Anybody tell you they never do that, they are lying. When things gone wrong and the doctor can't help, the priest can't help, well, then, it is the Obeah man you turning to. Every night I will light a candle for the spirits. I do it for the saints in the church and for the spirits at home. A little bit of everything never hurt anybody. The same thing goes for visiting other churches. We Caribbean people love to visit each other's churches. I am a Catholic, but from a very early age I went to the Seventh-day Adventist school, 'cause the principal was my father's friend. I know all the doctrines. I know all about it, but I have never been baptized. The same thing goes for the Anglican Church. But even then I would still also go to the Catholic Church. To me the whole thing is so ethical, why people don't decide to see themselves as members of one church. Just understand that they are all side branches of the original church. Some say that can't happen because everybody have different beliefs. But that is nonsense. What makes anybody believe that their belief is right and another person's wrong? At what point and where do you determine that my beliefs is wrong and yours right? 'Cause the bottom line for me is that when it is all said and done, it is all about a belief. So I am going to believe all the things that suit me, even though I was baptized in the Catholic Church.

Ben, like many other SXMers I interviewed, invoked what Caribbeanists have termed the *dual* or *multiple memberships* of Christians in the region. Daniel Crowley sought to capture this flexibility and pragmatism with regard to performing various societal identities when he stated that most West Indians feel "no inconsistency in being a British citizen, a

Negro in appearance, a Spaniard in name, a Roman Catholic at church, an Obeah (magic) practitioner in private, a Hindu at lunch, a Chinese at dinner, a Portuguese at work, and a Colored at the polls" (1957: 823). What we see as fixed identities, many West Indians see as "coats" they put on or take off, depending on the context.

While she most likely had never heard of Crowley, Ida argued similarly, claiming that performing contradictory and varied religious rituals was part of a wider Caribbean phenomenon, even if it had taken on an exaggerated form on SXM:

> In the Caribbean on a whole people are very spiritual minded. You'll hardly find people in the Caribbean that are totally atheist. And if they are they don't hide it, 'cause they know in the Caribbean, everything goes. I think those people are lost, but as a Christian I cannot condemn them. But anyway, because of the influences we have on SXM, from the different countries, islands, and what have you, there is a lot of information passed about among the people. Most of us don't have strong roots in one religion. We have the tendency of taking in bits of different religions and accepting all. So Christianity here is a very peculiar thing. This is so because of the many nations on this island. On other islands you won't find it that strong, though it is there throughout the Caribbean. You have people who will say yes they are Christian, but you will then find them practicing things of different religions. So they will be Christian but practicing Vodou and Science. For them there is no clear definition. This is due to the influence coming from different places and people. The other thing is that people, Caribbean people in general, do not like too much discipline. They do not want to be a total Christian, because there are certain expectations. So they rather be on their own and take in bits and use it to their own convenience. And this is what you find most of the time. In other countries, you will find that a Buddhist is a Buddhist, and he will not go in another person's temple or get involved with another religion. And therefore he doesn't know what it contains but condemns it. All they know is theirs. Here on SXM, most people are not like that. Many are not rooted but yet they are Christian minded. Most people in the Caribbean are brought up knowing the Word [Christian teachings], but regular church attendance, that is something else. To defend themselves, they can talk the Word like the best of them, hold a conversation with Billy Graham about scripture, if you know what I mean.

Two points can be drawn from Ida's comments. First, for most SXMers it was not a contradiction for Christians to practice Science. Most Christians did not regard Science as a religion but more as a spiritual philosophy that ties in to one of the conceptions of personhood to which they subscribed, in which people are accompanied in life by a host of spirits that they must placate. If they do so, these spirits will work to help them be successful in life. Science was highly regarded because many believed that by performing the appropriate rites connected to this spiritual philosophy, they would be more successful in the money tie system. What follows is a brief elaboration on Science's relationship to other spiritual philosophies.

Ben's comment that if the doctor and the church can't help, then one visits the Obeah man fits into the logic of Science, as Obeah is similar to Science in its belief that spirits exist and must be appeased. In fact many SXMers referred to the spiritual philosophies prominent on other islands as a kind of Science. This coincides with the findings of several Caribbeanists, who have noted the widespread use of the term *Science* in the wider British Caribbean as a pseudonym for Obeah and Shango: "The Obeah man has long been known as a professor; Edwards wrote in 1794, 'It is very difficult for the White proprietor to distinguish the Obeah professor from any other Negro upon his plantation.' This term is still in use. Much more modern, however, are science man, scientist, and scientific man" (Cassidy 1961: 242).

Building on this, others such as Stephan Palmié (2002) have argued convincingly that the term *Science* is an indication that practitioners of this spiritual philosophy wish to demonstrate that their tradition is not superstitious, static, or against modern innovations. Trial and error and a constant search for innovative techniques and truths that suit the times are important for practitioners of Science. The name *Science* or *Higher Science* in the Caribbean seems to have come about at approximately the same time as the European and North American practitioners of life sciences were rising to ascendancy in Western Europe and North America. Businesses trading in occultism during this time were not as forgetful as the established scientific institutions that prominent scientists such as Newton and Descartes engaged in alchemy and Rosicrucianism (Palmié 2002: 204). One such business, the famous DeLaurence Company, often sold its supra-scientific merchandise to West Indians, and such esoteric classics as the *Petit Albert* and the *Sixth and Seventh Books of Moses* were incorporated quite early into the repertoire of Obeah men and women of the region.[2]

Besides the heavy influence of Western-derived occultism, one can discern the distinguishable traces of African religious motifs in Obeah and Science. They are only traces, for the distinct African understandings of the sacred were not brought to the Caribbean as full-fledged religions, since the slaves came from various parts of Africa and had different religious systems (Mintz and Price 1976). All these systems were reconfigured and fused with Asian and Western occultism and, most of all, Christian elements.

Only on the larger islands and in mainland countries, where the descendants of slaves were better able to escape the condescending gaze of the colonizers, did some Afro-Caribbeans, helped by whites and Asian-Caribbeans, further concretize these philosophies into religions. They formed secret societies, such as the Candomblé and Shango houses, and were persecuted as late as the twentieth century for their beliefs (Mahabir and Maharaj 1996; Simpson 1978; Da Costa Lima 1977).

On such a small island as SXM, the creation of secret religious societies with abstractly formulated precepts was virtually impossible, and this may explain why Science did not evolve into a religion distinguishable from official Christianity. The Bible became one of the main books for practitioners of Science. Miss Maria once told me, "Somebody could read a psalm to blight you or to cure you. It all depends on which verses you read in the Bible." Science remained a way of life, and practitioners were not asked to renounce Christianity. After all, it was not considered a religion per se. Nonetheless, while Science is distinguished from Christianity, the Bible serves as the ultimate source of legitimacy for this spiritual philosophy. As Miss Maria explained:

> My son, you think that we here alone. Besides God, the greatest spirit of them all, you have all other kind of spirits around us. Mysterios [orishas] and defunto [the deceased], as we does say in Papiamento. Some defunto might be a favorite aunt or uncle who passed away. Some of them is complete strangers. Read your Bible and you will see. You got to deal with the spirits, 'cause they dealing with you. That is what Science is about. Religion ain't got nothing to do with it. Religion does talk about these things, but Science teaches you how to deal with them. In we culture we learn it from those who gone before us. My grandmother, who teach me a thing or two, was a God-fearing woman, so nobody can't come and tell me that God against Science. Anybody talk that foolishness with me, I telling them to back it up with scripture.

Miss Maria is no exception. On SXM the Bible is employed to lend legitimacy to, or promote tolerance toward, non-Christian philosophies of life. This brings me to Ida's second point: most Caribbean people have Christian beliefs without being regular members of a specific church. This provided an important clue to what was happening on SXM, pointing to a lacuna in many studies of Christianity in the New World.

Most studies of Christianity in the New World have actually been about devout members of denominations or about how these denominations are able to shape the lives of their members. In reading these, one is struck by the way Christianity in the Caribbean and the wider Americas is depicted as a religious battlefield in which the various denominations denounce one another's practices as heretical (e.g., Martin 1990; and Stoll 1990). In addition most studies show that Christians are even more intolerant toward practitioners of Vodou, Kardecian Spiritualism, Candomblé, and other spiritual pursuits considered demonic and backward.

In an effort to simplify and clarify matters, some scholars have tended to claim that the Catholic-Protestant struggles of the European Reformation are being fought out in the Americas (Martin 1990; Stoll 1990). This presentation of the matter reduces what is in fact a much more complex picture. In the Americas, "race," ethnic, and class logics cause Protestants and neo-Protestants such as Methodists and the Baptists to denounce one another as much as members of the various factions in the Catholic Church do (Harding 2000; Levine 1992). Liberation theologians are quite critical of Catholic Charismatics, whose emphasis on spirituality, they claim, lulls the poor into an acceptance of the status quo. They may feel more akin to Social Gospel preachers, who evoke similar arguments against Charismatic Protestant churches, where "miracles" take place every Sunday morning (West 2004, 1988). This commerce in miracles, they argue, takes attention away from the structural inequalities in the United States and the wider world. Moreover in the "dynamic" Protestant camp, Seventh-day Adventists will not hesitate to criticize what they perceive as the heretical practices of Pentecostals. Simple dualisms in which one has the hierarchical structure of Catholicism on one side and the dynamic creativity of (neo)Protestantism on the other will not do. Above all, as Ida's comments intimate, depicting Catholics as nominal believers and Protestants as devout ones is a problematic reduction.

Similarly, in most studies of Christianity in the Americas, only sparing attention is given to spiritual philosophies such as Vodou, and it is argued that "true" Christians will have little to do with them. The distinction that even many of these "true" Christians make between, on the one hand, Vodou and Kali Mai as spiritual philosophies that can easily live alongside Christianity and, on the other, Vodou and Kali Mai as codified religions is overlooked. Scholars such as Frederick J. Conway (1980) and Diane Austin-Broos (1997) demonstrate that overlooking this subtle distinction leads either to the idea of Christian denominations encompassing other belief systems or to the notion that religious creolization is an exception rather than a rule.

It is interesting to note that while it has become standard to argue that Pentecostals are the most exclusive of the Christian denominations, I did not find this to be true of many Pentecostals I encountered on SXM. My experiences confirm the findings of Conway and Austin-Broos on Haitian and Jamaican Pentecostals. Both follow a long line of anthropologists, including George Eaton Simpson (1978) and Donald Hogg (1964), who argued that before the arrival of Pentecostalism in the Caribbean, there were many indigenous movements that resembled Pentecostalism, such as the Shakers, Revivalists, and older forms of highly syncretic folk Catholicism mixed with Vodou. Therefore, both Conway and Austin-Broos aver that, despite all its external similarities with American styles of Pentecostal worship, Haitian and Jamaican Pentecostalism are creolized with these older forms. A study of Pentecostalism on SXM may reveal that this is also the case for many Pentecostal churches on the island. However, the Haitian and Jamaican situations are not the same as that of SXM, where the majority earns a living from entertaining tourists in search of hedonistic pleasures. How individual Pentecostals, and specifically Pentecostalism as an institution, relate to tourists is an interesting question. I did not conduct research on this issue. As an aside: it is quite interesting that while official Web sites on SXM tourism assert the presence of Vodou and Hinduism next to Catholicism and Methodism, the presence of Pentecostalism goes unmentioned.[3]

I do not want to argue that studies focusing on churches are incorrect, and no amount of intricate elaboration can sanitize the fact that many denominations in the Americas construct an evil Other. It may even be argued that when new members of religions undergo the process of affiliating themselves to a denomination, intolerance is sometimes directed toward those who choose to practice another seemingly conflicting religion. Moreover, this may be why churches, although creolized, have aligned themselves from time to time with exclusivist national politics of belonging and outright xenophobia and racism. In the United States, for instance, many exclusively white Southern Baptist and Pentecostal churches openly supported Jim Crow laws and anti-Semitism (Rose 2004; Telfair Sharpe 2000).

An examination of the issue of socialization into Christianity not exclusively marked by denominationalism, becoming "Christian minded without being rooted," may provide interesting insights into the general study of Christians, as it demonstrates the relationship between Christianity and the issue of belonging. It also may demonstrate the role of Christianity in the construction of a transcendental sense of society and the promotion of tolerance. Put differently, it may be useful to employ what is known as a typical ideal Durkheimian view on the social function of religion (Cladis 1992; Jones 1986; Durkheim 1983, 1954). This has to be complemented and modified in two ways. First, with a caution that in competitive societies, one may find alongside this typical ideal Durkheimian public religion competition-inducing ones (Horton 1960).[4] Second, as Bellah noted, in the Americas, public religions remained characteristically Christian oriented (Bellah 1967).

Bellah's theorization has to be complemented by Walcott's 1999 argument that in the case of many Caribbean islands, this public Christianity is creolized. It contains discernible Afro- and Asian-Caribbean religious motifs. That it openly incorporates other religious practices renders it assessable to non-Christians and circumvents Bellah's worry that public Christianity, in the case of the United States, may have to become more tolerant to deal with religious Others. In the Caribbean there is a growing positive acknowledgment of African and Asian cultural contributions to West Indian life. Building on these welcome additions, one can argue that religions with a public role become disruptive only when they are less creolized or their creolization is denied, and when particular groups employ them to promote their religious and social agendas and condemn members of society who practice other faiths.

The manner in which SXM society seeks to worship a transcendental version of itself is explicitly Christian infused. Nevertheless, issues of inner faith and conversion—Christian or otherwise—are addressed solely in the private sphere. Through this, Christianity's public role is one of promoting tolerance and acceptance of religious differences. On SXM most become Christian minded as part of a wider socialization process in which denominations do play a role, but one that is by no means the most important. In understanding the public role of Christianity on SXM, it is necessary to investigate the articulations among social, cultural, economic, and political fields that produce a Christian-oriented sense of the human condition that is then manifested in differentiated performances. This Christian-oriented sense of the human condition—what it means to be considered human and part of SXM society—has to be investigated for the implicit and explicit politics of belonging it conveys. Observing patterns among the varied public performances of Christianity can best do this. This observation is possible if one envisions SXM as a constantly shifting social whole that, although riddled with contradictions, manages to produce structures of feeling that make the varied Christian performances intelligible to all. All SXMers, regardless of their faith, understand one another when Christianity is employed as a metalanguage.

While it infuses all parts of society, Christianity socialization is nevertheless generation specific. Through conversations I learned that, unlike those who worked long hours in the tourist industry, children and the elderly were expected to attend church on a regular basis. Yaya told me during one of our many conversations: "I only does go to church on special occasions. Holidays and so. Church is for old people and lil' children, those who don't have to work. When I finish work at three o'clock in morning, you think I have time to get up and go to church? But I sending Veronica to church so she can learn about the Lord. It is good for her. When I was a child, every Sunday my mother would send me and Papito [her brother] to church. That is why I know how to behave."

Yaya's parents took Veronica to church, and she spent the day with them so that their daughter could rest. This was a prevalent pattern among SXMers, as the elderly were usually the ones who took children to church. Nevertheless, the majority of the working population and some members of the elites still upheld the idea of hearing the word of God on Sunday morning, and they often tuned in to sermons broadcast on the radio or on one of the American cable channels. Yaya commented: "You got to give the Lord he time on Sunday. During the week you so busy that you ain't got time, but on Sunday, well, you listen to your gospel and the pastor on TV. And when nighttime come, you go to Booboo Jam [a disco] to dance and enjoy the lil' free time you have." Yaya's juxtaposition of watching Christian TV on Sunday mornings with dancing kompa, calypso, and salsa in the evenings was also something I often observed. It tied in to how the local radio station actually organized its programming. Sunday mornings were strictly dedicated to gospel music, but as the day progressed, one got jazz, easy listening, and, as the night fell, calypso and merengue. During weekdays a similar division took place, as from 6 to 7 A.M., only gospel music was heard on the radio. After that devotional hour, the calypso and other Caribbean music that the tourists and most SXMers loved dominated the airwaves.

Yaya's comment that church was a place where children learned to behave was often repeated on SXM, as most reasoned that it was in Sunday school classes that the young learned Christian-based morals, tolerance toward all ethnic groups on the island, and love and fear of God. Many of the Sunday school teachers explained that they felt it was a lack of a love and fear of God that caused uncivil behavior on SXM and in the rest of the world. Here is what Agnes, a Sunday school teacher whose grandchildren lived in mainland France, had to say about the importance of Sunday school:

> In Sunday school, the children does learn how to behave. They does learn
> to memorize they lil' memory verse [verses of the Bible that are learned by
> heart], sing Hosanna, and learn that no matter what they do, Jesus looking

over them. They does learn to respect older people, the different cultures on the island, and themselves. That is the way it supposed to be. This island have many religions—the Indian bring his, the Chinese bring his—but in the end it is only one God. All children at this Anglican church does learn that. It ain't about saying my religion is better than yours. It is about praising the Lord, the maker of this world, your maker. A child who says, "God spare my life," when talking about something he would like to do later and who will thank Jesus for every meal is a child who know nothing moves without God's grace. That is a child who you can admire. But when a child don't go to Sunday school and ain't learn these things, they does turn out be a terror. You show me a terror on SXM, and I show you a child who mother didn't send him to Sunday school. Up where you live, is the same thing. I have grandchildren up there in France, and I know that a lot of children up there don't go to church. They don't even believe in God. That is why when you up there, you got to be holding you purse so tight and always looking over your shoulder, 'cause somebody might try rob you. They ain't learn no manners. My daughter always saying, "Mammy, when you coming to live by we?" I tell her, "Not me, my dear. A vacation is fine, but let me stay here where the Lord would have me be."

About the issue of national belonging and its connection to Christianity, Agnes was even more explicit, chastising the metropolitan French for being un-Christian:

Up there [France], the French man always talking about the foreigner this, foreigner that. That is because they don't fear God; they don't know that God make all people. Even if the people illegal in your country, God don't like that talk. Jesus himself said, "Suffer not the little children to come unto me." Here the children does sing, "Jesus love the little children, all the children of the world. Red and yellow, black and white, they are all precious in his sight. Jesus loves the little children of the world." So if Jesus love everybody, in Sunday school children should also learn to love everybody. On this island we have peace among all the nations because we are constantly reminded that God made Adam and Eve, not Adam, Eve, Steve, Harriet, and Jacob. We is one people. So even if I myself might not agree with everything those Indians believe, it is not for me to judge. That is in God's hands. If they ask me my opinion, then that is another story, and I ain't going to lie and tell them I agree with everything about their religion. I mean, I don't understand how they can say the cow holy and you mustn't kill it when you have so many starving people in India. Last night I see it with my own two eyes on TLC. To me, that is a sin. You have to be flexible about your belief.

Flexibility was the key to Agnes's Christian performance. She believed that religious doctrines should be constantly interpreted to fit the changing times. As with other SXMers, mass media's version of reality was summoned to lend truth-value to her arguments.

While Agnes stressed the importance of children attending Sunday school to instill an inclusive sense of belonging and respect for others, this was not the only way this was done. In a very literal sense, Sunday schools, places where kids learned to relate Christianity to inclusive ideas of belonging, were not confined to churches. Most social institutions where the socialization of youngsters took place functioned similarly to Sunday schools. At primary schools, after-school programs, and summer vacation activities, children of all faiths were encouraged to accept all SXMers, locals and newcomers alike, through the idiom of Christianity. Even though a formal distinction existed between Christian and public schools or youth activities, in practice, all employed Christianity as an encompassing idiom, a metalanguage to promote virtues and an all-inclusive sense of belonging.

Despite the layering of Christianity in the curriculum and pedagogies of these institutions, I never witnessed young children willingly performing the role of young pious souls. Morality, respect, and tolerance through the language of Christianity did not translate into Christian piety or the need for conversion. What they did translate into was knowledge of biblical texts and a freedom to interpret these to fit contemporary realities. The only constraint was that in public, one could not explicitly connect Christianity to exclusion based on religion, ethnicity, racism, or class discrimination. As a result of this, even non-Christians participated in bringing about the understanding of inclusive belonging through the idiom of Christianity. Shamiran, a social worker at one of the after-school programs and a Muslim whose family was from Palestine, taught young children about the Bible without feeling the least bit of contradiction:

> You mustn't take it so serious. I teaching them about David and Goliath, yes, but that don't mean I telling them to become Christian and lay down their life and become an apostle. I sure if Jesus was around now, he would refuse some of these rude children you have here, even if they say they going follow him for free [laughter]. For real, me teaching them about the Bible is just part of the job, and a way to teach them how to behave. I have children here who are Muslims like myself, and they does sing along just as hard as those who does go to Sunday school. And their parents don't mind, 'cause they know, and if they ask me I does tell them that religious faith is something private. What I teaching these children don't have nothing to do with that. No teacher here will teach children to disrespect another religion. If they do that, well then, they can be sure that that will be the last day on the job.

Shamiran's last comments are to the point, since during my stay on the island, I did not witness any schoolteachers or social workers disobey the taboo of teaching children to criticize another religion in public. After teaching them about the Bible, Shamiran would dance calypso and R&B with them and would not reprimand them for pretending to be Will Smith's character from *Men in Black* or other American actors in Hollywood action films.

In the homes of Christians, I witnessed little emphasis on having children enact piety. Children had to pray in the mornings and evenings and before meals were served, but these actions were rituals of socialization into appropriate moral behavior rather than attempts to get children to renounce worldly pleasures. When I asked Yaya how she justified refusing to send her daughter to church during Carnival time while still always commanding her to pray, she replied:

> You bold. You think I am hypocrite. Listen here, Francio, I don't want my child to be a preacher, but she must know about God and learn her manners. Still I always say, "Children should be children." They have to learn to free up themselves. So I will never stop Veronica from going to see Carnival. Veronica even playing Mass this year. Children have to learn to free up they self. Is we culture. Nobody can show me in the Bible where God say you mustn't play Mass. From young I playing Mass. My mother never stop me. I believe that once you dancing in a Christian way, God ain't got no problem with that.

After seeing how sexily Yaya danced and how she encouraged her daughter to do the same, I am sure that many theologians would disagree with Yaya's beliefs, but Yaya was her own biblical scholar. No religious authority could tell her how to interpret the Bible. Like most other parents I encountered, she also taught her daughter to interpret the Bible in accordance with the contemporary situation. For instance, she told me in front of her daughter that biblical doctrines concerning the subordination of women to men were outdated. In her opinion, they were from a time when women did not work outside the home to support themselves and therefore had to obey men. In a time of single parents such as herself, that rule should be scrapped. Her daughter and other children on SXM were growing up hearing their mothers and fathers constantly reinterpreting the Bible to suit contemporary needs.

While children were encouraged to enact a loose form of Christianity, for the elderly, performances of piety were considered appropriate and even desirable. They were a sign of spiritual maturity. There were very few older SXMers who were not faithful churchgoers. There was an enormous stigma attached to those who failed to uphold this unwritten rule. As was the case with the youngsters' activities, the activities that catered to the elderly were heavily imbued with Christian overtones. The men's and women's auxiliary clubs and other hobby associations were places where Christian-derived morals enveloped many discussions. At these clubs the members and other elderly visitors were expected to enact a pious performance: drinking alcohol and cursing were not done. Agnes, for instance, was quite cross about the rowdy behavior of an infamous elderly alcoholic nicknamed Bloody Mary, as she never attended church or Christian-oriented associations, choosing instead to engage with the middle-aged and young adults at drinking establishments and party centers:

> That woman is a disgrace. I don't even know her name, 'cause everybody does call her Mary. To me she don't have any family, 'cause if she had any family in Dominica, where she come from, they would send for her. Nobody want to see they grandmother cursing bad words and roaming the street stone drunk. My son, she don't have no respect for herself. When you young you can do those things, because you learning about the world, you learning why the word of God is correct. But as you grow older, you should turn to the church, live a godly life, and teach the young children why it is important for them to love the Lord and remember that nothing grows without him. The older generation have to teach the ones who coming up how to behave, and they can do that because they have been through life. If that Mary ain't learn why she should give her life to God yet and why she should set an example, well then, all I can tell her is "Cracko smoke your pipe" [here meaning a foolish person who doesn't understand the complexities of life].

What was quite telling about Agnes's justification was that she reasoned that after spending their adult years engaging in a partying lifestyle, as a mode of learning about why the ways of piety were correct, old men and women should become actively involved in the church, instructing children about the ways of the world. They, and not the children, should be the ones to express a deep conviction. This is an idea that I often heard. There were many stories about children who had been forced to behave piously and ended up being drug addicts and other social derelicts. Miss Maria had this to say on the matter:

> The Bible is book that does contradict itself. One place you read, "an eye for eye," and the other place it saying, "turn the other cheek." Children can't really understand what is what until they have been in the world. You have to know about the world, bump you head a couple of times, before you can understand the Bible. Young people still in the world, so they can't know either. I myself don't understand everything, but I have experience to know when the Lord speaking to me and to pick sense from nonsense. When you force a child to accept the Lord and he ain't ready, is only malice that can come out of that. You know that girl they call Rina, a druggie, she always roaming the streets of Marigot. Well, that is an example. Her par-

ents wouldn't even let her go to a school party, and you see how she turn out. The child didn't know anything, so she get hooked on base [crack]. It is sin. What her parents do is a sin.

Like Agnes, Miss Maria also spoke to the issue of the elderly having the task of teaching the young morals and acceptance of locals as well as newcomers:

> I believe a good Christian person is, not that somebody have to tell you that they are Christian, [but] when you see that person, you could know that that person have something good in them. I mean, all of we have something good, but really you're supposed to see it on their behavior. Is only those down in age who could usually do that. With the foundation, I does take care of children from the Haitians, the Dominicans, the Guyanese, all those people who here to make a living. And they breeding, boy, I tell you they breeding. Their children is SXMers. Whether their parents are Christian or not, that don't mean nothing to me. I mean, a lot of them Guyanese have another religion, but when they bring their children to Kids Care, they know me and Rebecca don't make no distinction. A good Christian don't make no distinction. I treating everybody the same, and I teaching their children to do the same thing. You know how many of them does stop me in the road and say, "Thanks, Miss Maria." When I go into some of those Indian stores, before I open my mouth about sponsoring an activity, the manager already will come and say, "Anything for you, Miss Maria." 'Cause they know once you contributing to this country, I contributing to help you and your children out.

The stance of Miss Maria makes sense when one realizes that on an island where many parents are busy earning a living, performing in the money tie system, it is the elderly who are counted on to instill morality in the young. In addition, the flexibility that the elderly displayed in accepting other religions was congruent with the messages of the most popular Christian leaders on the island.

On SXM, popular church leaders are those who can adapt the universal themes of Christianity to the particularities of a given surrounding to meet the expectations of their congregants. Priests and pastors on SXM must be aware that their flock consists primarily of old and young members who are not isolated from the workings of the wider society where the money tie system is dominant. Followers must engage with sons and daughters, mothers and fathers, aunts and uncles, schoolteachers and other civil servants, as well as with the tourists they meet through their daily experiences. Among these, there are many who do not enact pious performances of Christianity. They must also contend with a multireligious island. The most popular preachers are those who have best been able to interpret Christian scriptures to fit SXM society, who have been able to employ Christianity as a metalanguage of belonging that transcends religious and denominational exclusivity.

For example, Norma Reyes, a Puerto Rican leader of a Pentecostal church, employed a Christian metalanguage when interacting with her working-age members, most of whom were recently arrived newcomers from the Spanish Caribbean. One of the services I attended demonstrated her effectiveness: a Colombian couple who had been on the island only a couple of weeks approached the altar, wanting to give their lives to God. She prayed with them and said that just because they found Jesus in her church did not mean that they belonged exclusively to it. She told them that the Holy Spirit resides in all churches that praise God. She would guide them on the thorny road of life, but advised them that being born again Christians did not mean that they should give precedence to church worship over working hard to provide for their loved ones. Instead, they should make an effort to attend church whenever their busy work schedules permitted. She advised them to keep in mind, "No es la fé la que mueve montañas, sino la boca y el sudor. Jesús era un carpintero, él también tenía que trabajar duro. Jesús ama a los que trabajan duro para ayudarse en esta vida [It is not faith that moves mountains but actually the mouth, the ability to talk well, and sweat, hard work. Jesus was a carpenter; he too had to earn a living. Jesus loves those who work hard to help themselves in this life]."

When I asked her about her thoughts on her congregants visiting other churches, she told me:

> My brother is a Methodist priest. Do you think that I believe that he is not worshipping the same God as I am? I have a lot of Spanish people here who have mothers and younger sisters who are Catholics. How am I going to tell them that their family is on the wrong path, when those people depending on the money they sending back every month. Another thing, Pentecostalism for me is about spirituality, and spirituality does not belong to any church. When Holy Spirit descended during Pentecost, he did not descend on the members of any specific church. He anointed believers in Christ. On this island we ain't into that *baina* [confusion].

I encountered a similar ecumenism during a mass conducted by Father Charles, the Saint Lucian priest considered by many to be the island's most popular Christian leader. In his serene sermon, he employed Christianity as a metalanguage to explicitly promote equal belonging to the island:

> When our Lord and savior Jesus Christ started his public ministry, he told us, "Reform your lives. Change your mentality, for the kingdom has arrived.

The kingdom is here." He came to initiate the kingdom of grace and peace. We are a resurrected people. Let us rejoice in our resurrection, yet never forgetting that we are prone to sin. Verily, verily, I say unto thee, he is without sin I say, pelt, cast, the first stone. Let us go forth today remembering that with Christ, there is no slave, no white man; there is no gentile; there is no black man; there is no Jew; there is no local; there is no foreigner. It is a new covenant, a new Renaissance, a new beginning for all men.

After these words and the last peace sign, Father Charles led his congregation in singing Bob Marley's "One Love." When I had the opportunity to interview him, I asked him why he had chosen Bob Marley's "One Love" to end a Catholic Mass. He smiled and replied:

You're wondering, "What is a Catholic priest doing singing reggae music during the Sunday Mass?" But I tell you, I am afraid of the man who only reads one book or listens to only one kind of music. Such a man is even more dreadful if he lives on a tourist island such as ours. That would be an intolerant man, a destructive man, a man that points his fingers to his countrymen as well as to the tourists. Such a man would forget that God made him a man, and he would want to behave like an angel. Now I tell you, a man who tries to behave like an angel turns out to be a beast. SXMers should not engage in such reckless behavior. SXM people have to read many books and listen to many different kinds of music, become more universal, because we are living on an international island.

Even the Bible can be read in many different ways, which is exactly what Pastor Vlaun did. The name of his church is Acts 29, while the Acts of the Apostles only has 28 chapters. This name indicated new exegeses of biblical texts. Moreover, he argued that, within Caribbean culture, one could find hints as to how this should be done. Like Father Charles, he also played Bob Marley and the Wailers during one of his sermons. The song he selected was "Get Up, Stand Up." He told his congregation that they should pay special attention to this verse, sung by Peter Tosh:

We sick and tired of the hism skism
people die and go to heaven ina Jesus name.
We know and we understand,
the mighty God is a living man.
You can fool some people some time
but you can't fool all the people all the time.
So now you see the light.
You got to stand up for your rights.

Pastor Vlaun stopped the CD after these verses and told his congregation that while he disagreed with the Rastafarian beliefs that people experience their own Armageddon and that the blacks in the Caribbean experienced their collective carnage during slavery, he agreed with the Rastafarians that Armageddon and Judgment Day are not things yet to come. They are things of the past. Jesus is alive, and indeed heaven is not a place where one journeys to after death, but a place that can be created in the here and now. The earth we inhabit belongs to all.

Pastor Vlaun then went on to show through a biblical exegesis that what was written in the book of Revelation took place during Pauline times and that the creature called the devil cannot be blamed for the contemporary ills of the world. He said the devil was defeated in the past, and those American churches that were waiting on the Antichrist were deluded by wrongful exegeses performed by medieval scholars. He told his congregation that humans are no longer born as sinners, since Jesus died for us, but are actually persons who commit the most vicious and sinful acts on one another by their own volition. He advised them that no one can create a better society than they could, with the help of God. I was amazed at how he skillfully transformed the New Testament into an "old testament" on the basis of his assertion that Christ was the last Adam (the last person born a sinner):

> Every time you open up your New Testament, you have to remember you are in the transition period. And you have to get in context, 'cause unless you get in context, you will translate phrases and certain events in light of our modern world reality. And that will give you a wrong background reality. The New Testament is a unique period of the world, or the outworking of salvation. The scriptures have to do with salvation history. And the end of all things has to do with completion of salvation rather than the end of the world physically, all right. That is where a lot of mistakes have been made with eschatology. Once Christ became one with man, with his sin, and was crucified and delivered out of that, his own personal resurrection, that was the determining factor. He was the last Adam for the rest of humanity to come into that same fullness.

As beautiful and inventive as the exegeses of Pastor Norma Reyes, Father Charles, and Pastor Vlaun were, they were promoted or even possible only because they corresponded to the material conditions on SXM. I never heard any of them condemn the money tie system, tourism, or other religions. Their implicit understanding of Christianity, which lay behind their actions, was that this religion's public role was to bind all generations. The children and the elderly who were outside the tourist industry went to church, and through them, the vast majority of the middle generation atoned for having to entice tourists to live intemperately. Moreover, teenagers and young and middle-aged adults could live hedonistically and still claim to be Christian because the others, especially the older generation, actively pursued a pious life. The emphasis on individual conversion in public was most pronounced among those who had retired. Unlike the children, who faced the inescapable fact that most of them would have to perform in the money tie system later in life, the elderly could dedicate their efforts to living according to biblical precepts. In their old age, the middle generation would be expected to do the same. This communal understanding of Christianity, divorced of private belief, was well suited to the Christian performances most politicians and merchants found acceptable.

It was clear that high-ranking civil servants and politicians, as the main sponsors of schooling, welfare, and social work activities, had clear, though unwritten, rules about how Christianity should be manifested in public. These unwritten rules were made to coincide with the French and Dutch constitutions, where there is, first, a separation of church and state and, second, a clause that includes religiously based political parties, with the implicit understanding that this inclusion does not lead to religious intolerance. On both sides of the island, government funding went only to Christian-related activities that promoted multidenominationalism and religious tolerance. In other words, if organizations catering primarily to children and the elderly wished to be funded by government, they had to state clearly that one of their goals was to promote ecumenism and the inclusive belonging of all SXMers. Alex Richard, who held a degree from the Sorbonne and was a member of Pastor Vlaun's church and the main adviser to the mayor of French SXM, was quite clear on the matter:

> I do not have to spell out to you what has been done in the name of religion, especially Christianity. In my PhD thesis I wrote about Christianity in relation to slavery and the dehumanization of blacks in Haiti. And while religion is neither this nor that, it is not the opiate of the people or a liberating force, one has to be careful of mixing it with politics. That is why in the French system, there is a separation between church and state, and we respect that dearly on this island. What that means is that this commune will not fund any religious activities, but we will consider those that may be religiously oriented without being religious. So, for instance, we are seriously considering a project in which Father Charles is involved that will counsel drug addicts, 'cause we know that it will be ecumenical. . . . That is the only kind of project that the mayor is willing to even consider.

Though it could be successfully argued that Alex Richard's proposed separation between church and state is porous, the point remains that, according to this statesman, Christianity should be about inclusiveness. Christianity is thus positioned as a public religion, divorced of religious exclusivity, that encompasses all religions on the island. Church leaders such as Father Charles had to adapt their religious interpretations to those of the government. Another prominent political figure, Maria Buncamper-Molanus, state secretary of economics of the Dutch Antillean parliament and a member of the Catholic Church, was even more adamant about it. In the style of a politician claiming to represent her constituency, she stated:

> As far as myself and Sarah Westcott Williams [head of the government of Dutch SXM] is concerned, we go to church on regular basis. I don't know if others do so. But going to church don't give you an upper hand in this country. It doesn't make sense to campaign on that. SXM people will not vote for you if during your campaign you stand up and say that you does attend church every week. On the contrary, they will quicker distrust you, 'cause you are not saying anything important with that, in a country where the majority is Christian. And you making distinctions, mixing politics with religion. As the people does say, those two sharks shouldn't swim together; whether they are sharks is another matter. Anyway, I know that in other places, people think different about that. But unlike in Holland, our political parties are not based on religion. You don't have a CDA [Dutch Christian Democrats] or something like that. Parties on this island were established based on visions for the future of our people. All SXMers. So anything this government put money into will not be about one religion against the next. And we does set an example, 'cause even though most politicians are Christians, the island council meetings does start with a moment of silence so that everyone, regardless of their religion, can pray to God.

Maria Buncamper-Molanus and Alex Richard lived by their word, for I often met them in several different churches. Similarly, in their actions they made no distinctions between Christians and non-Christians. They were like the politicians who, as I suggested in the previous chapter, were skilled religious *bricoleurs*.

The tourist industry seems to influence expressions of Christianity in ways similar to the way the political establishment's actions influence them. Most businesses on the island are not Christian or, if Christian, are of the nonpious practicing sort. SXM is an island that sells itself as a hedonistic place, a fun retreat for wealthy tourists to come lay on the pearl white beaches and indulge in their fantasies. Tourists are encouraged by those who work there to spend their money gambling in casinos, dancing and drinking in discotheques, buying expensive jewelry and high-tech modern conveniences, and carousing in prostitution houses "specializing" in Latin, Eastern European, and West Indian women.

Many of the young pastors, most of whom are working class, work during the week in one of the sectors of the tourist industry. On SXM the churches are not big enough for most pastors to support themselves at the expense of their congregation. They have to engage with tourists and their employers, neither of whom tolerate performances of piety during working hours. One of the managers at a casino was quite frank, arguing that any person wishing to be hired should refrain from accentuating piety: "I believe in the Bible, but I don't want anybody in here telling the tourists, "Thou shall not gamble." Let them keep that talk for after working hours. Not in here if you please. Like the old people does say, there is a time and a place for everything."

The reach of the tourist industry extends beyond the workplace, influencing how sermons are preached in the church setting. One cannot be too critical in rebuking non-Christians or the worldly when one has brand-new ventilators recycling the air sponsored by a Hindu merchant in a church built from the blocks furnished free of charge by the womanizing owner of a construction company, and the collection plate is filled with money from the tips of tourists who have been encouraged to live intemperately. Norma Reyes's church was primarily built by donations from the business sector, and her congregants work in the tourist industry or are the children of those whose job it is to encourage others to live hedonistically.

This situation condones and simultaneously breeds specific forms of public Christian performances, especially among the working population. Violet, whom I mentioned at the beginning of this chapter, alerted me to this:

> But you ain't know that, Francio. *Christian* is a passport on this island. Once you is a cool Christian, nobody ain't bothering you; nobody ain't asking you if you have any papers [ID card or residence or work permit], where you come from. On this island we like cool Christians, those who will play they lil' number [lotto], curse they lil' bad word [swear], but still try to live right. That is the Christian we like and the Christian the tourists like to meet. Not those disgusting ones who constantly reminding you of death [heaven and hell]. Anybody come with that nonsense by me I setting him straight one time. That is why I had to teach that friend of yours [Mervin] some manners. You don't do those types of things. What he think, he is more Christian than we?

A similar comment was made by Clem, a petty entrepreneur who highlighted the money tie system and the somewhat privileged position held by SXM in the global capitalist world:

> Let me tell you something, Francio. The kind of Christians you looking for, well, we don't have that kind over here so. This here is money tie system

land. Come to think of it, I don't think that kind of Christian Christian
[pious Christian] exists, except in the Bible or somewhere where people cut
off. SXM is not a place that is cut off. You hear about the Big Apple, well,
this here is the Little Apple. That is what the people from the neighboring
islands does call SXM. Anybody on the island who receiving a paycheck
can't say that he born again. If he say that he is, he's a hypocrite, a stinking
dirty liar. Every month that he collect that paycheck, knowing that a lot of
drugs money does pass through this place, he sinning. Every time he say
thanks for that tip, knowing that it is from people who exploiting they own
people in the States, he sinning. We are all sinners. We trying to be Christian Christian, yes, but we can't be it as long as this island remains being the
Little Apple.

From this perspective the nonpious Christian performances of the
working classes are reduced to knee-jerk reactions to the necessities of
the tourist industry and the workings of the economy. While undoubtedly the influence of economics cannot be neglected, I believe that expressions of SXM Christianity do exert some influence on the economic
processes as well. Social anthropologists such as David Chidester (2005,
1996) have sought to warn us that the presentation of religion as occupying a field distinct from that of politics or economics is a modernist
fable that has little to do with the facts in most postcolonial societies. Yet
this fable has been so successfully adopted within and without academia
that elites and commoners alike still subscribe to it from time to time.
While Clem's comments seemingly represent this, several persons I spoke
to argued that Christian discourses might also be considered the all-
inclusive idiom of SXM society. Christianity's public role promotes tolerance. This is how the social worker Terry Gumbs phrased the matter:

Christianity can't be intolerant on this island. A Christian has to respect his
neighbor, no matter how much idols he worshipping. That's because of
how this island is. This is a tourist island. Here on SXM, because of the different cultures, you will discuss, argue, but at the end of the day you going
to drink together. Something you will hear on this island is that all nations
helped build it up. There are locals who feel this is their island, but even so
they have to, and will, show respect to the newcomers. It is an idea of give
everybody their space and respect. You don't have to be like me and I don't
have to like you as long as we respect and help out each other. Come to
think of it, this tolerance may also have to do with the Christianity or the
version of Christianity on this island. So Christianity might be the one causing all of this as well. 'Cause the general Christian idea among all the
people is that no one is perfect. What you hear quite often is: who is free of
sin cast the first stone. So people don't usually follow anyone blindly, not
even the preacher. 'Cause he also has his sinful ways. Besides this thing of
everybody having some fault, there is the feeling that God put us here to be

happy and successful. Yeah, I believe it is Christianity that keeps this island livable.

Terry's perspective becomes more visible when one realizes the extent to which Christianity as a metalanguage is employed to make all tourists feel welcome. The most telling example I witnessed occurred when a waitress employed Christianity to explain the homosexual lifestyle of a tourist couple. Two men who were flirting with each other straightened up when a waitress appeared in front of them. Casually she told them they didn't need to behave differently, because she had no problem with the gay lifestyle. Surprised, the men interrogated her, asking what had made her so liberal minded. She responded: "Sweetheart, in Genesis God said he made us all in his image, and since he made us all in his image, homosexuals are in his image too, wouldn't you agree? Now can I take your order? You guys look like good tippers who understand that a woman like me got to live too." This may seem an extreme example, and it is not representative of the types of behavior explicitly condoned or preached to young people by Christian institutions on SXM, but it does exhibit the stylized rhetoric typical of SXM and the wider Caribbean, which is often cloaked in a Christian idiom. By employing this idiom, which began in the colonial era, the hierarchical conceptions of society prevalent in the Caribbean are criticized.

Most studies on the Caribbean have highlighted the perennial struggle between hierarchical conceptions of society and "the embedded egalitarianism," to use Brenneis's phrase (1987), propagated in the region. There have been efforts to ground this contradiction in the primacy of gender (e.g., Wilson 1969), class (e.g., Williams 1991), and the ethnoracism complex (e.g., Smith 1991).

The works of Daniel Miller (1994), Sylvia Wynter (1984), and Stephan Palmié (2002) have circumvented this stance, offering a more general explanation concerning the juxtaposition of egalitarianism and hierarchy Caribbean-wide. They all argue that the dualism between hierarchy and egalitarianism in the prevalent racial, class, or gendered forms has to be understood as a way through which distinctions among humankind were constructed and legitimated in all colonial societies, and the Caribbean is by definition a region born of European colonialism. In other words, racism, gender inequality, and class discrimination are not the primary grounds of conflict, but they are the effects of the hierarchical distinctions between human beings created in the colonial era. From that period on, West Indian people have been struggling to instate another, more egalitarian order. In an interview, Sylvia Wynter observed, "From the very origin of the modern world, of the Western world system, there were never simply 'men' and 'women.' Rather on the one hand, Man, as invented in sixteenth-century Europe, as Foucault notes, and then on the other hand, Man's human Others, also invented by Europeans at the same time, as the anthropologist Jacob Pandian points out" (quoted in Scott 2000: 174).

Both the ideology of the fundamental unity and equality of all human beings and the hierarchical conventions used to legitimize the subordination of the vast majority of humanity are products of colonialism. In their battle to overcome their categorization as Man's human Others, the working classes in the Caribbean explicitly connected their stylized rhetorical forms of Creole speech to Christianity, since being Christian meant counting in most societies (Hall 2002; Chevannes 1995, 1994). With his usual brilliance, Derek Walcott captured this articulation when he stated: "[No] 'race' is converted against its will. The slave converted himself, he changed weapons, spiritual weapons, and he adapted his master's religion, he also adapted his language, and it is here that our poetic tradition begins. Now began the new naming of things" (Walcott 1993: 48). In the process of the new naming of things, Christianity and stylized rhetoric were employed together to criticize the unjust practices of the political and religious establishments. Within the works and politics of such figures as Edward Blyden, Paul Bogle, and the Bell sisters this becomes clear. Since colonial times West Indians have remained critical of established churches that are linked to those who have the political and economic might (Chevannes 1995, 1994; Catherine Hall 1992). They have strived to institute a society where political leaders will not privilege one church or religion above the other.

Christianity employed as metalanguage to promote social justice can also be understood as part of a wider New World phenomenon, especially during the civil rights movement. Think for instance of the fervor with which North American political activists such as Martin Luther King contested the social discrimination of African Americans and other minorities during the civil rights struggle. He was also critical of churches connected to Jim Crow politicians (Baker 1995; West 1988).

On SXM most members of the working classes, the majority of whom are newcomers, contest any form of exclusivity associated with Christianity by employing stylized rhetoric. I became aware of this at a popular Chinese restaurant. I was waiting for a takeout meal when two fairly young Jehovah's Witness proselytizers entered the establishment, trying to sell their Watchtower booklets. They approached two middle-aged women accompanied by a man who were sitting at the bar next to me. From the looks of it they were regulars, since they were quite amicable with the restaurant owner, Mamie, with whom they were exchanging the latest gossip.

Before one of the Jehovah's Witness "salesmen" could finish his pitch, the only man in the company of the regulars, in impeccable standard English, answered in a friendly yet brisk way, "I don't have any money." Refusing to be easily fazed, the elder of the two began talking about how the Watchtower booklet offered useful tips on how to live a life that is more in accordance with the will of God. He also connected it to the afterlife, asking if they knew where they were going if they, God forbid, died suddenly. It seems that his insistence really angered one of the women, Althea, as she forgot all her manners and blazed at him in a deep Creole twang:

> What it is wrong with you? You want to hex me into dying tonight? I got children to feed. You dotting or what? [*Dotting* is a contraction of "don't know nothing." It means someone who is ignorant.] You macoo? [Are you a macaque? Usually one uses it to refer to an idiot.] We are not interested. I look to you like I need salvation? Now leave and stop harassing we. Go and find yourself a decent job instead of harassing people with your tracts. All you ain't no Jehovah Witness. All you is Jehovah Wickedness. I know all about all you. All you won't leave you own children enjoy Carnival or listen to calypso music. Criticizing Caribbean culture. Leave before I really get vex with you. What happen? You ain't hear what I say? You tibbe? [Are you a retard?] Leave!

At that moment Mamie intervened and told the proselytizers that it would be better if they left, and that in the future they should not seek to sell their booklets in her restaurant: "I don't want no trouble in here. This is not a marketplace. This is restaurant. When you come in here, then don't come in here to sell your tracts. I don't go to your church to sell my nasi goreng. We must respect each other." The few customers who were in the restaurant were heartily laughing. Offended, the younger Jehovah's Witness forgot his standard speech and barked back, "Who the hell you think you is?" The elder of the two reprimanded him with his eyes, apologized for the inconvenience, said that he would nevertheless pray for them, and they both left the restaurant.

As soon as they left, Mamie and her friends began talking about the "hypocrisy" of the Jehovah's Witnesses and other young men and women who frequented church on a regular basis. In their opinion whenever one saw working-age adults actively involved in church life, that meant that they were either tricksters and hustlers or people who couldn't cope with life. They might also have been wealthy enough not to have to work, as it was reasoned that such people had to prove even more than the poor that they were worthy of entering the kingdom of heaven. Their verdict was that a Christian did not have to attend church regularly.

I asked them what made one a Christian. Althea turned to me and asked if I had been born. I found it a silly question, but I nevertheless replied, "Yes." Then she said, "Once you are born you are a Christian. We are all children of God, since we all belong to the Adamic race." She employed Christianity to promote the equal belonging of all humans. The other woman who accompanied her was somewhat uncomfortable with her reply and said that she did not agree. She retorted that so many SXMers live selfish lives, like the two Jehovah's Witnesses, criticizing others, but still wanted to be called, as she termed it, "Jah's children": "A Christian is somebody who is Christlike. Somebody who will ask her neighbor, 'Neighbor, how you doing? Can I help in any way?' and don't want nothing in return. My son, on this island, you don't have those kind of people. All you have is people who trying to be Christian and the ones who lying to themselves like those two Jehovah Wickednesses. It is they who are the most dangerous." Thus, from her perspective, the relationship between belonging and Christianity was articulated in the sense that all SXMers tried to be Christian but failed.

As the two women continued to bicker, the man, Timo, who had been silent burst out that he disagreed with both of them. For him, Christianity was in the heart. It was about believing in a power greater than oneself. It was not about exterior behavior, such as attending church on a regular basis: "A man can visit how much church he want. That does not make him a Christian. You is Christian once you believe in God. That is all it takes. Nobody can be like Jesus." For Timo, everyone belonged as long as they believed in God. The woman who had just been speaking was slightly irritated and said that his comment was not biblical. She then put down her Carib beer, opened up her bag, threw a very old and torn Bible on the counter, and demanded, "Read the Ten Commandments. That is what makes you a Christian." Noting her irritation, Timo picked up her Bible and in a very sarcastic tone said, "This one too old for me; you have to throw away that old raggedy thing. If it ain't King James, I ain't reading it."

Mamie and Althea burst out laughing. The owner of the Bible got furious and started swearing at Timo. Encouraged by the fact that he was winning this verbal debate, Timo took up the Bible once again and told her that she should not be angry with him since he could not read. This gesture added wood to the fire, and she ripped the Bible out of his hands and intensified her swearing, calling him ugly, stupid, and a good-for-nothing. Althea joined in taking the Bible and drew it close to her eyes, saying that the fine print was bad for her vision. Mamie, who turned out to be a Christian as well, tried to establish peace, saying that what really mattered was that they were not selfish. Selfish Christians were ones who constantly annoyed God with their trivialities, while good Christians understood that God was a busy man, so they should bother him only in times of utmost need.

This encounter demonstrated the enormous power of rhetoric in legitimating the Christianity of nonpious Christians and defending them from attacks by their pious counterparts, but also showed how such talk worked in their self-socialization into this nominal form of Christianity. This allowed them to draw a distinction between claiming to be Christian and performing piety. In the widest sense, all were included as the offspring of Adam.

As my awareness of the importance of the way people spoke grew, I began to see a wider pattern in the manner in which nonpious Christians dealt with those who tried to connect being Christian to practices of piety. Broadly speaking, their strategy consisted of three moves. First, they would be polite toward the performers of piety, while also making it quite clear that they did not wish to emulate this behavior. This would be done either in Standard English or a mixture of Creole and Standard English. If the performer of piety sought to convince them to join in his or her performance, they would employ indirect sarcasm. This was usually done in Creole. When this did not work, the last resort would be to curse and accuse the pious person of being un-Christian and hypocritical. This was done in a deeper form of Creole.

Most of the time the second strategy, implicit ridicule at performances of Christian piety, worked to create a truce between the performers of piety and those who did not wish to engage in this behavior. Consider the following example, which took place during a bus ride, whereby the passengers and the bus driver were able to silence a Baptist missionary from the United States through their use of implicit ridicule. The missionary, dressed in a white linen shirt and a tie and carrying a Bible, waved down a bus in which I was sitting. Since the back was filled, he went and sat next to the bus driver, whom he greeted with "How are you?" The bus driver replied in Standard English that, like the missionary and all other sinners, he was struggling since the Fall. The missionary, sensing an opportunity, jumped to explain that while he was a sinner, he had been born again, and that through Jesus, salvation in the afterlife was possible.

This was a mistake, as the bus driver then switched codes to a Creole that was still somewhat understandable to Standard English speakers, saying that the predicament of all sinners was actually Eve's fault. Eve had eaten from the Tree of Life and Death, accepted money from the serpent, and, to make matters worse, had had sex with the snake. The way he said it had the whole bus in a roar. The missionary tried to correct matters, believing that the bus driver was ill informed about the Genesis myth. The driver paid him no mind and continued talking about how the snake had made Eve tremble, and that since then, women love money and oral sex. He also said that the reason he didn't frequent church often was that the clergy hid these "truths" from the common folk. He claimed that if he had been informed about them, he would not have been fooled by his ex-wife, who was constantly on him for alimony and, according to rumors, had had a relationship with another woman.

One of the women who was sitting in the bus interrupted the two-way conversation, saying that if men can't take horns, they should not dish it out. Men were like little children, not grown-up enough to take responsibility for the results of prior actions. In her rendition of Genesis, Adam was having an affair with one of the cows, and to pay him back, Eve slept with the serpent. It was Adam who was the cause of the fall and not Eve. Other men and women entered the discussion, which was soon transformed into stories, theories, and gossip about infidelity. Biblical myths were recalled, such as the deceitfulness of Jezebel and David's lust for a married woman. The crux of the matter was that men and women were equally promiscuous, covetous, and prone to sin. It mattered little to which ethnic group a person belonged or whether one was local or newcomer. They also made the point that politicians, members of the economic elite, and church leaders were no better than ordinary folk. Where there was money and power, there was sin. This was especially the case on SXM, an island where the money tie system occupied the hegemonic performative space.

The missionary, sensing that his authority was not being taken seriously, gave up trying to proselytize, and he left the bus with a face red from embarrassment at the manner in which SXMers introduced sex into his seemingly desexualized proselytizing.

What this example clearly demonstrates is how nonpious performers tried to coerce their pious-playing counterparts into acknowledging that everyone who held a job or owned a business on the island was implicated in the money tie system. In public there was little space for issues of belief or conversion. Moreover, in the performances of the nonpious Christians toward their pious counterparts, power was concretized through the reminder that everyone was supposedly longing to have as much sex as possible.

In the bus driver's rendition of the Genesis myth, the serpent relied on money and Eve's love for oral sex to seduce her into being unfaithful. While one can recognize a sexist pattern here, where women are represented as the dangerous sex whose sexuality and material desires must be controlled to avoid social catastrophes, this reasoning was directly contested by resignifying Christianity such that these attributes were awarded to both sexes. One of the female passengers replied that the Fall of Man was actually Adam's fault, since he was the one who started fooling around and couldn't take it when Eve gave him a taste of his own medicine. Adam and Eve's infidelity was thus associated with the practices of locals and newcomers.

The enjoyment and pursuit of sex and wealth were extracted from the sphere of the sinful and ungodly and placed into the sphere of the godly. Though not mentioned in the bus, it seems that the only ones exempted were the elderly, and this may explain why their performances of piety were generally accepted. Christian doctrines and performances that sought to police sex and the unscrupulous drive for wealth were suspect because most SXMers were at least implicitly aware that, for all their theological and philosophical apologetics, Christian institutions that promoted desexualized and world-renouncing piety were deeply implicated in the social injustices that affected the commoners.

Nevertheless, most SXMers had a deep belief in God, who was fathomed as a force bigger than all mankind. SXMers knew that they were not in control of the global processes upon which their tourist economy was built. To boot, there was always the yearly hurricane threat, which could transform the posh hotels and marinas into a heap of rubble. As Miss Maria said: "God make us all. Man is nothing without God. No matter how big we mouth is, we know there is something bigger than all of us. That is the main reason why we religious on this island. The hurricane always there to remind us not to walk next to our shoes."

This understanding of human finitude, an important source of religiosity according to Lemert (1999) and Fortes and Horton (1959), did not, however, translate itself into prescriptions of pious behavior in public. Neither did SXMers' deep knowledge of the Bible lead them to renounce the worldly. Instead, belief and displays of deep Christian piety were reckoned private matters. Employing Christianity as a metalanguage was the way through which SXMers sought to construct a transcendental sense of their society that would include all the inhabitants of the island. These Christian discourses are best understood as cultural styles that captured the existing moods among SXMers. This new role of Christianity seems to be a global phenomenon that deserves our attention (Chidester 2005; Meyer 2004, 2003).

The general existing belief on SXM seems to be that no one occupies the high moral ground from which they can criticize the deeds of another. Comments such as "we like cool Christians here" and "a good Christian will not criticize his neighbor's religion" are symbolic of how most SXMers were socialized and socialized themselves into Christianity. Within the political, economic, social, and cultural fields, modes of Christianity were promoted that sought to guarantee peaceful living and recognition of the importance of the money tie system and tourism. In doing so, the tension between resolving the issue of belonging and the needs of the tourist industry was also being brokered by Christianity.

How this message was transmitted in the media will be the focus of the following three chapters. Radio was an obvious entry point, since it was the medium all SXMers tuned in to. Moreover, popular disc jockeys were hailed as celebrities and organic intellectuals. I will present the manner in which three disc jockeys, Fernando Clarke, DJ Shadow, and DJ Cimarron, have articulated the existing possibilities for resolving the issue of belonging by employing a Christian metalanguage.

CHAPTER 4

Clarke's Two Vitamin Cs for Successful Living

"Isn't it picture perfect?" Olga remarked, pointing up to the sky as she wiggled her hips, captivating everyone in sight with a kind of Ukrainian–Saint Martinian–Canadian dance to Short Shirt's calypso tune that was leaping out of the speakers. Olga had been born and raised in Canada by Ukrainian parents but had migrated to SXM and considered herself 100 percent local, as she would jokingly put it. Behind her humor there was a jab at well-to-do local women who felt that she was one of the "foreigners" who were stealing "their" best men.

Female newcomers, most of whom are working class, are labeled promiscuous and a threat to societal morality. Intra-gender and class intolerance is one of the avenues in which locals vent their xenophobia. Local women claim chasteness and respectability to justify their sense of being true SXMers. Immigrant women who supposedly "lack" these virtues belong less, if they belong at all.

But all that mattered little, since the sun was shining, three cruise ships were in, and Olga's beach bar, Olgies Perogies, was full. The tourists had arrived, and that meant bread and butter for most of the island's inhabitants and salmon and caviar for the privileged few. In between are those, such as Olga, for whom the tourists provide a bit more than just basic sustenance. Everyone on the island is trying to get ahead. Those in the lower classes are trying to get to the middle, while the middle classes want to be among the wealthy, and the wealthy want to be wealthier.

In their daily interactions, however, SXMers smile the friendly smile for the tourists, dance the dance of contentment, and talk about how happy they are and how much they respect one another. But when one knows about the existence of the money tie system, one realizes that SXMers are professionals at creating artifice.

I was at Olgies Perogies because I had an appointment with Fernando Clarke, the popular radio DJ who combines calypso and Christianity. Unfortunately Clarke hadn't time for me that day, because he was too busy entertaining tourists, who were delighted to engage with a small-island radio celebrity. I mused that both on and off air he is all about welcoming people and mollifying cultural barriers. Clarke refuses to accept the strictures of exclusive belonging based on gender or ethnicity and uses his radio program to advocate equality for all SXMers based on their overall participation in the tourist industry and by extension the money tie system, the hegemonic performative space constantly being enacted. For Clarke this space has led all SXMers to perform the role of honest yet cunning Christian calypsonians. Moreover, he advocates that this is the reality on which the issue of belonging should be resolved. Locals and newcomers belong equally because none can escape the demands of the tourist industry. All consent to performing and thus enacting the money tie system.

DJ Fernando Clarke hosts the Tuesday evening calypso show, which airs from 8:00 P.M. to 12:00 A.M. on PJD2, the oldest and most popular radio station on the island. The disc jockeys at PJD2 have access to state-of-the-art broadcasting equipment, including mixing tables, computerized music files, CD and LP turntables, and mini-disc and cassette recorders, and they are treated with the utmost respect by the administrative staff of the station.

Employment as a disc jockey at PJD2 requires that three criteria be fulfilled: one must master the required technical skills; one must be a popular and outspoken personality on the island; and one must and have the right connections. The last two matter for four reasons. First, like all other radio stations, PJD2 receives a large portion of its financing from selling advertising. If, off air, the disc jockey is already a much-liked person, this makes it easier for the administrative staff to entice businesses to advertise on the station. The DJ then lends his or her voice to the advertised product. In addition the DJ can also get his or her friends or relatives to advertise on the radio. The DJ then shares in the profit. Second, through trial and error, the management of PJD2 has come to the conclusion that DJ popularity leads to a substantial audience. A DJ who can skillfully handle him- or herself verbally can captivate listeners. Third, someone with the right connections—familial, financial, political, and cultural—is more likely to have access to privileged information, a vital aspect in all mass media. Fourth, since one cannot live on a radio disc jockey's salary, five dollars an hour, it is mostly well-to-do persons who are able to take on such a role. As such, they view radio broadcasting as a hobby, a vocation, or a means to a specific end: an avenue to promote their business or other personal interests.

The manager of PJD2 reported that he has no qualms with DJs promoting their business ventures via the radio, but political, ethnic, or religious-oriented fundamentalism is inexcusable. The vast majority of the advertisers are Asian and North American businessmen. They profess non-Christian faiths or are nominal Christians. Therefore, the management of PJD2 has to take its DJs sensibilities into account if they wish to keep these advertisers as customers. The advertisers, along with those who are directly or indirectly connected to the largest political parties, will fund Christian-oriented radio—promoting Christianity as an all-inclusive public religion—but not disc jockeys who wish to condemn the hedonism of the tourist industry and the private expressions of other religions as ungodly.

During my stay on the island, a disc jockey at PJD2 was fired because he openly sided with and explicitly encouraged listeners to vote for a particular political party.[1] At another radio station—Radio Saint Martin—a disc jockey was also laid off for refusing to apologize for playing a taped sermon of an American evangelist who accused Islam of being demonic. When I asked Jeanette Mingau, the manager of that radio station, about the event, her reply was that since many merchants and inhabitants of the island are Muslims, such statements are not condoned on the radio.

Disc jockeys on PJD2, as on other radio stations, can broadcast only programs that create a politics of belonging that does not exclude any of the groups that live on the island. Fernando Clarke exemplifies what the PJD2 management seeks from its disc jockeys.

Clarke is a celebrity on SXM. Everyone knows him and everyone wants to know him. He is even famous off the island. Clarke is one of the best-known stand-up comedians and theater actors in the lesser northeastern Caribbean. If he holds a show, it is sold out. He even performed at Harlem's Apollo Theater, where the crème de la crème of Caribbean comedians came together for a special hurricane relief benefit.

Besides his socially charged comedy, which has earned him the nickname the Philosopher of Humor, he is also a much-sought-after calypso composer and master of ceremonies for beauty pageants, church activities, weddings, and other social events. He is known as someone who is always around wherever a "pan is knocking," wherever there is party. He doesn't attend church on a regular basis but claims that God knows how strong his faith is. He claims that regular church attendance will come at a later age, as he put it, "when I old and gray, trembling with the Bible in my hand." Although he was baptized a Methodist, for Clarke all denominations are equal, and he joins various congregations occasionally. For instance, Clarke is the annual host of the Seventh-day Adventist gospel talent show. In addition he often teams up with Father Charles, a popular Catholic priest, as a master of ceremonies for weddings and anniversaries.

Clarke does his best to cultivate this seemingly paradoxical "Christian partying man of the people" image, which he portrays brilliantly during stand-up shows and other artistic activities. His persona is that of an always cheerful God-fearing man who works hard, loves to party, and appears happy with the little that he has. His knowledge is folk based, mixed with biblical verses, and he always seems to have a trick up his sleeve to mesmerize others. Although he does make progress financially, he never really makes big strides, because he sometimes forgets his Christian-derived morality—honesty, solidarity, tolerance, and being one's brother or sister's keeper—and is duly punished for it. As such, he is the shrewd Christian calypsonian par excellence, a Christian operating according to a prudential logic instead of the categorical imperative.

But this "low-key man of the people" image does not fit well with other significant aspects of Clarke's life. He is a manager at the RBTT (Royal Bank of Trinidad and Tobago) and is part of a class of transnationally oriented banking professionals. Before his employment at the RBTT, Clarke worked for Barclays and ABN AMRO. He has been stationed in England, the United States, Barbados, and other places with strong economies. Currently he is in charge of a section of the loans and mortgages department of the RBTT. Despite all his "simple folk trying to get ahead" talk, I saw Clarke as an upper-middle-class professional who had the right social, cultural, and symbolic capital—status, educational credentials, and networks—which he could convert to financial capital.

As a result of Clarke's artistic and professional capacities, his close friend, Don Hughes, the owner of PJD2, personally asked him to host a midweek calypso program. Clarke accepted his friend's offer, knowing it would be a win-win situation. With Clarke hosting a midweek calypso show, PJD2 was assured of a large weekday listening audience. In addition, Clarke's presence would entice RBTT and other enterprises to buy radio advertising. In turn, the radio program provided Clarke with an opportunity to showcase himself and his art, increasing his fame throughout the northeastern Caribbean. Clarke's broadcasts can be heard from Puerto Rico to Saint Lucia, and he receives sporadic fan mail from islands in between, including Saba, Saint Kitts, Nevis, Guadeloupe, and Dominica. He is proud that there are French SXM inmates on Guadeloupe who have sent him letters, thanking him for bringing the island feeling to them via the airwaves.

All social identities involve role playing. Whenever people meet they have to present the appropriate social identifications while also canceling out others that are ill suited to the occasion (Travers 1992; Goffman 1967). In short, they have to perform. Since people are unable to access the "soul," they are forced to rely on others' performances—their actions and speech.[2] Moreover, viewing even religious identifications as performances frees one from the bias of understanding religiosity as commencing with belief and faith (Meyer 2004; Asad 1993; Luhrmann 1989). How and if one believes are effects of religious practices in interaction with other social performances.

On the evening Clarke and I met at PJD2, about two weeks after our encounter at Olga's, his lower right arm was in a cast. Since he'd been fine the last time I had seen him, I assumed he must have fallen or had some kind of accident doing his calypso antics. As it turned out, he had been in a fight with a drug addict. After a calypso concert, he caught someone trying to break in to his car. Enraged that the thief was so bold as to curse him for arriving too soon, he hit the man hard enough to fracture his own wrist. "I had to hit the man, because he continued trying to break in while I stood there being nice," Clarke said. "I was talking to him, telling him, 'Partner, don't do that.' " I took the opportunity to cynically ask him whether he was more a "turn the other cheek" guy or an "eye for an eye, tooth for a tooth" Christian. He started to laugh and replied, "Don't let nobody fool you. Jesus would have done the same thing. You ain't see how bad he get on in the temple when they was gambling and carrying on in there. I use my fist. I believe Jesus was using a whip. I am a Christian, but I ain't no fool."

His words were telling. According to Clarke, meek and mild Christians who always behave properly are insipid. In his rendition, the Gospel Man, in the generic sense of the term, must at times behave rashly, must be a Christian calypsonian. God did the same, and Jesus' behavior in the temple when he chased out the moneychangers and swindlers is an example to all. Many theologians might not agree with his reading, but Clarke used it to vindicate his behavior toward the would-be thief and to make clear that his brand of Christianity differs from the "love thy neighbor no matter what" perspective. His Christianity has been influenced by the lessons of calypso: one needs to operate according to a prudential logic.

After talking about his broken wrist and the audacity of drug addicts on the island, Clarke began unpacking his record cases. "My God," I thought, "this man must have been collecting calypso music since the age of two!" There were very old 45 singles and twelve-inch records as well as a newer batch of CDs, cassettes, and DAT recordings.

When I asked him how he became a lover of the music, he told me every God-fearing West Indian child got his daily dose of the "two vitamin Cs": Christianity and calypso. His mother administered the Gospel while his father was the high priest of calypso. Clarke's mother instilled the prevailing Christian-based social norms of honesty and concern for others, while his father taught him the other ways of the world, where cunning was of crucial importance. Both were adept in both of these systems for understanding life, but the dominant gender conventions within his nuclear family dictated this division of tasks. His recollections of growing up in Aruba in the 1960s reveal a striking similarity between Aruba and SXM: the socioeconomic order influences the manifestation of Christianity on the island. Aruba is also heavily dependent on tourism, and like SXM, the island is a playground for wealthy Western tourists.

From as early an age as he could remember, Saturday was calypso day at his home and in the homes throughout the neighborhood of San Nicholas, where he was born and raised. After five days of hard work and commands by "superiors" at school, in the hotels, or at the oil refinery, Saturday was the time to unwind, to play calypso and laugh about life. On these days his father, a blue-collar technician at the oil refinery, became a DJ and took his place behind his brand-new Zenith stereo, which was still partly covered with plastic wrap. All the greats of calypso, from Sparrow to Stallion, were blasted through its speakers.

Everyone was encouraged to dance and move his or her hips. It was time to party. Clarke recalls that one could not be a geek, dance without rhythm, or act shy and refuse to sing. People who did these things were ridiculed and taught that dancing and singing calypso is living. The ability to listen and understand the messages is directly related to this full-body participation. In other words hearing is not divorced from the other senses. What one hears and how one interprets what one hears are informed by the dance that one engages in, inter- and intra-subjectively. Baumann (1995), Blacking (1990), and other ethnomusicologists have written extensively about this mode of listening, in which the five senses and rhythmic movements of the body are involved. Clarke learned that calypso is about recognizing that, despite everything else, life should ultimately be about joy. Displaying joy is what makes people open their hearts to others. It is what made the North American foremen respect Clarke's father in the oil refinery and was why his mother got so many tips from Western tourists visiting the island.

This social performance, partly engendered under situations of duress, made Clarke's parents at times "invisible" to their enemies or "superiors," and thus, when their ill-wishers and "superordinates" least expected it, his mother and father could pay them back for wrongs or subordination suffered. Scholars ranging from historians (e.g., Schueller 1999) to sociologists (e.g., Snow and Anderson 1987) to social anthropologists (e.g., Gwaltney 1980) and novelist-philosophers (e.g., Selvon 1993) have written about these conscious social performances of subordinated groups in the Americas. An important lesson among the working classes in the Caribbean is that success in life involves being able to smile and have a joyful demeanor. This is where dignity lies. In Clarke's opinion this early socialization helped him realize that dancing and singing calypso are an expression of this understanding. As with other pan-Caribbean musical genres, calypsos are musical documents conveying these philosophies of life (Mahabir 2002; Rohlehr 2001).

Besides hearing calypso on his father's records, Clarke also heard Aruban radio programs, which had a wide listening audience. Clarke was a fan of the Baba Charlie calypso show. His father and others listened to these programs to know what was hot and new in calypso. While they sipped their gin and scotch and ate journey cakes and salt fish, they tuned in and laughed at the jokes the DJs cracked in between the record playing. The shows were characterized by critical social and political commentary concealed in humor. No one was exempt from blame for the situation on the island or in the wider Caribbean. In Clarke's words, "Everyone, from the prime minister in his Cadillac to the old lady selling her lotto on the side of the road, had something up they sleeves." Everyone was skilled in artifice. At that early age Clarke was exposed to the power of the radio DJs and, through them, to the strategizing elements that are necessary when one lives in a tourist paradise.

This Saturday calypso ritual had been around since time immemorial, and Clarke did not feel the need to analyze it. He simply felt that this was the time for those who worked the hardest and took the most flack to unwind. It was a time for them to remember how and why to smile. The *how* related to physical and bodily pleasure, while the *why* was indicative of calypso's political and social role. As is the case with other New World cultural expressions, both went together (Kelley 1997). No one explicitly questioned calypso's dominance on Saturday, except the priests and pastors. But even their complaints failed to lead to a change of heart or a termination of calypso performance.

Many priests and pastors, most of whom were North American or Western European, were not happy with calypso and what they deemed the rambunctious lifestyle associated with it. According to these men of the Lord, hip grinding, rum drinking, excessive partying, and especially the theatrical display of sexual prowess were at odds with the way of Christ and his apostles. They were also at odds with what they considered civilized behavior.

Judging from Clarke's account, the priests and pastors conceived of Christian living as ideally involving righteousness and a renouncement of worldly pleasures. There was no place for hedonism, let alone cunning. They realized that the Christianity of these small islanders was a Creole affair: respectability and piety should always be accompanied and overruled by shrewdness when necessary. As Clarke put it, "From young they teach me that God helps those who help themselves. Manna ain't going to fall from the sky. That was back then, back in Moses them days. Even if your actions ain't all that clean, [it's all right] as long as he see you making an effort."

In other words, Clarke learned that the biblically derived ontological idea of man's sinful nature had to be married to the concrete realities of survival. In the marriage of the two and in the judgment of and privilege given to actions based primarily on those realities, sinful behavior was not excused but rather was made acceptable. Furthermore, God made it a habit to strike at those who seemed to live clean, pious lives; all their cleanliness and hallelujahs, Clarke's mother and others would gossip, didn't amount to much in the eyes of the Lord. It was up to them, like Job, to figure out where they went wrong. Despite the upstanding Christian performance of these "Jobs," these people were usually knocked down a peg or two when it came to ridding themselves of ill fortune. Though they admired the priest and pastors, these clergy were ill suited for spiritual warfare in the Caribbean. Such tasks required a specialist in Obeah, Santeria, or Vodou, but one who was also "Creole enough" to accommodate their Christian sensibilities. These specialists could provide a spiritually grounded explanation for the predicaments of dutiful but ill-favored Christians. Difficulties were rarely blamed on the afflicted individuals but instead on envious persons or disquieted ancestral spirits. Those who were blamed were accused of employing evil magic or of having gone to a specialist who could work such a spell. At other times it was said that ancestral spirits were angry about current affairs.

Underestimating the impact of creolization, the missionaries felt that they were going to teach the Arubans how to live in a godly manner. From the pulpit, many of these "civilization bringers" preached fire and brimstone, rebuking the calypso lifestyle. Others took another route, promoting the ethos of unconditional love, advising Arubans to follow Christ's example and turn the other cheek. Love would conquer all. Such approaches failed to attract large congregations, however. Most young and middle-aged adults rarely attended church. Religious leaders watched as the churches got emptier and emptier.

Instead of confronting church leaders, many congregants, especially children, middle-aged women, and the elderly, simply chose to switch to another church or denomination. Visiting churches across denominational lines was not unusual. People often did this to demonstrate working-class solidarity, emphasizing that egalitarianism should counter the hierarchy of "my group is better than yours," dominant in the wider society. Even if people believed their denomination was better than that of their neighbors, they would still attend other services when invited.

Clarke also emphasized the ecumenical idea that there is only one God anyway. Because of this one God ideology, Clarke's mother, though having him baptized a Methodist, made him attend various churches, including the Church of God, a Catholic church, and a Seventh-day Adventist church. If someone asked kindly, Clarke's mother would send him to that person's church. The more blessings a person had and, in material terms, the wider his or her network was, the more steadfast he or she was in life.

Some congregants confronted church leaders when they were dissatisfied, but respect for men of the Lord, especially Western missionaries, was still a commonplace. The interaction between the common folk and the missionaries was marked by shows of paternalism and racial deference—in short, the realities of white superiority, a term that denotes "a system of power relations that structures society" (Dawson 1995: 203). Generally speaking, in the West Indies class and race went hand in hand (James 1969, 1963). Those who owned the most or occupied the higher stations in society were usually those with a lighter complexion, and the most important positions were always occupied by whites. Missionaries represented the economic and political might of the Western colonial powers but also ideas of race and civility. Hence, those in Clarke's neighborhood who might have confronted these missionaries would have had to deconstruct various ideological barriers based on inequality. They would have had to go against the established system, the privileged readings of the institutional and conceptual conditions of subjectification, whereby having a lighter complexion and occupying a higher position supposedly translated into being the bearer of truth. But this system was always contested. Conceptual and institutional conditions were never unequivocal.

Pioneering, sharp-tongued women like Clarke's mother spoke their minds and made it clear to priests and pastors that the only ones who could give them any commands about how to live their lives were God and their deceased mothers and fathers, who spoke to them in dreams. They knew their Bibles too and knew that God speaks to only a select few. A popular argument among them was that David danced, so what was wrong with them carrying on, if they did so decently? Then, one of two things would generally occur: either the religious leaders would start to show respect for their lifestyles and to understand the Bible according to their interpretations, or these congregants would quit the church until someone appeared who was more to their liking.

Naturally there were pioneering figures on the other side as well: priests and pastors who genuinely sought to build equitable or less hierarchical relations with the people they had come to instruct in the ways of the Lord. These men, in their own ways, enacted the role of Christian calypsonians. They became somewhat legendary, and Clarke has fond memories of them.

In addition to the supposedly noble intentions of some of these priests and pastors, pragmatism as well as their own idiosyncratic ways of being Christians might also have been at work. Clarke recalled a Dutch Catholic priest who was enormously popular because he publicly displayed that his feet were indeed made of clay. He would often be found drinking, sometimes to the point of drunkenness, with the men in the local rum shop. During Carnival, when calypso was king, he danced on the side of the road. Although most hymns sung in his church were Gregorian chants, he had quite a congregation, some of whom had been baptized as Protestants.

There was also a Methodist minister from a larger British West Indian isle, a handsome and well-mannered gentleman by all accounts, who made it his business to stop by and play a little steel pan with the men on Saturdays. That simple gesture of playing pan and taking a sip of rum with the "boys" ensured that young Clarke and others in the neighborhood would visit his church on Sundays.

It is safe to say that the defiant stances of the working and lower middle classes, coupled with a similar lifestyle and theological understanding among the well-to-do, made the more attuned priests and pastors on Aruba aware that calypso and Christianity each had its day. If Saturday was dedicated to calypso, then on Sunday the Gospel reigned supreme. Dressed in his starched shirt and linen trousers, young Clarke regularly attended Sunday school, where he learned biblical verses by heart and sang praises to the Lord.

The verses Clarke memorized were mainly from the Old Testament, favored because they were considered adventurous. Noah and his ark, Moses and the promised land, Jonah in the belly of the whale: all the stories that captivated a young child's imagination. Through these tales, Clarke became aware that a moral yet demanding God was constantly watching over his shoulder: "It was not a question of choice. You had to believe in him. If he let a whale swallow Jonah, no telling what he would do to you."

Despite God's terribleness, Clarke, like everyone else in the neighborhood, bothered little about dutifully implementing Christian ethics in his daily life. He explains it this way: "Belief was number one; practice, number three or four." According to Clarke, no one doubted the power of God and the idea that if they did wrong, they would be punished, but they reckoned that God could not keep up with all the mischievousness of his people and that he simply let a lot of wrongdoings slide. Through the Old Testament, they learned that mankind had to really overdo it for God to intervene.

There were many examples of corrupt politicians and wealthy businessmen who succeeded through all kinds of artifice. Listening to the Baba Charlie calypso show and to the conversations of older people and his peers taught Clarke that God punished the corrupt politicians on Aruba or the rest of the world only sporadically. Old men would tell jokes, saying that God had lazy angels. Some were so busy eyeing the beautiful women that they forgot to record the deeds of the wealthy. Their slackness allowed these "big fish" as well as the small "guppies" to avoid punishment. From his mother Clarke learned the importance of doing one's best to live according to God's laws but not overdoing it to the point of jeopardizing one's chances at worldly success.

Sundays were also marked by a change of music in the home. Clarke's mother and others in the neighborhood played Mahalia Jackson and other North American gospel artists rather than calypso. On Sunday, the mothers were the designated DJs. The Victoria radio station, whose religious format was unpopular during the week, had a large listening audience on Sunday. Neither Clarke nor the other children were required to sit down and pay attention to the religious broadcasts, but there was no escaping them, since wherever you were, in the house or the yard, gospel music and church sermons enveloped the air. The Christian soundscape that permeated the neighborhood meant that at least some messages were heard.

Clarke's father, like most of the men and young adults on the block, disappeared quite early on Sunday, right after the first phase of the gospel music onslaught. Like elsewhere in the Caribbean, on Aruba church attendance and related practices were primarily female activities (see, e.g., Austin-Broos 1997 on Jamaica). In the afternoon, gospel music mania died down. If the kids behaved themselves well, they were rewarded with a worldly treat. Hordes of kids accompanied by their elder siblings or responsible teenagers headed to Principal, the nearest movie theater.

The mothers took the opportunity provided by the "babysitting" of Principal to visit one another and catch up on the latest gossip. After the children returned from the cinema in the evening, it was time for them to go to bed. If Clarke's parents were in a good mood, he and his older siblings could take the transistor radio into the bedroom and listen to some music.

Sunk into these thoughts and smiling about the good old days, Clarke lost track of the time. He suddenly realized that it was time to begin his program. Off went the automatic recorder and up went the lever, whereby the people at home could hear Clarke's voice. His accent changed completely. Gone was the "proper" speech with its slight Yankee accent. In typical West Indian fashion, Clarke had mastered both Standard English and its local Creole variety. The switch to the latter illustrated his awareness of what was necessary to play the role of a calypso disc jockey: to provide authenticity to the format of his program and to entice others to participate. The switch also indicated his awareness of what was necessary in playing the role of informant to me, making me wonder to what degree I had been "played." This is at issue whenever informants relate part of their lives to anthropologists (Gwaltney 1980). However, with Clarke, his role as a public performer added an extra dimension to this issue.

In Clarke's recounting of the early part of his life story, the impact of socioeconomic class formations played a pivotal role. Clarke presented himself and the ideas on Christianity and calypso that shaped him as products of the working-class way of life. However, as he began the broadcast, it soon became apparent that Clarke's radio audience, the contemporary aficionados of the calypso way of life, did not adhere to clear-cut class distinctions. He seemed to be quite fine with that. This is understandable, since on SXM, where everyone works in the tourist industry, class ceases to be a self-evident master category that persons employ when relating to one another. Instead inter- and intra-class cultural categories, such as those described in the following section, become prevalent. Put differently, leisure-based lifestyles combined with consumption patterns are the privileged mode of identification. Defining oneself in class terms is not fashionable. Only when addressing international issues do class and *"dependencia"* versions of Marxism become explanatory tools. In the everyday interactions on the island, class formations are better looked at as effects that reveal certain social dynamics rather than an overarching explanatory ground.

Target audiences of particular radio programs do not materialize out of thin air (Spitulnik 2000; Barber 1997). Usually they are crafted by the disc jockey under the influence of the managerial staff. This is done contextually, however; as a rule, there must be a specific relationship between the audience and a radio disc jockey that the DJ and staff want to encourage, and this goal influences the format that is employed. By *format,* I refer to the linguistic style of presentation, the role of music, the disc jockey's interaction with the audience, the societal topics that are addressed, and the manner in which these topics are discussed. In short, *format* encompasses the whole layout or design of a radio program.

On a small island such as SXM, it is not lucrative for a team of experts to think about these issues and develop a strategy to be implemented, followed by the necessary monitoring techniques. The owner of PJD2 told me that on the island, "one plays it by ear." What he meant is that, generally speaking, the crafting of an ideal audience is left in the hands of the disc jockeys. Once a program is successful and has sufficient sponsorship, no one in management will interfere with it. If a program does not appeal, it is simply cut from the roster. With Clarke's connections and popularity, sponsors and advertisers were queuing up for him to endorse their businesses.

I was always amazed at the manner in which Clarke constructs an audience, interweaving this with the right format. Though he gives it an extra flair, it is a format that I was to encounter time and time again with other calypso disc jockeys. It consists of a performative model of being a calypso disc jockey and a mode of address whereby one seeks to persuade a wide listening public to tune in.

The performative model is based on mimicry. By exaggeratedly mimicking the linguistic slang and style of argumentation of a rummie and a fortune seeker, Clarke seeks to entice those who perform these roles more often. A *rummie* and a *fortune seeker,* two similar lifestyles that I discuss in chapter 2, are emic terms used to describe persons whose preferred leisure activities consist of frequenting neighborhood snack bars, drinking establishments, casinos, lotto shops, and prostitution houses. Their day is incomplete if they have not visited one of these. Playing games of chance, drinking strong rum, and constantly talking about just missing the big lotto prize are essential ingredients of the rummie's and fortune seeker's ideas about having a good time. These are not the only distinguishing traits of the rummie and fortune-seeker lifestyles. They are also known for the way they embody these identities. Rummies and fortune seekers demonstrate an enormous amount of bravura. Making covert, vulgar jokes concerning sexual escapades, gossiping about love relationships gone sour, exhibiting continual sarcasm toward the rampant corruption in politics and the rising cost of living, and deliberating over the cunning that is necessary to get ahead in the money tie system are typical among rummies and fortune seekers.

Not all rummies and fortune seekers are blue-collar workers. For instance, one of the most notorious rummies on the island was a medical doctor who also had an MA in economics. After work he could be found with his shirt wide open, hanging out with friends belonging to various social classes. Another example is the late Dr. Claude Wathey, a successful politician who was renowned for his unapologetic performance of the rummie lifestyle.[3]

Nevertheless, there is a strong confluence between these social categories and being working class. As a result rummies and fortune seekers often engage with tourists, which is a source of delight for many of the latter. Many tourists enjoy interacting with workers who perform more watered-down versions of the rummie and the fortune-seeker lifestyles during working hours. They embody the honest hedonism ideal with a touch of ruffian, which many tourists expect to find on SXM. The most daring or adventurous tourists solicit such performers to take them to the local establishments where they hang out after work. At these places they are treated to rawer versions of the rummie and fortune-seeker lifestyles. As long as they are willing to pay for a fair share of the food, drinks, and casino chips, they are made honorary members of that particular rummie and fortune-seeker "club." In exchange for opening their purses, the tourists are given the feeling that they have connected with the ordinary folk on the island, a connection that usually ends after the holiday.

The music that is usually played in the establishments that rummies and fortune seekers frequent is calypso and other pan-Caribbean genres such as bachata, merengue, zouk, salsa, and kompa. On a Tuesday evening many of these bars will have their radio or TV tuned in to Clarke's calypso program. This is because he will comment on the most talked-about occurrences of the week in a humorous fashion, filled with indirect criticism toward abusers of all classes. In other words, he will mimic the way these issues are discussed among rummies and fortune seekers. Clarke knows what to talk about and how to talk about it because he is a frequenter of many of these establishments. He employs various working-class-based innuendos to connect with the majority of rummies and fortune seekers. Clarke hails them to tune in and participate through slick verbalizations such as: "Remember back in the days when all we had were marbles or a wicket and ball to play cricket? Nowadays our ungrateful children want Nintendo and Sega. When we tell them we don't have it they ask us, 'Mammy, what happen to all them tips from the tourists?' Call in and speak your mind. Tell me where it is hurting." He combines this with shout-outs to the most outspoken performers of the rummie and fortune-seeker lifestyles. He also mentions particular establishments, providing free advertising for them.

Two qualifications regarding rummie and fortune-seeker performances must be made, however. First, the question of language and musical preference divides rummies and fortune seekers. Although most SXMers are fluent in Creole English, not all transmigrants who perform the rummie and fortune-seeker lifestyles in their spare time employ this idiom. In establishments with a predominant Haitian and Dominican clientele, Haitian or Spaniol is the lingua franca, and bachata or kompa music are played much more than calypso. Because of these language and music differences, the establishments rarely tune in to Clarke's program.

Seemingly, Clarke deems these establishments so inconsequential that he does not bother to include bachata, merengue, salsa, zouk, or kompa in his program. He could easily do so, since other calypso disc jockeys have made this move, and he is versed in Spaniol and Haitian. I did not verify the main reason for this omission. All I can deduce is that Clarke does not need additional rummies and fortune seekers to tune in on a regular basis. He already has a steady and loyal audience. And as the adage goes: if it ain't broke, don't fix it. In addition, his love for calypso and its importance in his stand-up performances may be influencing why he remains exclusively faithful to this genre.

The second qualification I must make is that I encountered some working-, middle-, and upper-class SXMers who considered rummies and fortune seekers crass. They saw such performances as overdone: too much cunning, too little virtuousness. Many considered it inappropriate for Clarke to endorse this type of living on the radio. Understandably, most of these do not feel invited to tune in to, let alone participate in, Clarke's calypso program.

Nevertheless, the mode of address that Clarke as the calypsonian employs to entice a listening public is reminiscent of the one he uses with the wider fan base that attends his stand-up shows and theater performances. These shows have a strong antiphonal, call-and-response character to them, with Clarke taking on multiple guises. There is no real Clarke behind these, only a series of personae.

As is the case with his theater presentations, he works to establish a dialogue with his public. Through this dialogue, a form of participatory interaction, Clarke ideally hopes to lead his public toward a specific understanding of wider societal issues. Hence, those who reply during his live performances often feel compelled to do the same during his radio broadcasts as call-in respondents. They need not adhere to or be outstanding performers of the rummie or fortune-seeker lifestyles. Olga, the owner of the restaurant where Clarke and I met, is someone who in her spare time does not frequent bars, but she does call in to converse with her friend on the radio.

When members of the more affluent classes call in—people who may not identify with, or may even be somewhat disapproving of, the rummie or fortune-seeker lifestyle—the interaction takes on implicit class dimensions: "How is business? That mattress can still handle all of that money? When are you going to share some of that money with us? Remember the Lord said its better to give than to receive."

Olga and other relatively wealthy callers usually reply in the same sarcastic tone, saying that things are slow, that they themselves are having difficulties getting by. Clarke may then ask them to contribute whatever they can spare to a particular charity or a barbecue ticket or raffle that is being held at one of the hang-out spots of rummies and fortune seekers. Put on the spot, they usually reply that in the interest of the island they would be happy to do so.

Clarke's performative model of the calypso disc jockey and his mode of address are not random, for they fulfill his wish to be heard by various sectors of SXM society. Clarke is motivated by the desire to make his star shine brighter. For him fame brings the yearning for more fame and, concretely speaking, more ticket sales for his live shows. Nonetheless, this is only part of the story. I also witnessed how his exaggerated performances and interpellations demonstrate a double message in every interaction: the honest hospitality that accompanies the "what's in it for me." In this he reminds SXMers that the money tie system is a social fact, a performative space in which everyone participates.

Clarke rarely prepares a specific subject to address on his program. His main objective is to entice the audience to participate. He touches on various contentious subjects that he knows to be current among rummies and fortune seekers. Quite often these same subjects intersect with major societal concerns. Of the subjects that gain the most attention, the one with the widest appeal is the one he selects. This subject will then be dealt with in the hour dedicated to serious societal affairs.

As a result of Clarke's appeal for audience participation, PJD2 often resembles a transit hall when he is on the air, with people from all walks of life coming and going. Some fans bring newly acquired CDs or rare "oldie goldies" that "he just has to play," while others stop by to exchange small talk. Also more business-minded fans come to ask him to promote a charity, barbecue, or fete they are organizing. They give him some free tickets to give away on his program, and if he thinks the event is for a good or interesting cause, he will improvise a five-minute interview.

In addition to these visitors, some also use the phone to interact with Clarke, to react to the "bait" he throws when humorously touching on certain societal topics. The night I was there, however, it was neither the visitors nor the callers who had the scoop that would assure him a successful broadcast but rather his "freelance journalists." "Freelance journalists" is the nickname I gave to Clarke's buddies who are professionals in performing the rummie and fortune-seeker lifestyles and regular visitors to the station. These men and women know the latest gossip and, thus, what is likely to captivate the attention of their counterparts in the corner shops and snack bars. All calypso disc jockeys have their freelance journalists. Some become regular coanchors for those listening in at home.

About forty-five minutes into the program, a group of these journalists appeared: three men in their early forties carrying a six-pack of beer and a Coke. The six-pack was clearly for them to remain "nice" (drunk), as they say on the island. They brought the Coke for Clarke, since he does not usually drink, in contrast with his talk about rum and guavaberry.

"Boy I telling you, you going to get ants in your belly from all that soda," one of the men jokingly remarked as he opened his Carib beer.

The way these three men installed themselves in the broadcasting room indicated they were accustomed to sitting in during his program and that they intended to stay for the whole show. There were chuckles of anticipation, as they could not wait to feed Clarke the latest tittle-tattle. With all the sweetness and exaggeration that accompanies hot gossip, these men told Clarke about a well-known local personality who was caught cheating. His wife, a local as well, proceeded to beat him and his mistress, who was from Saint Kitts. According to them she was angry about his extramarital affair and that he had spent his hard-earned money on his mistress instead of on her and their children. As if this was the first time they had heard the story, they accompanied Clarke as he laughed his heart out. The scene was reminiscent of young adolescents enjoying themselves at the expense of others. To make it even juicier, one of the men enacted how the Casanova sought to protect himself from his wife's wrath.

Clarke seemed to be waiting for this opportunity. He took to the microphone with a new élan. He began by admonishing men on SXM that they should not forget that fornication is a sin, quoting the Old Testament: "The ways of man are before the eyes of the Lord." To avoid any misunderstandings, he proclaimed that he was not talking about Jacques, saying the man's name who supposedly had been caught in the act. Hence, no one should say that he was trying to pick a fight. He was simply making a general comment.

After clarifying that he was not gossiping but was busy with social commentary, he continued, "Guys, be careful. You never know who you getting into bed with." He then played a song by Black Prince, an artist known for his humorous songs full of smut and self-ridicule: "De Letter," one of Prince's classics about a conquest gone foul. In this particular song Black Prince tries to court a beautiful woman who shrugs off his clichéd advances. In the chorus she tells him that the only way she will have an affair with him is if he gets his ex-wife or -girlfriend to write a letter of recommendation. Furthermore the ex has to mention a telephone number or address where she can be reached for confirmation. Since Black Prince knows that no ex of his will write a letter of good conduct, he gets his cousin, who is a homosexual, to do it for him. After reading the letter, his potential conquest seems pleased with the female overtones in it. Full of confidence, Black Prince tells the listener that he is going to let the woman pay for her boldness and insolence in bed. As the song ends we learn that during the "deed," Black Prince realizes that he is lying in bed with a transvestite.

Following this song, Clarke played a tune by Shayne Balley about a woman who threatens to physically abuse anyone who sleeps with her man. While Clarke was playing these two songs, the phones began to ring incessantly, as women, mostly locals, felt that he had invited them to react. Most of these callers claimed that men were reckless and couldn't keep their penises in their pants. Local men were like dogs that needed to be trained; otherwise their instincts would take over and they would start straying to the worst sluts, who were usually characterized as newcomers. Here is Shayne Balley, who the callers felt was on their side:

This song is for all them hungry girls them
If I only
This is a warning
Had too many drinks Carnival night
me and that girl almost had a fight because the watching me man and I
    can't over stand
Girl move your ass I find you rather out of place
And you're ugly in this
you're like a disgrace
But me man think that I am drunk
and them girls think that they could front
so they holding me man and I can't over stand
But I building up courage and I walk up to the stage
I say "Darling I have a problem"
Me maybe drink me Carib and me stout
but me no put water in me mouth
I have a problem that's my boyfriend
You better let him go right now
before I share out some stout
I have a problem that's my boyfriend
Let go me man.

Clarke interacted with these callers, agreeing that it did seem as if the nature of man was so weak that at times his brain was overridden by the one-eyed old man. On the basis of callers' comments and requests, he played "Stay Home" and "Who Let the Dogs Out?" "Stay Home" is a song about how a woman trains her new man, whom she calls Rover, so that he will not commit infidelity. It refers to sex and mentions a particular magical brew of herbs that should be used when preparing a man's food, to guarantee that he remains tame. In contrast, "Who Let the Dogs Out?" is an anthem in which men are heartened to take the negative connotation of the word *dog* and resignify it to mean a man who is sexually

active and proud of it. Thus, while women use the term *dog* to insult
men, men invert the term, rendering it less powerful.

> I have a little rover
> frisky Casanova
> Rover always playing
> man he always straying
> As he get the itch like a bitch in heat
> Rover out the gate and he on the street
> When he doggy hormones start to scratch
> Rover gone again and leaves me to catch
> So I give him stay home in the morning
> stay home in the evening
> Stay home in the night time that's always the right time
> When man get the urge and they want to roam give them stay home
>
> Girls: Yes.
> Listen up. I giving out the recipe now.
> What I put in this special brew I know your bound to ask.
> A little country bukie, cunu munu I used to keep in a flask.
> Compelling powder and shinning bush, a little this and that,
> a special something that folks call. . . . Shit I telling you flat.

The comments of the singer, T. C., about preparing a special herbal
brew to keep men in check seemed to strike a chord with male listeners.
On the island rumors abound about women having secret recipes that
make their men more plaint. These various recipes go by the collective
name of "blijf hier," which, translated from Dutch, means "stay here."

Several rummie and fortune-seeker performers from the community
took the opportunity to reveal personal experiences, weaving stories
with fantastic plots that seemed more like fiction with only a few grains
of truth; others with more truth than fiction. Let me give two illustra-
tions. The first caller had a typical SXM accent, indicating that he was
possibly a local. He retold an experience he had had with a woman who
had sought to use blijf hier on him. He began by bragging that as a single man with a good job, he had his share of sexual adventures. There
was one woman, however, who seemed to have some sort of control over
him. Before entering her house he was "mister macho man," but as soon
as he had been there for a while, his manly shield "melted like butter."
After confessing this to a close friend, it was suggested that she might be
putting something in his food, and indeed, every time he arrived at her
house, she had a plate of food ready for him. Since he "liked his mouth,"
he ate everything she fed him. His friend gave him a special little silver

spoon to use to test the food. If it turned black upon touching the food, he could be assured that she was using blijf hier on him.

He took his friend's advice, and during the following visit, he carried the little silver spoon in his pocket. As always, she had a bowl of steaming rice and red snapper waiting for him. This time, however, he feigned being tired and said he would eat the food later. What made him even more suspicious was that after two and a half hours, the rice was still steaming. He went to the table, took a spoonful of rice, and fed it to the woman's cat. The cat went berserk and ran out of the house. Meanwhile the spoon had turned black. Days later he was told that the cat was still circling the Catholic Church. He thought that had he eaten the rice, he would have probably asked the woman to marry him. The moral of his story was that women can't be trusted, especially those who never curse and are always aiming to please.

The second caller had a discernible Dutch metropolitan accent. I assumed he was a Dutch expatriate who had taken to island life. Bars and corner shops that were frequented by legal and illegal immigrant women searching for a good man were his hangouts. He was a pro in the game of chatting up women, and he had plenty of fun without being sucked into marriage or a steady relationship with what he called gold diggers. Like all pros, however, he was not immune to the boomerang effect— what goes around comes around.

One particular evening he had been introduced to a Dominican woman who seemed out of place in the pub setting. She did not openly solicit his attention or that of any of the other men present. Striking up a conversation, she claimed that because of poverty she had had to migrate to SXM. Her father had died when she was quite young, and as the eldest she took care of her mother and her younger siblings. She also had two young children whom she supported, since their good-for-nothing father had run off with someone else. Since she was not into whoring and didn't want to make her poverty an excuse to work in that sector, she made a living cleaning the houses of the rich. It didn't pay half as much as being an exotic dancer would have, but at least she maintained her dignity.

The metropolitan expatriate was taken by the simplicity, honesty, and attractiveness of this Dominican woman. Even though she did not ask, he began giving her money to send to her family in the Dominican Republic. He even paid for her plane ticket home when she told him that her mother was ill. In the months that followed he began to fall head over heels in love with his Dominican Cinderella. He even contemplated asking her to move

in with him. He probably would have done so if she had not inadvertently
blown her own cover.

A few weeks after she had returned from the Dominican Republic, he
found her at her home, sobbing. He could hardly understand her through
her weeping. After he had managed to comfort her and calm her down,
she told him that her father was gravely ill. It was then that he smelled
foul. The first time they met she had told him about growing up without
a father. He confronted her with her lie, and she was dumbfounded. She
claimed that she was referring to her stepfather, whom she considered to
be her real father. This alleged stepfather didn't have much, but he always gave her mother what he could. Her digressions and improvisations
proved useless. He cursed her and ended the relationship. For him, as for
the previous caller, women in general could not be trusted.

The songs Clarke played after these verbal performances were
"Obeah Man," "Hairy Banker," and "You Ain't Going." "Obeah Man"
deals with a man who outsmarts a woman trying to put a magic spell on
him. She is unaware that he is an Obeah high priest. "Hairy Banker" is
about a man who spends all his money on a woman who has him
wrapped around her finger. *Hairy bank* is a folk term for vagina. Lastly,
"You Ain't Going" tells the story of a macho man who, while feigning
bravado, seeks permission from his wife to hang out with his male
friends. Here is a portion of "Obeah Man," followed by one from
"Hairy Banker":

> Melda dear you're making wedding plans
> carrying my name to Obeah man
> All you do
> You can't get through
> I still ain't going to marry to you.

> Me pocket empty
> empty
> 'Cause all the money
> money on me
> in the hairy bank
> where all the money gone: in the hairy bank
> where all the money dey [there]: in the hairy bank
> Hairy Mary take me money
> hairy Mary she contrary.

Now it was the women's turn again. A fortune-seeker performer
called in, saying that she had no sympathy for men, especially local men,
who were being taken for a ride by immigrant women. She mentioned
knowing locals who left their wives for Colombians and Dominicans

who worked as prostitutes. As a casino dealer who frequented brothels as "pit stops" before heading home, she had seen many of these women dancing on poles only to be brought into respectability by these men. Without any shame, they would parade with these women in the middle of town. They were so in love that they didn't notice that they were being ridiculed behind their backs. Everybody on SXM knew everybody else's business.

The caller's comment that she visited brothels should not be viewed as odd; on SXM I had a lot of contact with young female casino workers who would hang out at brothels and strip clubs after work. When I asked them about it, they told me that when one works the night shift, these were the only establishments open after work. Their presence there did not cause any hostile reactions by male customers. At times these girls would give the strippers tips to dance for them.

The caller relished the opportunity to speak her mind on the radio and claimed that the show's focus on blijf hier was problematic. She said that local men wanted to treat women like servants, and that local women told them to do their share of household chores and to help with the raising of their children, but poor immigrant women did not. According to her, the latter would even have a basin with water ready to clean their men's feet when they got home. Exempting men from household chores made them unaware that they were being milked for everything they had.

Clarke responded by stating that he knew from experience that it was expensive to have a mistress on SXM. They were all about " 'Me love you, Papi. You bring money for me pequeños en Medellín. Amour, the rent has to be paid in two days, ai Papi," all of which he pronounced with a characteristic Colombian accent. He said that local women should smell their men when they came home late at night to protect themselves. He mentioned perfume brands used by the different ethnicities, playing into local stereotypes. If their man smelled cheap and strong, he had been with a Colombian. On the other hand, Jamaican women loved syrupy-sweet scents. If he smelled expensive and had white sand on his shoes, he had been with a tourist.

Clarke followed these observations by playing "Everybody Peeping," a song that addresses the suffocating gossip in Caribbean societies. This was followed by "Who the Hell Is Kim," which relates the tale of a man who mistakenly calls out the wrong name (Kim) while having sex with his steady girlfriend:

I don't understand this
Girl I love the dirt you walk on

Hey listen T. C. didn't mean to cause you pain
I was only trying to come up with a baby's name
and that is the honest truth simple and plain
I will never ever talk in bed again
What you think about Kim and if it's a boy then Slim
a baby just like you.

Finally he played a calypso classic entitled "Lying Excuses," which humorously depicts a cheating man who desperately tries to improvise after getting caught in flagrante delicto by his wife:

Darlin, Sugar Dumplin, don't look so sad
The woman you catch me with in our bed
didn't have nowhere to lay she head
Casually she sat on the bed
And ask to massage she legs
That is all, that is all, that is all
I wouldn't lie to you.

After this round of guy bashing, Clarke provided an unexpected twist to the broadcast. He informed men that anything they could do, a women could do better. In storyteller mode, he talked about how his ex had taken him for a ride. One day he came home early from work to find his woman yelling loudly. His children ran up to him, telling him that there was a naked man in the house. Clarke didn't hesitate for a moment: he ran up the stairs to protect his wife. Upon entering the room, he saw that his wife was lying there naked, out of breath and perspiring heavily. As he headed toward her, he saw that the closet door was ajar. Inside he found his best friend, stark naked as well. Then Clarke delivered the punch line, saying that he trusted his wife so much that he angrily admonished his friend for frightening his children while his wife was having a heart attack.

He went on to talk about the infidelity of many local women who were just as unfaithful as their husbands. Husbands shouldn't feign surprise when they see that one or two of their children resemble the young, single Curaçaon living next door or the Chinese grocer from down the street. On SXM extramarital affairs were the rule rather than the exception. Many respectable local women had "sweet boys" from other islands. Their husbands spent their hard-earned money on the family, while, in Clarke's words, their wives bought Gucci and Naf Naf for their "Yardies" (Jamaicans).

Ending the discussion, Clarke declared that it was time for all SXMers to stop the excess and to clean up their acts: "We all make mistakes, but

Figure 8. Whatever happens, let's not forget that this is one happy cheating island.

we must not overdo it; this is one happy cheating island. We must remember that the Lord is watching." He then played "Bazodee," "Forkin," "Old Woman Alone," and "The World Needs More Love." "Bazodee" is a song about a woman who forgets her marital responsibilities because of the sweetness of the calypso music. The synonym for calypso music in this song is *iron,* a word that signifies drums but also the phallus:

> I find me self in a jouvert band
> with a sexy man
> can't remember me husband name
> could not remember me husband name
> because he iron have me so bazodee
> the iron have me so bazodee
> the iron have me so . . .

The same ambiguity is at play in Edwin Yearwood's "Forkin," which can be understood as a song in which someone complains that an unknown stranger is weeding his garden with a fork, or as one in which a "woman's garden" (i.e., her vagina) is forked (i.e., fucked) by a stranger:

> Somebody: somebody Bold
> Somebody: forkin me land

Somebody dig me dirt
Every time I go to work
Somebody forkin forkin
Now please don't you get me wrong
I working me land so long
I done work it all night long
but still when I gone somebody forkin.

The third song, "Old Woman Alone," symbolizes the "sweet boys"
who choose local older women for material gain:

Tell me who?
Do unto others as you would like them to do unto you
So just put your foot in a elderly person shoe
and remember one day you'll get old too
old woman alone we taking home
old woman alone in we Lexus
old woman alone in we big bus
I went and encourage jaggo
he say he have three he no want more
I went and encourage snakey
he say he car full up already
old woman we taking home.

The last song, "The World Needs More Love," is about the problematic state of the world today. The solution is not to have high aspirations
but to show love to the people in one's life:

When I take a look at the world today
I see disaster children gone astray
babies having babies
without going to church
I asked myself many questions
and I got no answer
the world needs more affection
we got to dig deeper
wash away your hatred with love
and you feel better
just walk away from your anger
and you will live longer
the world needs more love
love up with your baby
drink up and be merry
chin up don't you worry
I know life is not easy. Hug up in the party
link up with somebody
mash it up and be irie.

Clarke's show ended late, so he offered me a lift to my apartment. In the car we spoke about his radio program. During the drive I began to understand how his format, in combination with his personal views concerning the precariousness of being dependent on tourism, led to his inclusive politics of belonging. It was the combination of these two factors that dictated why he tackled the issue of inter- and intra-gender feuds between locals and newcomers in the manner that he did.

He began by explaining that a competent calypso disc jockey must know his genre and must be able to improvise. Furthermore, he must thoroughly analyze his society. These components—knowledge of calypso music, improvisation skills, and societal analysis—must be flavored with a heavy dose of humor to get one's message across effectively. A calypso disc jockey must know what to say and what to play to bring people to a level where they can laugh about things and about themselves, where they can realize that they are not without fault and should not harshly criticize others. Calypso is part of lived reality where everyone is implicated and no one can escape blame. In accordance with Clarke's biblically derived wisdom, he might sum his philosophy up this way: "Let those who are without sin cast the first stone."

Clarke told me that one of his secrets is to make victims feel that their resentment is justified. He pointed out that in the beginning of his show's section on relationships, local women were calling in, angry about the behavior of their male counterparts and critical of newcomer women who, in their opinions, acted like whores. Local women faced humiliation by their husbands' infidelity and the promiscuity of the newcomer women.

By siding with them and playing relevant calypsos, Clarke's actions were interpreted by the female callers as sympathetic. When he felt they were sufficiently confident, he turned the argument around, reminding them that they were also unfaithful. He mentioned the "sweet boys" from Jamaica and other Caribbean islands who supplied illicit sexual services to respectable local women. He told them they should not be surprised if the women they were discriminating against were having sex with their husbands. In Clarke's words:

When the French [metropolitan] woman treats her illegal Haitian [servant] like shit and she constantly arguing with her man, she shouldn't be surprise to find him in bed with Sophie [the Haitian domestic] screaming, "Papa bon Dieu." If you do good, good will come to you. Do bad and expect it back. God don't like wickedness. We all know that we are sinners, and no matter how much SXMers believe in God, they will sin. Man ain't no angel, but we must not abuse it. That is, practically speaking, what my program is all about.

Then Clarke became serious for the first time the entire night. He told me that for him, the gravest threat on a multiethnic island like SXM comes when people interpret conflict along ethnic lines. He believed this would have devastating effects on the tourist economy. "Tourists come to SXM to meet friendly people, people who live peacefully," he said. "If they want tensions, all they have to do is drive to the Bronx or follow the Bosnia drama on CNN." On the basis of this conviction, he transformed any topic that was brought to him during his radio program involving locals and newcomers so as to make clear to all SXMers that everyone is always complicit, that no ethnic group is morally privileged. According to Clarke, the appropriate politics of belonging for SXM is one where all belong equally. It is a politics accompanied by a conviction that Christian-inspired ethics should mediate against the excesses of artifice dictated by the money tie system. It is best observed in the balancing of calypso and Christianity, both of God's prerequisites for successful living.

I was intrigued by Clarke's inclusive politics of belonging. Here was a man who contested the exclusionary pronouncements found in the nationalist rhetoric of affluent local women who believed they belonged more than their newcomer counterparts because, unlike these newcomers, they supposedly lived more chaste lives. Clarke used his program to contest this idea by positing an alternative view: all SXMers, locals and newcomers, males and females, cheated. Clarke implied that this lack of virtuousness was caused by living within the money tie system. He argued that this shared reality should be the basis for a more inclusive politics of belonging. All SXMers belong equally, since none can claim the moral high ground. Clarke never mentioned the money tie system explicitly but did allude to it several times. For instance, he spoke about the sexual services rendered by young Jamaican newcomers, lower-class men who are both used by and use older well-off local women, many of whom are married.

In other instances it was Clarke's public who implicitly mentioned the toll taken by the constant enactment of the money tie system. There was, for instance, the tale of the rummie who met a Dominican woman who took him for a ride. He found out that he was being used only because she had forgotten her first lie. She told him that she had grown up without a father and then solicited money to visit this long-deceased father who was now supposedly ill.

For Clarke, shared complicity in the money tie system and a shared lack of respectability resulted in equal belonging. Though I admired Clarke's politics of belonging, I also felt that it seemed to obscure the class and gender inequalities that resulted from performances in the money tie system. Some are more to blame and have more to gain from the money tie system, and presenting this from a class and gender perspective could at least offer partial revelations.

But class and gender were not the prime explanatory categories most SXMers employed. I needed to understand matters from Clarke's perspective, which was tied to that of the wider society. By doing this I would award his discussion on promiscuity and chasteness the importance it deserved. Moreover, this move made me aware once more that class consciousness and class status are not natural forms of identification and understanding (Hall 1991, 1988; Laclau 1990, 1977). The same goes for a critical appraisal of one's gender as a product of patriarchy and placing this as primary (Gorelick 1991; Wharton 1991). Ethnicity, religious preference, and other social identifications are not secondary issues underlying the primacy of gender. Gender divorced from these other social identifications is, in Jane Flax's words, "a category that feminist theorists have constructed to analyze certain relations in our cultures and experiences. The concept must therefore reflect our questions, desires, and needs" (Flax 1992: 454). Like class, the concept has much purchase and is necessary, but several translations of one's experiences into political and scientific terms need to occur before one views oneself or society in class and patriarchal terms. Whether this concept gets adopted by an individual depends on the success that organic intellectuals (self-taught intellectuals) have in constructing a convincing ideology through which persons in a similar socioeconomic position reinterpret their realities. This reinterpretation gives them a different view of their common condition and ways of altering it.

As an outside observer, one could view Clarke as an upper-middle-class male who benefits from patriarchy. This does not necessarily mean that he identifies himself as such. Clarke is a male banker, but there is nothing to make him identify naturally with other professional men such as hotel managers, school directors, or lawyers. Intellectual work and processes of translating his experience into the political concepts of class and gender must first be undertaken for him to see himself in such a way. Even then there is no guarantee that he will view his class and gender positioning as primary. There is always choice.

The more I challenged the remnants of my biases of class and patriarchy as givens, the more I could see why Clarke sidesteps these issues. By focusing on universal promiscuity and the impossibility for any group to lay claim to chasteness, he challenges the exclusionary rhetoric of local women. Clarke points out that although all SXMers may wish to live honest lives, their repetitive enactment of the money tie system guarantees that virtuousness will be secondary to cunning. In such a milieu, the only *morally* acceptable politics of belonging is one that takes the overall *immorality* of all SXMers into account. In other words, SXMers have to accept a politics that marries the Christian ontological idea of the inescapable sinful nature of mankind to the realities of the island's tourist-based economy. "Sinful" acts such as infidelity are hereby not excused but are deemed unavoidable because of the concrete material circumstances. Clarke's message, based on how he understands the societal performances of SXMers, seems to corroborate the findings of some anthropologists researching Christianity: sinful practices are becoming ever more attractive and are even highlighted while in rhetoric they continue to be condemned (e.g., Meyer 2004, 2003). There is even a symbiosis between these two ideas.

Clarke's description of the money tie system can be read as an indication that it is the dominant performative space on SXM. Clarke does this by inviting rummies, fortune seekers, and his onstage fans to participate in a program dedicated to discussing infidelity on SXM. Through this discussion he seeks to show that honesty is usually secondary to cunning. It matters little whether one is a local or a newcomer, male or female, rich or poor: SXMers cannot escape the reality of enacting the money tie system.

For Clarke successful living revolves around being able to perform several identities at once, without any being primary. The only givens that he seems to accept are the anatomical differences between males and females. Nevertheless, these do not, for him, form a sufficient basis to differentiate performances of chasteness or promiscuity along gender lines. Clarke seems to understand that gender conventions regarding heterosexuality are not based on one's sexual organs or other anatomical differences. Men are not naturally more promiscuous than women, regardless of the fanciful ways that such a myth is presented. Anatomy is a limit, but as such, it says nothing about the varied societal performances that can be enacted.

In addition, in leading SXMers toward this understanding, Clarke employs inter- and intra-class and inter-gender categories. Rummies, fortune seekers, and fans of his onstage comedic performances are not easily reducible to specific class categories. Many rummies and fortune seekers are lower-class workers, but lawyers and doctors perform these lifestyles as well. Clarke does not treat the wealthy rummies differently from their less-well-off counterparts. Nor does he privilege one gender over another. His aim is to demonstrate that gender, class, and ethnic categories are of little consequence when it comes to promiscuity and chasteness. Everyone who lives on SXM is implicated in the money tie system. He asserts entanglement and connectivity. There is no space for claiming a single autonomous identity.

He makes his message powerful by employing calypso. The socially charged calypsos illustrate the contradictions of the lived reality of SXMers. Thus, the divide between victims and perpetrators, in this case local women and their newcomer counterparts, becomes difficult to sustain.

Clarke preaches that Christian-derived ethics, such as solidarity, tolerance, and brotherly or sisterly love, should act as a check to SXMers' promiscuity. The negative results of enacting the money tie system on male-female love relationships should be balanced by adhering to these ethics, though never to the extreme. In this constantly enacted performative space where cunning remains dominant, virtuousness should check immoral behavior when things get out of hand.

From Clarke's pragmatic perspective, tourism is definitely a mixed blessing but should not be challenged. His commonsense response to the tourist industry is similar to most SXMers'. They ask why they should hope that Westerners, who neglect their own impoverished fellow citizens, would be benevolent toward them if tourism ends. This common sense is based on media, hearsay, and their personal experiences. SXMers tune in daily to cable TV programs, where they observe the squalid conditions faced by a growing segment in the United States. In addition, many SXMers travel frequently to the North Atlantic countries or have close kin who live there. They know that bag ladies, crackheads, and other poor urban inhabitants exist in these countries. Many have families in the United States who struggle daily to keep their heads above water.

Many SXMers come from countries that do not have a booming tourist industry, countries where endemic poverty is the rule rather than the exception. They look to the remittance-based Haiti, the Dominican Republic, and Jamaica to see what happens when, as they put it, "the West forgets" or is only interested in cultivating safe touristy spaces such as Montego Bay.

For Clarke an extra dimension plays a role in his pragmatic stance. Because of his profession, he is aware of patterns of investments in the lesser Caribbean, which does not attract large-scale Western investors in non-tourist-related fields. As far as SXM goes, agriculture, industry, and service sectors unrelated to tourism are nonexistent. In addition, the island has no natural resources. Besides structural aid from France and the Netherlands, tourism is all that SXM has. Tourism, and by implication the money tie system, is thus seen as a necessity. SXMers "consent" to performing the calypsoing Other so that even the poorest newcomers can enjoy standard health care, education, and, more important, food on their tables. For poor newcomers SXM is heaven when compared with the hell lived by most in the Global South.

Calling for an end to this performance through the complete substitution of honesty and righteous living for cunning is incongruous with the necessities of the tourist industry. In Clarke's reasoning, shaped by his growing up on Aruba, Christian living should always be balanced by being able to perform the role of the calypsonian. In touristy Aruba, like on SXM, Christian-derived ethics are also second to the calypso lifestyle. On both islands this is so because of the survival needs of a people for whom tourism is their only means of income.

Through the marriage of the ontological idea of mankind's sinful nature to the contextual importance of tourism, privileging the latter, the most important aspect of SXM's Christianity can remain unfettered, that is, belief in God. Clarke learned as a youngster that it was not a matter of choice; one had to believe in God. Everything stood or fell through his grace. The Caribbean's blessings in the precariousness of global capitalism were explained as coming from the merciful hand of God. What's more, God did not unconditionally encourage following the precepts of the Bible over those of calypso. A balanced attitude toward both, where calypso has a slight edge, was considered to be God's unspoken commandment to the island's inhabitants. After all, God was a part-time calypsonian.

CHAPTER 5

DJ Shadow's Prescription for Rastafari Individuality

In the popular Western perception, Rastafari is still synonymous with the Caribbean downtrodden. So too is roots reggae, or conscious reggae, as they call this genre on SXM. DJ Shadow, a handsome brown-skinned Rasta with deep dimples who always dresses in the latest fads, shows this to be a far more complicated affair. Here is a man whose family is one of the wealthiest local clans on the island. They own substantial real estate on SXM and neighboring islands, such as Anguilla and Saint Kitts; lease their property to American and European hoteliers and merchants; and own motels, construction companies, import and export agencies, car rental agencies, and apartment complexes. DJ Shadow himself earns his living as a sophisticated West Indian who organizes festivals and concerts where top Caribbean and North American acts perform. Thus, here is a Rasta man far removed from the hardships and invisibility that the Masta Rasta (Bob Marley) and his Wailers had to overcome to achieve global stardom. Nonetheless, DJ Shadow also performs the One Love ideology—the assertion of a universal human identity, a privileging of individuality above national and ethnic differences. And in a multiethnic and multireligious country where, through conscious reggae, Rastafari messages of egalitarianism have transcended the closures of the deeply faithful and class is not a primary identification, DJ Shadow's version of Rasta is embraced by most.

I was at the PJD2 radio station, which was owned by the Shadow's uncle, to ascertain the semantic richness and specificity of his One Love

ideology and what this means for his politics of belonging. As always DJ
Shadow opened his broadcast with a recorded prayer from DMX, an
American rapper-turned-actor. This, he said, was to let his public know
that the first part of his show, the conscious reggae hour, was dedicated
to "spiritual matters," meaning societal issues connected to existential
queries: "Everything that happens in a society starts and ends with how
a man sees himself, 'cause how he sees himself will determine how he sees
others. So everything is spiritual, you overs? [a Rasta term that denotes
a change of heart and following this up in one's practice]."

DMX's prayer was accompanied by an entrancing dub rhythm. If I
had not known that the original track had been recorded a cappella, I
would have sworn that the music and prayer belonged together. DJ
Shadow was quiet and in a somewhat meditative state as DMX prayed
a "thug prayer," the prayer of a hoodlum thanking the Lord for caring
for him despite his wrongdoings and imperfections:

> Father God I am just learning how to pray
> First I thank you for the life of everyone that's here with me
> Then I thank you for the love you gave me
> Why?
> I don't know
> I don't deserve it, and it hurts inside
> Many a nights I have cried, and called your name out loud
> But didn't call you when I was doing good, I was too proud
> And still you gave me love, I wasn't used to that
> Most people that gave me love ended up taking it back
> That's something new to me, so I'm asking you for time to adjust
> Let me make it there, I will be one you can trust
> What I stand for, I put my life on it, I do
> I guess what I asking is, show me how to stand for you
> And I will rap for you, sing for you, teach for you, reach for you
> I will love you like you love me, unconditionally
> And I will always be prepared, for whatever the mission will be
> Give the nutrition to me, and I will properly digest it
> And when I give it back, I'll show you word well invested
> And whenever I go, before I go, let me give thanks to you my Lord, for
>   my birth, for every day that I've lived
> You gave me love most of my life, I didn't know was there
> In the name of Jesus, I give you my life 'cause you care.

As DMX's prayer finished, DJ Shadow took to the microphone and
began addressing his public. His address was wide as he greeted youngsters hanging out at street corners, members of the police squad, fire
brigadiers, hotel personnel, construction workers, bank clerks, store as-

sistants, managers, and even visiting tourists. DJ Shadow was calling out to SXMers from all walks of life to tune in to his program. But his address went further as he also sent shout-outs to potential listeners living on the neighboring islands of Anguilla, Saba, Saint Eustatius, Saint Barthélemy, Saint Kitts, and Nevis.

I wanted to question him about his public but had to wait, since the background music accompanying his shout-outs was setting the mood for the theme he would address during the show. The tune accompanying his greetings and luring in listeners was "Between Joy and Blues," by Ziggy Marley and the Melody Makers. In this song, life is likened to an enormous sea, and for this reason, humans have to be aware of the implications of the choices they make:

> Here we are in this ocean
> between life and death, truth and lie
> between faith and trust and hypocrisy
> between sick and cure
> between joy and blues
> So choose well make sure you don't lose
> Pick your choice, choose well
> 'Cause when your life is on the line, well then it's life that you can lose.

Finishing up his introductory greetings, DJ Shadow rewound the Melody Makers tune and told his listeners that it was dedicated to Riddim, a notorious biker who had tragically died in a motorcycle accident. He expressed his condolences to the family and reiterated that life can end so suddenly that it was therefore of utmost importance that SXMers choose every step carefully. The two songs that followed up "Between Joy and Blues" also touched on the theme of how life means constantly having to make choices. The second song, "In the Garden of Life," made a distinction between the garden of righteousness—or, positive path in life—and the garden of wickedness. The song claims that even though we are free to choose, God rewards or punishes us depending on which garden we choose. The third song, "Untold Stories," by Buju Banton, added another dimension, making it explicit that many important choices are made under conditions of Babylon, the Rastafarian term for Western-dominated capitalism. One chooses, but not under conditions of one's own choosing. "Untold Stories" is about how those with insufficient material means are unable to make choices to move on to greener pastures:

> Who can afford to will run
> But what about those who can't?
> They will have to stay

Opportunity a scarce, scarce commodity
In these times I say, when mama spend her last and send you go a class,
   never you a play
Its a competitive world for low budget people
Spending a dime while earning a nickel
With no regards to who it may tickle
No love for the people who a suffer real bad
Another toll to the poll, may God help we soul.

The first two songs present a unified version of being human, which signifies having to choose and face the consequences of one's choices. These songs speak to what can be envisioned as a universal human predicament across class, national, ethnic, religious, and gender lines. In the third song, however, a differentiation is made: some humans are better able to act on their choices than others. For those who live in poor nation-states and do not have sufficient means, personal choice means something different than for the affluent who live in wealthier states.

Did anyone hear these texts? DJ Shadow sought to make sure they did. He sang along with choruses and reiterated what he considered the most important verses. Besides what his efforts demonstrated, my own experiences in listening to conscious reggae with SXMers have taught me that many listen to the texts as well as the music.[1] Trevor, for instance, could recite whole verses of Peter Tosh and Capelton and philosophize about these, but when asked to do the same with the songs of popular North American R&B artists, he fell short. He knew the choruses or parts of verses. "That was just commercialism," he would say. The reason for this distinction is that from an early age, most children are socialized to connect the texts of certain types of music to larger societal experiences. (See the work of Carolyn Cooper, Gordon Rohlehr, and Brenda Berrian, respectively, on the Jamaican toasters, Trinidadian calypsonians, and Guadeloupean zouk singers who function as the organic intellectuals who produce these texts.) This socialization is done in many subtle ways. When speaking to one another, adults often quote artists and song texts to lend extra credence to their arguments: "like Bob Marley say" or "listen to Sparrow song." Youngsters do the same with their favorite heroes. And to do so, they have to know what the songs are about.

Conscious reggae concerts, and for that matter calypso festivals as well, are the recurring spaces where SXMers are socialized to take the texts of certain music forms seriously. These are spaces where life stories and stories about life are told. And to really understand these stories requires full-body engagement. One dances and sings along. Through this engagement, one hears the text. There is no passive reception. The artists build up their songs in such a way that they compel their audiences to participate and become co-performers. Call-and-response, break beats, musical and vocal improvisations, and crescendos whenever important messages are given are the general patterns of conscious reggae. The rhythms especially entreat the audience to engage and let down their guard. To do so, these rhythms evoke a sphere in which the world of worries is temporarily forgotten. They create a happy feeling, a collective effervescence in which there is a seamless, though temporary, reconciliation between the individual and the collective. Everyone's individuality is the improvisation on the general structure of the collective rhythmic performance.

However it is created, this happy feeling contrasts with the serious texts of conscious reggae. The words say, "Rebel. The system is rigged against the poor," but the rhythms say, "System or not, one must enjoy life first." On a touristy island such as SXM, the majority obey the commandment of the rhythm. The texts are secondary, producing rebels who only rebel verbally, who never go against the money tie system or the tourist industry. I would learn that DJ Shadow is a radio architect, producing rebels with a pragmatic cause: to keep SXM peaceful and prosperous within the bosom of capitalism.

But that was a future realization. Right now I was in the studio, conversing with the Shadow about his wide appeal. As Buju Banton's "Untold Story" played, I asked him to give explicit the reasons for his choice to address such a wide variety of SXMers. He replied that as a result of his time slot, when people from all walks of life tune in, and the segmented nature of his call-ins and requests, he has to address a wide public. He also wants a varied audience:

> I can't pinpoint exactly who listens to me. And I can't only judge it by the calls I get. I mean, yes, I can see that a lot of youths on the island or say, for instance, Statia [Saint Eustatius] will send an e-mail asking for a song or a big up [a shout-out to friends], but that is only a small portion. It is very surprising to meet older folk and older head who says, "You know, that prayer you played yesterday, I really like. Where did you get it?" Then I know, that is a midforty, midfifty person listening who will never call in. And when I walking through Front Street, a teenager will say, "Shadowman, what going on, like the program today?" If I was to guess, my main audience will be between fourteen and fifty years. What I want is for everybody to listen to my program. From the young girl to the old woman. That is a joy to me.

He also said that listeners from neighboring islands are of commercial importance for many businesses on the island, which is why he tries to draw them in: "Radio is entertainment and radio is business. I have to entertain the masses. I can't entertain one set of people. And the more people I entertain, the more business my uncle does. When those people in Anguilla hear me big them up and stay tuning in and hear that Rams [a wholesale and retail supermarket on SXM] have sale, it is there they going buy they stuff on Saturday." (Many Anguillans take the ferry and do their weekend shopping on SXM).

As I was tapping my feet and singing along to the tunes he selected, DJ Shadow commented approvingly, "I see you still know you tunes." He continued by saying that if one wants to engage SXMers from all walks of life, one has to play conscious reggae. Through conscious reggae, the egalitarian tenets of the Rastafari spiritual philosophy are delivered to all generations. Talking about the theme of the show, he said:

> The show today dealing with choices. We all got to learn to choose well. Riddim choose wrong and he die. I mean, too many young people dying senselessly. This is something the people talking about, 'cause Riddim was known, and he ain't the only one. Some youths want to play "Bad John," so they disobeying they parents and playing Evel Knievel on these pissy-ass roads we got here. Now, when you blazing on a bike down these little roads, and some of them have big-ass holes, accidents bound to happen. So I got to say something about it. I want tell them and their parents something. And I believe if you want to reach young and old with seriousness, you got to choose consciousness. When SXM people hear consciousness, they know it is about serious matters. It is a music that does reach all people. I mean, come on, when we was younger, we too used to listen to consciousness. And we still listening. We both have locks [dreadlocks] and the livity [egalitarian philosophy] of Bob, Steel Pulse, and Jacob Killer Miller rub off on us. Like us, you have lot more brothers and sisters, even those who gone corporate [working in banks and other financial institutions], who can't forget the Rasta business. And even our mothers. I mean, you know how many old heads might not like the whole chalice business [smoking of marijuana], but they know their Jimmy Cliff, Peter Tosh, and their Bob Marley. They too does tune in, 'cause Rasta ain't a youth thing alone, you overs? Rasta business is about equality, and which of our mothers ain't into equality?

DJ Shadow was on track about conscious reggae being the music of all generations. One of my earliest childhood recollections is that of my mother standing behind the stove as she moved and sang along to Bob Marley's "War." According to her, that was Marley's best song, as it spoke to the timeless issue of man's oppression of man. I learned to listen to the texts of conscious reggae partly because of her. And though many things have changed, conscious reggae's mass appeal has not. On SXM, it is the music of young and the old, local and newcomer. It also transcends religious differences. I encountered Christians, Muslims, Buddhists, and Hindus who were into this music. Philosophizing about this, DJ Shadow claimed, "Rasta business is all people business. Them boys might worship Shiva, but they still love Marley, 'cause Marley sing that the caste system must done. Rasta is international, nondenominational, seen?" (Here, *seen* means, "Have you gotten the point in a way that it leads to a new understanding?") I had to agree with him that on SXM, various religious groups embrace Bob Marley. And though the Masta Rasta sang that the caste system must done, his music has enticed people who are not necessarily anti-caste or anti-capitalism to shop at Indian-owned stores.

Important things were happening for his public during our conversation and the broadcasting of the first three tunes. He struck a chord by beginning his program with condolences for the family and friends of Riddim. The phones began to ring as people called in to make requests or just to mention that they agreed with him that life was all about making the right choices. I noticed that those who called in belonged to several generations. Some callers, however, were somewhat off track, as they were requesting merengue tunes during the conscious reggae hour. Their excuse was that they were "thieving a chance" to call when their managers were not paying attention or when they had few customers. No matter the caller or the request, DJ Shadow was polite and friendly. He jotted down the requests, made jokes if it was a regular, and, if necessary, carefully explained to some that he could not play the requested merengue tunes, since they didn't fit into the show's theme. He told them that he would still mention their names on the radio and play another fitting tune. For all those who simply called to offer condolences to the family of Riddim, he mentioned their names and, after the third song, played the Twenty-third Psalm in a reggae rhythm.

The musical rendition of the Twenty-third Psalm was followed by a short commercial break, after which DJ Shadow returned to the microphone, saying that when choosing between the various options that life presents, one has to be aware of the negative influence of "politricksians" and "false prophets," political and religious leaders who claim to know what is best for others. He claimed that they seek to create divisions among SXMers. Protecting renegade youths on motorbikes from

injuring themselves is not about enacting more rules and tougher legislation, but more about questioning the sincerity of leaders:

> As Buju a say, the Lord is him shepherd. That is the only shepherd we need,
> people. The politricksians and the false prophets rules is not from Jah. Jah
> rules inside of we. Them man, them just want divide the place with they
> tribalism. Man, know thyself. A lot of youths, in fact a lot of we, would not
> go astray if it wasn't for these false shepherds. We don't need more rules.
> We need to listen to Jah. I telling you, people, do not drink the politrick-
> sians' and the false prophets' bush teas. Jah say, "Seek and learn for your-
> self." We ah going run these tunes fi real.

After this short comment, he played songs by Mutabaruka, VC, and
Bob Marley. The first two tunes, "People's Court, Parts I and II," by Mutabaruka, enact a court case presided over by the black working classes,
who put political and religious leaders on trial for keeping the masses
dumb to exploit and rule them:

> All rise
> Judge 1,000 years presiding
> Your honor we have here Mister Religious Belief and his henchman Mis-
> ter Demonenation [denomination]
> Mister religious belief and Mister Denomination I see you also have
> been promising Black people, but you are even worst than the politi-
> cians
> You promise them good living after they die
> Yes you say their reward will be in heaven
> It would appear to me that both of you have been in heaven already and
> have gotten yours
> Every little open land have a tent for a few months, then a massive
> building later
> Did the Bible not say that your body is the temple of God?
> And did I not hear you teaching them to pray and I quote "lead us not
> into temptation"
> When since the Lord lead people into temptation that you should be ask-
> ing him not to do it
> You have made women look inferior in all your religious books
> From Eve till now you have blamed women for the downfall of the
> world
> You blame Delilah for Samson stupidity
> You have even placed a sin on sex, saying Mary was a virgin all her life
> With these images what do you expect from our people?
> Remember the Baker [Jim Bakker]
> Remember the one who was swagging hearts [Jimmy Swaggart]
> remember the one who was using his mouth to orally-rob-earth [Oral
> Roberts]
> All of these collecting souls under false pretense.

The VC song, entitled "By His Deeds," which followed, criticizes seemingly devout Rastafarians and other Christians who are constantly scheming about how to get ahead at the expense of others:

> Sitting on your church on Sunday
> Thinking who you're gonna screw Monday
> Who you're gonna thief
> Who you're gonna rob
> Take it as me tell you, I say you can't fool God no
> Everyday you bawl out Jah Jah
> Call yourself a dreadlock Rasta
> While you terrorize the people on your lane, 'cause a so you a get
>   wicked when you lick the coke
> If you are a warrior tell me what you fight for
> And if it's justice, put up your lighter
> But if a vanity, jewelry, and such, remember that you will soon get hurt
> By his deeds shall a man be known: a man ask you for a piece of bread
>   you give him stone
> By his deeds shall a man be known: natty up your head and still you
>   worship Babylon throne.

The fourth song, "Rebel," by Bob Marley, is about heartening the working classes to refuse the inferior social positions awarded to them. While listening to these compositions, I was able to see the issue of inclusive religious belonging and the inter- and intra-state inequalities being addressed. With Mutabaruka's "People's Court, Part I" and Bob Marley's "Rebel," there was a direct attack on most third world leaders, who, they claim, oppress their compatriots for material gains. Nevertheless, Marley and Mutabaruka sing that these political leaders are actually operating under the auspices of Western-dominated and capitalism-promoting institutions, such as the World Bank and the IMF. Similarly in "People's Court, Part II," it is third world religious leaders who are accused of lulling the masses with the opiate of institutionalized Christianity. This causes them, according to Mutabaruka, to resign themselves to their situation and also to subordinate the female sex. Mutabaruka also implicates internationally renowned American evangelists such as Jimmy Swaggart, because they are the role models for these leaders.

While Marley's and Mutabaruka's songs present a dualistic analysis, the oppressed on one side of the spectrum and the oppressors on the other, VC's "By His Deeds" disrupts the duality. This song actually addresses the fact that even among the working classes and lay members of religious groups, one finds many oppressive persons. No class holds a monopoly on good or bad deeds. This latter idea ties into DJ Shadow's notion of personhood.

DJ Shadow and I continued to talk while the music played. I asked him to explain why he had referred to political and religious leaders as "politricksians" and "false prophets," and what he meant by his advice that SXMers should not drink their "bush teas." I was also curious about his comments that Jah's rules are inside us. He replied that he feels some SXMers have the bad habit of blindly following religious and political leaders. According to him, they do this out of a fear of life and of making choices on the basis of their own convictions. Because of these fears, they hand over their authority to others and render themselves vulnerable to the manipulative and exploitative behavior of political and religious leaders. He wants them to realize that these fears are unfounded and that they don't need these leaders:

> I and I [my inner divinity and I] want to burn the fear out of the people.
> A man who afraid to choose for himself is a man who fear life. People have to realize that life is good, and Jah give us a compass so we can decide for ourselves. You don't need anybody telling you what to do and which way to follow. You see for me, the pastor and the politician are twins. Pastors I relate to the past. That was when man used to follow prophets. Old Testament style, seen? Now man knows better, so automatically I and I blocking it out. And politicians is just pollution, Star [my cosmic friend, meaning we are stars walking on the face of the earth], polluting the people brains. We can't deal with pollution or with the past. They both should have no meaning in this present time here.

In claiming that all people have their own compasses with which to navigate life and in referring to himself as "I and I," DJ Shadow was adhering to a well-known tenet of the Rastafari spiritual philosophy that posits human beings are made up of an earthly Self and a divine counterpart, God within. Therefore, there is no reason for anyone to worship a god outside him- or herself. Many SXMers I knew were equally eloquent in voicing this idea. This is what Trevor replied when I asked if he saw Jesus as the son of God or as God himself: "Fire 'pon that nonsense. Your body is the vessel. We are all sons of God. We are all his sons. Yessus [Jesus] is also his son. But he is not the only son. We are all sons. In us Jah can judge us."

As DJ Shadow continued explaining what he meant by "I and I," I realized that his concept of "I and I" contains a third "I" that is silent. According to him, it is our personal devil. Thus, his notion of personhood is "I and I and I." The self is deemed somewhat autonomous, though it still has to reckon with the influences of the God and devil within. The philosophy of Science, with its idea of multiple selves and its definition of good and bad as dependent on circumstance, has influenced this conception. He mentioned the importance of his grandmother in leading him to this notion of personhood:

> My grandmother was a women who could do things, you know what I mean? She was into her Higher Science. I can remember sitting in her lap and she telling me that I should never forget that the devil used to be an angel too, so he ain't all that bad. She used to tell me that when you read your Bible and they say that Lucifer was cast down to earth for disobeying God, you must remember that it was about power. God had all the power, and Lucifer wanted some of it. So they fight, and God's general, Michael, defeat Lucifer and banish him to earth. She would say, just like how the big men does fight for power over the heads of the small man, the same thing took place in heaven. In the same way, we too have a God and a devil inside, fighting to have power over we. Both of them want we soul. Now what is important for me is this life, and not so much the other life. Nobody ever come back to tell me how it was. So what I believe we must do is respect both of them and use them to get ahead. But we must always remember that we will never be able to fully control them. So when I say "I and I," sometimes it means me and my God, but if you're fucking around, it means me and my devil ain't going take your shit. This is my version of "I and I," my Rastafarian individuality, you overs?

He then took off his T-shirt to show me his tattoos, which are symbolic of this understanding. On the right half of his chest he has a tattoo of Jesus Christ, the common Michelangelo type, with the inscription "only God can judge me." On his back he has an iconic image of a red devil with horns with the words "he used to be an angel too" underneath. Though he made no mention of it, his philosophical perspective also has some Catholic elements in it. As SXM's Science is intrinsically connected to Christianity, the idea of an internal God and devil is a particular reworking of the Christian idea of having a good and a bad angel on every pair of shoulders. The difference is that here, they are not explicitly thought of as being messengers of higher forces.

Realizing that his idea of having a personal devil next to a personal God would be considered unorthodox by many performers of Rasta on the island, he told me that even in Bob Marley's Jamaica, there was no consensus as to what constituted true Rastafari faith. He argued that no one has a right to decide that:

> I went to Jamaica and hang out with a lot of Rastas. I had reasoning with them, but all of them had a different explanation about who Selassie I

[Haile Selassie the first] was. Some say Selassie was God. Some say, "No, he was just a king." Some say he was the spirit of Jesus who come back. Some say he was a prophet. All different versions. Remember this, Star, this what my grandmother, rest her soul, used to say, "There is no religion in righteousness. Religion is a way towards righteousness." You overs? I know that Jah would never expect me to follow some of the foolishness that in the Bible if it hurting my interest. No false prophets have to come and tell me nothing. I got to decide what my version of Rasta is and how this religion of mine will lead me to righteousness. Here on earth, I got to choose between what my God and my devil advising me. I got to choose, like every man got to choose for himself. Sometimes what my devil is telling me is more to the point. So I got to choose it. Now, you have a lot of Rasta who will say that whole business about having a devil inside of you is bullshit. But there they wrong. You know why? I am talking about my Rasta. Like a lot of Catholics, I believe that San Miquel does help me when I ask him for something. Now, does that make me less of a Rasta? No dread. My Rastafarianism is eclectic. You have to respect every woman, man, and child. If you are judgmental, then you are being impure. Being judgmental means judging a man for what he believes. From my principles, I can't tell you what you believe is right. But I can't tell you what you believe is wrong, either. There is only one judgment to be fallen on you, and that is the judgment of Jah, the Lord. Jah going decide when the time comes, but right now, I got to decide and live for myself.

Many Caribbeanists who have studied Rastafari corroborate DJ Shadow's claim that it consists of various mutually exclusive doctrines (Chevannes 1994; Mansingh and Mansingh 1985). Because of the decentralized structure of Rastafari religious groups and the nonexistence of a central or overarching authority, no one can say what is and what is not in accordance with Rasta. Rastafari is better understood as a spiritual philosophy whereby certain ideas recur with some frequency.[2] Herein God, not strictly theologized, is the ultimate judge, and no person can claim that he sanctions a particular religious practice above another.

Through this notion of personhood, based on a combination of Rasta and Science, DJ Shadow advised SXMers to stop drinking the "bush teas" made by the politricksians and the false prophets. He mentioned, in passing, that even though, in accordance with PJD2 policy, he cannot criticize particular politicians and religious leaders by name, SXMers know that most cannot be trusted. Though he made no mention of it, what probably also played a role was the potential harm that speaking out against influential politicians could do to his family's business ventures. Even DJ Shadow has to be political with regard to what he says:

When you sick and you grandmother go pick some bush to make some tea for you, she always makes it in such a way to cure your sickness. You might stand with the cup to your mouth for hours 'cause you don't really like how it taste, but when you see that she ain't leaving your side until you drink it and her eye turn to that belt, well then, you just swallow it as fast as possible and say a prayer behind that to ask God to help you. To help *you*, you overs? Not to help the politricksian who say, "Don't worry, man. I going take care of it." You see what I saying? Your grandmother bush tea always make especially for you. And old folks always say, "Don't drink anybody else's bush tea, 'cause that is for their sickness. That ain't for you, dread. So what I telling the people is not to drink the politricksians' and the false prophets' bush tea. Yeah, they going say they want serve the people, that it is God who spoke to them, but you have to realize everybody looking out for themselves, taking care of their business. So who you're going trust? The ones who are in power are fucking up. And the ones that want to get in, want to get in to do the same thing. So who you going trust? Trust yourself. Deal with yourself. Deal with your own God and devil. If everybody do that, I bet you a lot of malice what a go on will cease. That is Jah's prescription. Now, I can't mention names on the radio, 'cause that is against the rules, but what I can do is play certain tunes and say certain things so the people remember why they don't trust the politricksians we got here. SXMers know that most of them full of tricks.

That religious leaders encompass both locals and newcomers while politics is run by locals matters little to DJ Shadow. He feels that in the end, regardless of who they are, they are untrustworthy: "All of them is crooks. All of them. All of those 'mister jacket and ties' is the same to me. I don't care where they come from. The local politricksian and the preacher from Saint Kitts, all of them just in it for the money, as far as I can see." In our conversation, he then criticized the local fringe politicians, headed by the Baineses, who were championing a politics of belonging in the form of more political autonomy from France and the Netherlands. This, according to him, was just an excuse to get power, and it would lead to divisions among the island's inhabitants:

You have dirty politricksians with a little bit of conscience, and you have those who just don't give a damn about anybody else; they just greedy. We have some of them crackpots here who luckily the SXM people will not vote for, although they in politics for the longest while. When you sit down and listen to their politricks, is about we the people of SXM, we the SXM nation, need more autonomy from Holland. And on the French side, is about the French man got to respect we. Now they say they doing it for all SXMers, that we are one nation, but when you listen carefully, 'cause them man so dumb they does contradict themselves, they saying the locals must come first. Now that is to me just causing tribalism. And their definition of local is they and their friends. I telling you, Star, them politricksians bad, bad, bad.

I wanted him to elaborate a bit more about his views on the politics of belonging of local fringe politicians and about their striving for more political independence from France and the Netherlands, but he had to return to disc jockeying. With a few quick words, he alerted his listeners that a short commercial break was due: "I got to make some money, so I will be right back with you. Don't you dare touch that dial." He then got up and motioned me to join him to get a drink and catch some fresh air. I decided to postpone the question about political autonomy until the conscious reggae hour was over, since it was not directly connected to the theme of the program.

As we walked back to the station with our cans of soda, I asked whether he ever feared that a popular personality would rise up on SXM who would be able to embody both political and religious leadership. Someone who talks as slickly as DJ Shadow does could probably pull such a thing off. He laughed and said he did not, for he deemed SXMers too smart to fall for that. "You ever hear SXM people say, 'Them two sharks shouldn't swim together?' Now why you think that is? Is because the people know that both of them is crooks, con artists, swindlers. You overs? All I doing is making the people more aware of what they already know. Why you think the people like me? Is because I does speak the truth."

I definitely recognized the voice of SXMers in what he was saying. SXMers claim that God made separate basins for political and religious leaders so that these two, likened to sharks, cannot swim together. On SXM, as in other parts of the Caribbean, most believe there should be an absolute separation between church and state and between the official representatives of both institutions. Christianity is SXM's public religion, but one that is divorced from the edicts of a particular church or a political leader. Put differently, the public sphere is Christian inflected but is not dominated by a particular Christian church.

Many SXMers expressed their distrust of politicians, claiming that they also operate under the logic of the money tie system. Underneath all their words of solidarity and their assertions of taking up office to serve the people, politicians too are considered performers seeking money and power. A single mother of two who worked in one of the island's casinos put it this way: "This here is a *de vez en cuándo* [once in a while] democracy. The majority rule during election time; after that, the minority can take over again. So whenever them *sin vergüenzas* [good for nothings] want my vote, they have to pay." And many politicians have readily complied, paying for votes, implicitly underscoring their and all SXMers "identities" as cunning performers in the money tie system. Though most SXMers play along with the politicians, nearly all told me they would not endorse candidates who want more autonomy from France and the Netherlands. They felt that the island's dependence on tourism is too precarious for that, and they distrust such politicians, whom they believe would abuse their power.

A similar atmosphere of distrust was discernible around priests and pastors. Many of the people whom I interviewed referred to religious figures as con men, exploiting the emotionally weak for material gain. Nestor, whom I introduced in chapter 1, had this to say: "All preachers is con men. You have to be a con man to make someone believe you in just a few minutes. Them preachers are sweet-talkers. Them tell people to wait for their rewards in heaven, while they driving a Lexus in the here and now. It is only people that suffering from the Hawaiian disease Lakanuki [lack of nookie, i.e., sex] that can live the Christian life. Look at Sugarwater [the neighborhood Baptist who has a speech impediment coupled with slight mental retardation]."

This distrust of religious leaders seems to be part of a wider Caribbean phenomenon. Some Caribbeanists have argued that this distrust is an outgrowth of the historical development whereby Christianity itself was creolized and accepted while the dominant Christian institutions and the majority of the clergy who headed these were distrusted because they often supported the oppressive edicts of the political establishments and employed two standards of judgment (Hall 2002; Chevannes 1995, 1994). This led to the ironic development whereby Christian ideas became the idiom in which many of the working class voiced their desire for social justice and equal civil belonging and rebelled against both established churches and the political establishment. "People's Court, Part II," the Mutabaruka song played by DJ Shadow during his program, is only one of the many musical documents in which this can be heard. Christianity has provided a language to express ideas of social justice, one not necessarily connected to performing the role of the pious churchgoer.

In chapter 3 I argued that SXM's contemporary Christian metalanguage contains ideas born in the past but merged with compromises deemed deeply necessary in the here and now. Understood this way, the historical relationship between Christianity as a metalanguage of resistance adjusts to the contemporary needs of the tourist industry for cheap laborers from abroad. This Christian metalanguage sanctifies the unwritten social consensus between the elites and the working classes, which dictates that religious differentiation should not be voiced in any hierarchical terms. It also condemns hierarchical ideas of national belonging uttered by some locals as un-Christian. Christianity as a metalanguage stands for an all-inclusive religious and political belonging. Nevertheless, those who use a Christian metalanguage to criticize the performative space of the money tie system and openly place the blame of socioeconomic inequalities solely on the shoulders of elites are ostracized. On SXM's radio stations, blame for negative excesses in the performative space of the money tie system must be attributed to all parties. Put another way, when radio disc jockeys speak out against social injustices, they must do so in a manner that implicates all SXMers and therein reiterates social unity. DJ Shadow was about to show me that he knows this unspoken rule and adheres to it on his radio program.

When we returned to the studio, DJ Shadow informed me that he was coming to the end of the conscious reggae segment. He once again sent out greetings to his public and returned to the theme of making choices for oneself and not handing over this task to religious and political leaders. He told his listeners that it would be easy to put the blame squarely on the shoulders of the politricksians and false prophets, but it is wiser to realize their own faults as well. Instead of blaming others for the choices they make on the people's behalf, his listeners might better take responsibility: "Youth and Youth out there, brethren and sisteren, you have fi choose for yourself. Don't blame the politricksians and the false prophets for choosing wrong when you give them the power to choose for you. Jah say, 'Who is without sin cast the first stone.' Here is Culture with, 'If you're looking for revolution,' they say, 'try and find the right man,' for there are no innocent people out there. So cast the stone at yourself. Iser the Wiser."

In the last segment DJ Shadow played the hit "Revolution," by Culture, followed by songs from Jack Radics, Beres Hammond, and Sanchez. "Revolution" refers to the overwhelming influence of Western-dominated global capitalism and suggests that none can claim to have clean hands and therefore point a finger at the other. Everyone is to blame. The group Culture proposes a revolution that starts with a mental change and people caring for others:

> If you're ready for revolution try and find the right man
> There is no innocent man in this society
> For all that I am I am a Rasta man
> Trying to heal all nation of the wound in their heart man

> I would rather prefer to teach the children than to bust a gun man
> I rather even go to children hospital and put on my uniform and be a
>   nurse man, or a doctor man
> If you're ready for revolution try and find the right man.

On the other hand, Jack Radics's composition "Chains" speaks about the necessity of re-creating society in a way that will allow the down-trodden to choose freely. The third song, "Come Down Father," by Beres Hammond, makes explicit that mankind will not be able to create a society to its liking without adhering to the godly tenets of fraternity and being one another's keeper. The last song, "Never Diss the Man," by Sanchez, is about asserting the powerlessness of mankind with regard to the major issues in life, such as the unpredictability of death:

> You could be living this minute
> The next minute you are gone away
> So say a prayer and chant psalms
> Prayer a day keep the evil calm
> You don't have to go to church or to be Christian to call on Jah name
> Shout out the name Jahovah in the valleys
> Shout out the name of Jahovah on the hills
> Shout out the name Jahovah on the plains, or even if it rains
> Call on tha name, call on Jah name the same
> Never diss the Man with handle, the one who's got the title
> The one who sits high and He looks down low.

The chronological order in which these four songs were played re-vealed Shadow's brilliance in using music to get his message of overall complicity across. With "Revolution" it is averred that everyone is im-plicated in the capitalist way of life, but all are responsible for their ac-tions and are able to bring about change. The revolution is one of self-reflexivity and performing charitable works. While everyone is implicated in the capitalist way of life, the second song, "Chains," reminds us that the rich have more choices regarding their participation in this system than the downtrodden. While this understanding can lead to aggressive actions or at least division into ideological camps, "Come Down Father" and "Never Diss" once again emphasize the equality of all the actors in-volved, claiming that one needs to have faith in the hope that justice will prevail and that the path to accomplishing this is through the realization that, existentially, we are all in the same boat.

These songs were followed by another commercial break and a news bulletin. Then DJ Shadow completely changed gears, turning to calypso, interspersing music with double entendres alluding to sex. Unlike

DJ Fernando Clarke, DJ Shadow does not tie his calypso songs to a specific theme, nor does he endorse Clarke's philosophy of the two vitamins Cs, calypso and Christianity, whereby calypso, as a symbol of cunning, should be given precedence. Instead DJ Shadow focuses on selecting music, uttering feel-good sound bits, and playing requests.

During the remaining hours of the show, I asked DJ Shadow what he had been up to since the last time we met and how his experiences have helped shape his philosophy of Rastafari individuality. I also got the opportunity to talk to him about his views about fringe political leaders who champion more political autonomy from France and the Netherlands. It was at this time that he was most explicit about his encompassing politics of belonging.

Since DJ Shadow had said very little about nationalism, I asked him how he feels about the hierarchical distinction some locals make between themselves and the newcomers. He replied that he finds such talk nonsensical and thinks it is exacerbated by fringe politicians. He chided most religious leaders for not speaking out enough and for not condemning hierarchical ideas of national belonging, suggesting their silence might be connected to denominationalism, which is also a form of hierarchical belonging, positing individual churches as the most liked by God:

> Instead of them talk about the tribalism these politricksians promoting, they only preaching about Mary had a little lamb and Moses and Joshua and David. I telling you, Dread, they in it for the money, plain and simple. False prophets. They 'fraid that if they talk about the tribalism of the politricksians, the politricksians will talk about their tribalism and tell the people Catholic, Methodist, Anglican, is all the same. That God don't favor any religion. That there is no religion in righteousness but that religion is way toward righteousness. You overs? And they don't want that.

At this point Shadow began talking explicitly about nationalism. He stated his belief that hierarchical ideas of belonging expressed by some locals are tied to their ideas of being a distinct nation. This is especially true for those who fail to benefit from the money tie system. Under the influence of fringe local politicians, such as the Larosso brothers, people are encouraged to see themselves as belonging to a nation, distinct from the newcomers, who are viewed as representatives of other nations. At the same time, these politicians encourage newcomers to see themselves as belonging to a multicultural SXM nation that encompasses several nations:

> Even though I say we SXM people smart, I have to admit that some of us too trusting. You have some of these politricksians, college boys, who like to use big words like *autonomy, decolonization, the UN Charter*, stuff like

that. They don't get much votes but they dangerous. They telling "locals," those, you know, who ain't doing so well because they love to gamble and run woman, "Look man, you are the original, so you should come first. Don't worry. Vote for me and I going to stand up for your rights." And you have some of them men believing them, instead of looking at where they went wrong. These same politricksians will go to the Haitian who the big man them slaving and he going to tell them, "Vote for me, man, and it will be out of many cultures, one nation." And some of them Haitians and Jamaicans and Guyanese who flee poverty and want to send more money home for their children might believe them. Now all these people, they fool. They telling them, "We as your representatives, we going to stand up for your rights as a nation and demand more autonomy." I can bet you anything, if Holland stupid enough to grant them it, I bet you they going to create laws so they and their kind can rob the country dry. They going say a local should manage things. But that is because they are the locals.

Because of this political possibility, DJ Shadow feels that SXMers should move beyond the idea of nationalism, although most SXMers do not take the categories of "local" and "newcomer" too seriously. He went on to argue that an excessive belief in nationalism is a symptom of being out of balance, of the mistaken idea of feeling superior to another: "That nation business is just hate business, devil works. Whenever you have a nation, you have an enemy, [and then] you have war. Is like that because you going to believe you better than the other man. I mean, Bob Marley spoke about this. Listen to 'War.' There the man is basically telling you that that is nonsense. Madness, B [*B* is a shortened version of *brother*]. Jah create us all. That nation business is just tribalism, the illusions of the politricksians."

Both DJ Shadow and Marley's song "War" are critiquing "the imagined community of the nation," a social construct born in the Americas. According to Anderson, the social discrimination directed at the Euro-Creole elites by their metropolitan counterparts, combined with travel and the proliferation of printed journals primarily dedicated to local topics, led them as a public to imagine themselves as members of a "community" separate from the colonial powers (Anderson 1991). As they fought successful wars of independence against their respective "mother countries," they established the first nation-states in the world.

Several Caribbeanists have challenged Anderson and other scholars with similar conceptualizations, suggesting that nationalism was not solely created by Euro-Creole elites (e.g., Hallward 2004; Sanchez 2003). Nationalism was instead the product of masters and slaves, as well as those belonging to every other social category in between these two extremes. The case of Haiti, which was the wealthiest colony in the New World when it began its struggle for independence and which became the second nation-state in the world, stands as irrefutable proof. The rise of nationalism and nation-states is also related to the rise of liberal egalitarianism, the ideology of the unity and equality of man. This ideology may have been written down by white Europeans and Euro-Creoles, but it was inspired by radical social processes involving both the poor and the rich.

To stay competitive in world markets, however, the leaders of these new nation-states, who were mostly wealthy Euro-Creoles but also sometimes black planters, retained institutions such as slavery, encomienda, and indentured labor, with their necessary racism and ethnic discrimination, even while proclaiming the unity of man. Racism and ethnic discrimination were not an aberration in the construction of nationalism, as several studies have shown that, despite the passing of time, racism and ethnic discrimination in their many incarnations remain integral to most if not all official expressions of nationalism and nation-state projects.[3] All nations are characterized by their ethnic and racialist views concerning the character of the chosen and the excluded (Brown 2000; Gilroy 2006, 2000).

This insider versus outsider logic also plays itself out between dominant and subordinate groups within a nation. In discussions concerning the issue of national belonging, the ethnic and racial basis of official nationalism is usually camouflaged in the form of civic nationalism, which is ideally based upon voluntarism and ethnic neutrality, and multicultural nationalism, which claims that one should respect the rights of all "ethno-racial" groups or nations within the larger nation. Under the guise of neutrality (civics) or respect for difference (multiculturalism), elites among the dominant ethno-racial group still decide what constitutes difference and how this should be classified, accepted, and judged.[4] That is what DJ Shadow accused the local politicians of doing. As he put it, "I am not for more political autonomy from Holland. That to me is just more nationalism. I think the world has had enough of that. I and I am not endorsing that tribalism."

Relying on his own experiences, DJ Shadow has arrived at conclusions similar to those of scholars who have critiqued the concept of nationalism: "I don't have to go to school to see that that is nonsense. All I have to do is look at the next man, and I know that he ain't so different from me. He too got to shit, eat, and sleep [he laughs]. Any man who can't see that have to get his head checked."

While print and travel might have encouraged his elite Euro-Creole predecessors to imagine nation-states as natural communities, conscious reggae and travel have led DJ Shadow to realize the inverse. Like them, he holds grudges against the "mother countries" in Western Europe, but unlike them, he does not champion equality and independence while legitimating the subjugation of the poor and the disenfranchised. In a world in which the masses in the politically independent Global South are suffering from the adverse effects of capitalism, he feels nationalist projects and independence movements promise few or no material benefits.

DJ Shadow is well traveled, having resided on various Caribbean islands, in the United States, and in several countries in Western Europe. All these places were spaces of awakening for him that led him to understand that nationalism and related hierarchical ideas of belonging engender violent divisions among human beings. Instead of employing the mutually exclusive categories *local* and *newcomer* to designate differential and hierarchical belonging, DJ Shadow feels all SXMers should better understand themselves as "Rastafari individuals" and be aware of the violence committed by those who see themselves as belonging to distinct nations.

DJ Shadow lived in Curaçao, the Dominican Republic, Saint Kitts, Jamaica, and Trinidad. His stay on these islands strengthened his understanding that SXMers share many similarities with other West Indians, especially in regard to everyday practices. The islanders have borrowed one another's creolized cultural products and on each island have made something unique of their mutual borrowings. This is especially true with music. For instance, with calypso music, which first emerged in Trinidad, Shadow has observed unique versions of this genre on every island. He asserts that in this borrowing there is the intention not only of mimicking but also of proclaiming difference: "Calypso comes from Trinidad, but everybody plays it differently. If you give each Caribbean island the same song to play, each one will intentionally play it different. So SXM calypso is from SXM." He also pointed out calypso musicians in Trinidad borrowing from other islands, making the whole origin story problematic: "I mean, when you look at it, Trinidadian calypso get influence by the Jam band style from Dominica, so what is what?"

According to Shadow, one can make the same point about conscious reggae. What was important is that conscious reggae composers have written songs that promote transnational alliances among the structurally oppressed, primarily dark-skinned West Indians and inspire them to keep struggling for social justice. While Marley and other reggae artists have championed national independence in songs such as "Zimbabwe,"

DJ Shadow consciously omitted this to make his point about transnational solidarity:[5]

> Consciousness don't cater for that national thing. Marley, Tosh, Burning Spear, Buju, them man is not national. Them man is international. It is about the black man redemption, about the small man struggles. You overs? The small man in the Caribbean, and let we be frank, most of them black, struggling ever since with Babylon. But still they ain't give up yet. They still smiling, and that is their strength. So when Bob say, "Lively up yourself and don't be no dread," he telling them, "Remain happy. Don't let Babylon enslave you brain." A sad man is a man who lose the battle before it even started.

According to DJ Shadow, nationalism has sought to obfuscate this and other commonalities among the inhabitants of the Caribbean basin. Caribbean people are, as he put it, "children of the sun. Caribbeanness is defined by the sun." He used the word *sun* in a metaphorical sense. For DJ Shadow, the word signifies a stance in life that radically asserts joy coupled with an uncompromising sense of somebody-ness and an unrelenting ambition to get ahead: "Caribbean people have an aura about them. They love to party. Bacchanal is their thing. They have a strong sense of pride and don't accept injustice. They don't want to sit in the back of the bus [this is an allusion to the Rosa Parks incident]. They want front seat. You overs? We SXMers are no exception." When I asked him where these attributes came from, he replied matter-of-factly that they stemmed from the African, Asian, and European ancestors of Caribbean people. However, as with his metaphor of the bus, he explicitly highlighted the experience of blacks in the New World: "Listen, Star, we don't have to travel to really know Africa, Europe, or Asia, because they are here. We born from them. All of us have to acknowledge our black grandmothers, even the whitest of us. If it wasn't for her titties, Star, think about it. You overs? [DJ Shadow is alluding to the role played by many African women in breastfeeding both blacks and whites.] If she didn't survive, none of us would have survived."

DJ Shadow was doing two things in the context of our conversation. He was employing the stereotypes of the eternally joyful and the ambitious West Indians to show me the self-resilience of most Caribbean people, who have constructed themselves thusly in the midst of unspeakable horrors. His characterization is congruent with the West Indian transnational identity discussed in the first chapter of this book. By claiming that Africa, Asia, and Europe are in the Caribbean and that all have to acknowledge their black grandmothers, he was referring to the legacy left by the ancestors and the importance of those who survived slavery. He was voicing what Caribbeanists have termed the *shipwreck experience* that binds the West Indies and the *presences* that roam about in the region (Mintz 1996; Walcott 1993; Stuart Hall 1992).

The *shipwreck experience* is a metaphor used to convey the well-documented horrors of colonialism in the Caribbean. Millions of people from Africa, Asia, and to a lesser extent Europe were forced to leave their homelands for the Caribbean basin on ships, chained together by their ankles. Many had their prospects strangled by indentured labor contracts or were trying to escape religious persecution (Mintz 1996; Walcott 1993). Most of the identifications and practices that they were accustomed to performing were unsustainable in their new homelands, because most of the institutions and contexts on which they were based were nonexistent:

> The transplanted peoples of the Caribbean had to be homogenized in some ways to meet the economic demands imposed upon them, at the same time that they were being individualized by the erasure of the institutional underpinnings of their pasts. These were the achievements—if we choose to call them that—of Caribbean colonialism. The movements of people by which such sweeping changes were facilitated were massive, mostly coerced, and extended over centuries. I do not think that there is much with which they can be compared, in previous and subsequent world history. Those who came in chains could bring little with them. The conditions under which they had then to create and recreate institutions for their own use was unimaginably taxing. This was, of course, particularly the situation of those who came as slaves. It was different, and somewhat better, for impressed or contracted Europeans. But the Irish deported by Cromwell, the convicts and the *engages,* the debt and the indentured servants from Britain and France, cannot be said to have been truly better off, so far as the transfer of kin groups, community norms or material culture are concerned. Nor, for that matter, were the Chinese who would be shipped to Cuba, the Indians who went to the Guianas and Trinidad, or the Javanese who went to Suriname in the subsequent centuries. (Mintz 1996: 297–298)

This has led to the situation in the Caribbean that Africa, Asia, Europe, and the Arawak and Carib world are "presences," traces of the old, transformed though nevertheless discernible and lingering in all cultural expressions. The African presence particularly, though often repressed, remains an important structuring element. During our conversation, DJ Shadow highlighted its importance. Scholars such as Stuart Hall have also averred that this structuring element has to be recognized throughout the Caribbean:

> "Présence Africaine" is the site of the repressed. Apparently silenced beyond memory by the power of the new cultures of slavery, it was, in fact,

present everywhere: in the everyday life and customs of the slave quarters, in the languages and patois of the plantations, in the names and words, often disconnected from their taxonomies, in the secret syntactical structures through which other languages were spoken, in the stories and tales told to children, in religious practices and beliefs, in the spiritual life, in the arts, crafts, musics, and rhythms of slave and post-emancipation society. Africa, the signified which could not be represented, remained the unspoken, unspeakable "presence" in Caribbean culture. It is in "hiding" behind every verbal inflection, every narrative twist of Caribbean cultural life. It is the secret code with which every Western text was "re-read." This was—is—the "Africa" that is still alive and well in the diaspora. . . . Everyone in the Caribbean, of whatever ethnic background, must sooner or later come to terms with this African Presence. Black, brown, mulatto, white—all must look "Présence Africaine" in the face, speak its name. (1992: 229–230)

Although "African traces" are of utmost importance, contemporary Caribbean people and their cultural expressions are an embodiment of all the presences in constant reconfiguration. All traces play a constitutive role, and racial taxonomies offer no privileged indication of the different Caribbean groups or their cultural expressions. In telling fashion, Édouard Glissant dismisses any possibility of arguing that although Caribbean people and their expressions are in the making, in a "state of becoming," as Stuart Hall would phrase it, one could nevertheless claim to discern groups on the basis of racial criteria or singular roots: "Whatever the value of the explanations or the publicity Alex Haley afforded us with *Roots*, we have a strong sense that the overly certain affiliation invoked there does not really suit the vivid genius of our countries" (2000: 72). Several other studies have shown that these reconfigurations were made and continue to be made in a milieu characterized by colonial, neocolonial, and internally based structural inequalities (e.g., Palmié 2002; Besson 2002). Especially for the working classes, re-creating themselves positively and struggling against these structural inequalities have gone hand in hand.

The presences, reconfigured into Caribbean cultural expressions and enmeshed in projects dedicated to social justice, have also given birth to xenophobic nationalist projects and hierarchical ideas of belonging. DJ Shadow personally experienced xenophobia and at the hands of "autochthon" elite and working-class Curaçaons when he attended secondary school on Curaçao:

When you left here as a young man and you go to school in Curaçao, MAVO and HAVO [high schools], back in the day they would call you an Ingles stinki [uncouth Englishmen], tell you ain't got no culture. And I am an Antillean just like you, B. I carrying the same passport you carrying. I don't have anything against them personally, but that mentality has got to go. They feel that Curaçao is the head. Curaçao is number one. Like they would say, "Yu di Korsow" [son of the Curaçao], and consider themselves better than everyone. No one is better than another. Jah ain't create nations, seen. Too much of them under the spell of they politricksians, who robbing them while the eyes open.

The labeling as "Ingles stinki" in the experience of DJ Shadow and other Dutch Windward Island students who primarily spoke English is a telling example of the adverse effects of the presences reconfigured in the ethnic biases of Curaçaon nationalism. It is an example in which the "présence Européenne" is clearly discernible, or in DJ Shadow's terms, "the Western sensibility driving them mad." Let me clarify this. If one unclogs one's mind from the idea of race, one realizes that what these predominantly dark-skinned Curaçaons were doing in calling their Windward Island counterparts "uncouth Englishmen" had its roots in the historical opposition that Western European thinkers, in the late nineteenth and early twentieth centuries, posited between Europeans who spoke Latinate languages and those who spoke Germanic ones. These linguistic and cultural differences, combined with assertions of religious superiority, were used to make and substantiate ethnic and racist claims. French and Spanish thinkers posited that Latin Europeans were more cultured and that Catholicism was a more spiritual religion than the Protestantism of Northern Europeans. German and English intellectuals averred on the other hand that Northern Europeans were bearers of Protestantism and a work ethic that made them the natural leaders of the world. Historically this opposition was also played out between Latin American and North American intellectuals (Skurski 1994; Rock 1987).

In their nationalist scheme, political leaders on Curaçao have used these ideas to claim that the island's "autochthons" are bearers of a superior Latin Caribbean culture while the inhabitants of the Dutch Windward Islands are part of a less refined English Caribbean. This is one of the ways they have sought to legitimize the occupation of fourteen of the twenty-two seats in the Dutch Antillean parliament. Thus, Curaçaon parliamentary officials have the ultimate say as to matters of other Dutch Antillean islands.[6] This, of course, is a conjecture, but not a far-fetched one, bearing in mind the strong links between the Curaçaon elites and their Latin American counterparts.

In DJ Shadow's opinion, the United States is made up of the same presences as those in the Caribbean and also underwent the shipwreck experience. "They basically experience the same thing." For him the only differences are in size and might: the United States is larger and has surpassed Europe in political and economic power. This is, according to him, the main reason why many Europeans dislike and ridicule North Americans: "Europe build America, so basically America is the baby brother of Europe. Yet they clash because baby brother don't want to listen to big brother and want to take over. But I ain't in that with them, Boo [brother]. I love New York, and they treat me nice over there. And when they come here, most of them does behave well proper. Yes, [the United States] is Babylon capital, and yes, Bush is a war man, but you gotta give Jack his jacket."

As with the West Indies, however, the United States also remains a victim of nationalism camouflaged in a multicultural rhetoric of belonging. Here too one finds politicians seeking to delude the ordinary folk: "They too living the scenario of their politricksians. Clinton was bad too, but Bush is a dirty motherfucker." While living and studying in Miami and New York, DJ Shadow lived in a country where race combined with ethnicity seeps through all areas of life. The first time he was pulled over by a police officer and thoroughly searched, he knew it was because of the color of his skin and his accent. One of the cops who pulled him over was dark skinned, showing, according to him, how many black and white Americans have "the racial thing in them."

While ideas of race combined with ethnicity are not exclusive to the United States, it was there that DJ Shadow became fully aware of their impact in structuring and legitimating power relations. This is an argument that has been put forward by several African Americanists (e.g., Higginbotham 1996; West 1993). In Western Europe, Shadow came face-to-face with the continent he identified as having bred this evil.

In 1993 DJ Shadow traveled to Europe. He stayed there for six years, residing in Amsterdam, Berlin, London, and Madrid. What made the most impact on DJ Shadow was the bureaucratic efficiency in these Western European countries. He chided the government officials on SXM for their inefficiency and explicit clientelistic attitude: "I live in Holland. I realize that if SXM would run the way Holland is run, everything would be on the straight and narrow. But here they take so much different corners and forget the main road, so they end up on a side street and can't get back out."

Nonetheless, while he admires Western European societies for their bureaucratic efficiency, he criticizes them for not using their power to right the historical and contemporary wrongs they have caused. He claims that while these countries are well off, they do not do enough to alleviate the disparate conditions faced by most in the Global South. For him, this state of affairs is also internally visible in the racism that immigrants hailing from the Global South face. Many Western Europeans still wish to consider persons that are "taxonomically" identified as non-European as intruders who have stormed their shores without any historical precedent. There too, the Shadow averred, one finds a hierarchical if not exclusionary politics of belonging:

> You see it there every day the way they stigmatize Moroccans, Turks, Surinamers, Africans, basically the third world massive. They want to forget that they went to those countries first and loot them. They want to forget that they went to Africa and took people from anywhere they could get them. They sold them. Families that were together were scattered. They needed big strong bucks to do the work that they needed to do. They who started this thing. Now they want to forget. When they see these people in Europe and see the poverty in the world, they should know it is not only about them.

What DJ Shadow was articulating was that "the involuntary association," as Wilson Harris termed it, between lighter-skinned Westerners and the darker-skinned peoples of the Global South during the colonial era was constitutive of what both have become:

> In the selection of a thread upon which to string likenesses that are consolidated into the status of a privileged ruling family, clearly cultures reject others who remain nevertheless the hidden unacknowledged kith and kin, let us say, of the chosen ones. The rejection constitutes both a chasm or a divide in humanity and a context of involuntary association between the chosen ones and the outcast ones. The relationship is involuntary in that, though, on the one hand, it is plain and obvious, privileged status within that relationship endorses by degrees, on the other hand, a callus upon humanity. And that callus becomes so apparently normal that a blindness develops, a blindness that negates relationship between the privileged caste and the outcast. (Harris 1998: 28)

The discrimination inflicted on immigrants from the Global South is, for DJ Shadow, an indication that this relationship has not been properly acknowledged. He uses the horrors of slavery as a trope to bring home the point that colonialism has entailed the dehumanization of third world peoples in general, and persons of African descent in particular, and that this needs to be acknowledged as a crime against humanity, a wound that should also bother lighter-skinned Europeans, although their ancestors did not undergo this humiliation. In his seminal work *The Black Atlantic*, Paul Gilroy presents a similar argument: "Locke's colonial interests and the effect of the conquest of the Americas on Descartes and Rousseau are simply non-issues. In this setting, it is hardly surprising that if it is perceived to be relevant at all, the history of slavery is somehow assigned to blacks. It becomes our special property rather than a part of the ethical and intellectual heritage of the West as a whole" (Gilroy 1993: 49).

DJ Shadow feels that the Othering of non-Western immigrants in racial and ethnic terms is also at play in the manner in which many "autochthonous" Dutch treat their Dutch West Indian counterparts. While Dutch West Indians have the same legal rights as those in the Netherlands, many "autochthons" still consider them foreigners. DJ Shadow thinks that if the Dutch Kingdom is to function effectively and justly, the same standards and politics of belonging should apply in all Dutch territories. The parliament in The Hague should act on behalf of its citizens in the West Indies when the politicians there fail to do their jobs correctly. While he is also critical of the French, he feels at least the citizens of these overseas territories enjoy the same social benefits as those in Paris:

> The French have the racial thing too, but when you go to any French island, drive around on the French side and you can see that they helping out, that they keeping things crisp. On the French side the politricksians can thief but they still have to be fair, 'cause them boys in France watching them and will intervene if they have to. On the French side they have to thief and rule the same way they does thief and rule in France: never too openly so they don't get catch. But the Dutch does sit down and don't put all their effort into regulating the problems that they have here. I don't think they put effort into making sure that the SXM government is just and that they do the just and right thing. They just let them do what they want, and when they realize things getting out of hand, then they clamp down on them. Regulate it before they fuck up. That is what irritates me about the Dutch.

For DJ Shadow, talk about neocolonialism by elected officials on SXM is just a cover-up for the fact that they too have embraced the tenets of nationalism. He sees the metropolitan Dutch as belonging to a different nation from that of the politricksians: "The Dutch should not worry when they hear we politricksians say SXM should be left alone, that they have rights as a nation. No, that would give them more leeway to fuck up the country even more. All of we are Dutch. The Dutch Antillean is Dutch. So if they aren't doing it right, somebody has to show them, whether they call it neocolonialism, colonialism, or whatever. If they ain't doing it right, Holland should step in."

To me there is a paradox in DJ Shadow's last comments about Dutch SXMers being Dutch. I asked, wasn't this rejecting nationalism at the front door and welcoming it through the back? He noted my concerns but smilingly countered that my confusion was due to my not being "real," meaning realistic. For all his critique of France and the Netherlands, he said he feels that under the present global conditions, SXM should never dream of severing its constitutional ties with these Western European countries. And he sees more political autonomy as the beginning of that process: "Once you start that thing about autonomy, there is no way back. The only way is forward, independence. And I don't want to go there. I like it here. This is just fine with me." He then reiterated his fundamental dislike of nationalism, and he claimed that more political autonomy, followed inevitably by constitutionally breaking with France and the Netherlands, did not entail leaving nationalism behind: "Like I tell you already, that nation business is just tribalism. I following Jah and not the scenarios of the politricksians. I and I for unity, seen. When them politricksians say SXM must rule itself, and people believe them, then they falling into the same trap of the nation business. That there is a dead end."

According to DJ Shadow, the trap of "the nation business," nationalist projects, is dangerous. Countries that have desired more political autonomy and have eventually become independent have not done well. In fact, he argued, independence has worsened the lives of the poor in these countries. In his explanation he did not allude to the trade embargoes and unequal trade relations between the United States and Western Europe and independent Caribbean countries such as Cuba, Jamaica, Haiti, and the Dominican Republic. He was explaining the internal conditions in those countries and not the external reasons that led to them:

> Personally I have seen what has happened to independent countries. I don't want my child growing up in it, even though my family ain't hand-to-mouth. It is a matter of the principle, 'cause life is a funny thing. Today you up, tomorrow you down. You overs? In the Dominican Republic I saw factories among factories, and there is no middle class. There is just rich and poor. And the poor is constantly living off of credit. The poor have to go and credit a food, some rice, corn, sugar, and salt. That's poverty. That's some hard-ass living. I drive some places on the island where as far as your eyes can see is zinc roof alone, no tile floor, outhouse. You understand? That is poverty. And this is an independent island with all these resources, and nobody want to touch them. Take Jamaica. This country produces everything: clothes, shoes, aluminum, but nobody want to touch them. They have no value, internationally speaking. Their money ain't worth shit. Why would you want to do that to your people? You see where I coming from?

Many SXMers I spoke to expressed similar views. They too felt that embarking on the road of nationalism, in the form of more political autonomy from France and the Netherlands, would be unwise. The working-class newcomers especially furnished me with example after example of the abject poverty that they faced while living in independent countries. Others told me about being victimized partly because they belonged to the internal enemies of the nation.

DJ Shadow was now on a roll, philosophizing with conviction, and all I had to do was sit down and listen. He continued by saying that even if SXMers influenced by fringe politicians want to take the risk of more political autonomy and eventually full political independence, their island has its size against it:

> This island is thirty-seven square miles. The Dutch side is the smaller part: seventeen square miles. Let's say the Dutch side wants to go independent. Out of that seventeen square miles there is a pond. Let's say about five square miles out of that seventeen is taken up by water. You're down to twelve square miles of land. How are you going to go independent with just twelve square miles of land? Where are you going? You can't travel to the French side as you feel anymore. I don't see the logic in it. To me it is ludicrous; it is ridiculous; it is foolish. If they ever think about something like that, if SXM go independent, I leaving. For real, it don't make sense staying. I don't see how you going to survive.

He then touched on SXM's precarious dependence on tourism. He said that this is a public secret, just as the money tie system is the secret reason why most SXMers reside on the island. They would, therefore, not hesitate to leave if they got wind that fringe politicians had convinced the parliament in France and the Netherlands to grant the island more political autonomy or full independence. He admitted that he, too, would leave without hesitation:

> What do we have [without] tourism? Nah, man, I don't believe in that, because there is nothing generating but tourism. After 9/11 SXM feel it 'cause Americans didn't want to take the plane no more. The next thing you know, you get another lunatic like bin Laden say he going to sink a cruise ship this time, he don't want any planes no more. Where you think they coming? Cruise ships stop float, they ain't coming here no more, so what we going to eat? What we going survive on? That is our only means of survival. We don't have any factories. That is why I telling you I leaving if any politricksian even think about doing something like that. But not me alone, I telling you, almost everybody going to leave. We SXMers, all of us, local and newcomer alike, have a nationalism for the good times, [but] we don't believe in staying on a sinking ship. We all know that deep down it is all about the money tie system. Even though we love this country, even though

I love this country, it is my home and I don't want to leave it, but I will if I have to. First and foremost, I have to take care of myself and my family.

DJ Shadow then argued that under the present constitution, there are concrete benefits in being part of France and the Netherlands. It means an ability to travel the world unperturbed by immigration officers and to settle in greener pastures if SXM's tourist economy declines. Under the present conditions, he did not feel as though he was living under an oppressive French and Dutch regime:

> Things good right now, so I don't see why we should change it. You know the saying, "You must never bite the hand that feeds you"? Well, that is what I am about. Curse the hand, yes. Tell it when it fuck up, it fuck up. Tell it when it being unfair. But don't bite it. This is not a colonial thing or a slavery thing like in Kunta Kinte days. Them days long gone. This is one country run by two entities, but living on the Dutch side, I can drive to the French side all day, everyday, without a problem. Nobody can't tell me nothing. And if the gendarmerie tell me I can't go over there, something is wrong. Something got to be seriously wrong, because there is no border, no checkpoint. Ask a French man [French SXMer] and he'll tell you he love that French passport. I telling you I don't believe in giving up my Dutch passport, my right to be a European citizen. If SXM go independent, you are no longer a European citizen, you're a SXMer. I need to travel, B. Ask anybody and they'll tell you they love that European passport, 'cause when things go bad, they can leave and go somewhere else to feed their children.

Was it all a question of making the best of present conditions and thus nationalism? Yes. DJ Shadow has a solution to nationalism, though, which is his version of the unity of man. If every person recognizes his or her divinity within, his or her Rastafari individuality, nationalism would be overcome. Nevertheless, he believes that nationalism and the issue of belonging that it induces would be replaced with others through which men and women would once again be lured to discriminate against one another:

> Fi real, Star. The solution is simple if every man see himself truly, see that he have a devil and the God inside, a lot of this tribal business would done. All man have to see that. They have to be overs that. Then Babylon going fall down. But it ain't going to be over then. Life is struggle, and that is a never-ending story. Mystically it is a continuing struggle between good and evil, between God and the devil inside of us. You got the devil over here and his troops and God over there with his. Like I say, it's a never-ending story, so something else will come up.

After these last words, DJ Shadow and I parted ways. His program had one more hour to go, but he admitted that he was tired and would just like to relax and not talk about politics anymore. I understood, as I too was exhausted, and bode him farewell. Coming out of the studio and waving down a bus to take me home, I thought, if there is a mystical battle raging in all of us, maybe SXMers like DJ Shadow are wise to play it safe. Perhaps they should be ideologically against embarking on the road of nationalism and should assert the recognition of Rastafari individuality on the island but remain pragmatists, safely in the bosom of France and the Netherlands, where the winds of capitalism are, relatively speaking, rather mild.

As I reflected back on our meeting, I realized that DJ Shadow is the ultimate politician—someone who is able to entice others to follow his or her vision for the future—and deep down, he probably knows it. No politician I had met on the island, both those with and without political backing, was as skillful as he is in addressing people from all walks of life.

After that memorable day in the studio, I encountered DJ Shadow several times, both out- and inside the radio booth. Through the many encounters I had with him, I understood why it is possible for him to entice a radio public encompassing various socioeconomic classes and generations. For example, while performing as a disc jockey at a beach party, DJ Shadow was the embodiment of the rummie, cracking jokes and playing calypso and zouk tunes to his audience's delight. It was all about having a good time and enjoying life. He made everyone feel at home and promoted a sense of inclusiveness. Life seemed, if only for a few hours, simple and uncomplicated.

The tourists and the local audiences who were in attendance recognized in DJ Shadow the postcard image, presented in tourist billboards and promo films, of the happy-go-lucky West Indian. A middle-aged Nevisian woman told me that whenever she is housekeeping at the hotel where she is employed, she and her colleagues tune in to his radio program because he plays the latest dance hits, which alleviates their work burden. But DJ Shadow also appeals to those who spend hundreds of dollars to stay in the hotels SXMers clean. A wealthy American tourist I spoke to at this beach party told me that during these gatherings, he had a sense of belonging and acceptance that was at times stronger than the one he felt at home. The performances of SXMers seemed to work wonders on the spending habits of the American and European tourists.

At another venue, a calypso extravaganza, DJ Shadow transformed himself into a verbally violent version of *Native Son*'s Bigger Thomas. Since these calypso extravaganzas are spaces where critical political and social commentaries are usually expressed, DJ Shadow took the opportunity to make an appeal for more social justice and to criticize the political establishment. He sang two self-composed songs, "Justice" and "They Fool We Again." "Justice" is about the inequalities between the elites and the working classes on the island:

I want Justice
I looking for Justice
I want Justice
Equal Justice. When the poor man fail and commit he crime
He going through hell just to do he time
When the rich man them, they run their scheme, they living life as dream
I want Justice
Equal Justice
Justice: for one and all whether you White, Black, Indian, Chinese
Justice: all I asking in for is just a little Justice for one and for all.

"They Fool We Again" discusses the way politicians promise their constituents heaven at election time:

Deceitful business
They promise we this and promise we that and nothing doing again
Promises is only promises: when they get in office they going fix we business
Promises is only promises: once they get in power they say we could go for the future
But when I take a stock of the truth what I really see it bothering me
One race controlling the currency
The next corrupting democracy
They fool we again. They fool we again. They fool we again: waving up the banner, one Love joint together
They fool we again. They fool we again: things looking so bad who will guard they guard?

These songs, which DJ Shadow had recorded a few years earlier, were classics that had topped the SXM charts and had also been hits in the neighboring islands. The melody, rhythm, and lyrical arrangement of these songs were so catchy that even if one was hearing them for the first time, one could easily sing along. I gathered from their reactions that the majority of the audience had seen DJ Shadow perform these songs several times. They knew the cues and sang with loud voices that SXM society needs to be fairer and that uncertainty in politics needs to be eliminated. The politicians were taking the brunt for allegedly turning a blind eye and even readily encouraging these practices. But the question was, What did the audience make of all of this? By carefully observing their behavior, I got some clues.

With a baked chicken leg in one hand and a daiquiri in the other, an old school friend who resided in the United States and had accompanied me to the concert said, "That's right. The boy right. You give them hell, Addie." ("Addie" is Shadow's Christian name.) But there was a telling difference between her bodily movement and her words encouraging DJ Shadow to criticize the establishment. As she moved her hips to "They Fool We Again," there was not a trace of anger or urgency on her face. Her mouth was saying one thing; the rest of her body, another. It was a mix that I can only describe as socially critical with a heavy dose of hedonism. She reminded me of my conversations with DJ Fernando Clarke, who told me that through calypso, many West Indians learn from an early age to be critical of societal injustices without losing themselves to a quixotic form of social activism. As I mentioned earlier, one of the typical traits of Caribbean music is that, while the words are political, the music acts as a counterpoint. The latter reminds Caribbean people that everything is not political, not reducible to strife; living life also brings its joys. Life is not black and white but various shades of gray. Thus, it is all a matter of knowing that society is unjust but that rash actions are unwise.

My friend exemplified this understanding, as did the majority of the audience. After his performance, DJ Shadow simmered down and stopped performing his Bigger Thomas, working-class image. While drinking a Guinness, he greeted fans and exchanged pleasantries with acquaintances and friends. When I asked him about his relaxed posture, he replied, "I am Caribbean man. When I done speak my mind, I want party. Take a whine, free up myself. The Bible say a man can't live by bread alone. I say a man can't live by warring alone, Seen."

When I spoke to my friend and others at the venue about DJ Shadow's performance, I was told that the reason they liked him was that even during his most damning critique of the establishment, he seeks to promote unity among all SXMers. In the words of one of these people, "He know 'bout life," meaning, "He knows life is about give and take."

DJ Shadow metamorphosed again when he performed as the master of ceremonies at Junior Gong's concert, one of the heirs of Bob Marley's legacy of immanent social critique. At this concert DJ Shadow was the righteous Rasta, criticizing Babylon and promoting Rastafari individuality and livity (messages of radical egalitarianism). The audience, teenage Bob Marley wannabes, were elated with his performance. He touched a nerve every time he said, "We a going chant down Babylon tonight" and "A inity we want." (*Inity* is an explicit wish for unity and equality.) The teenagers I spoke to felt that DJ Shadow is a genuine "rebel man." Many told me that they were loyal fans who listened to his program daily.

These examples demonstrate that DJ Shadow has a broad-based public that he is able to entice. His secrets to success are his wit, his talent at attracting an audience, and his keen insight into the workings of his society. He talks the revolutionary's talk but walks the pragmatist's walk. For all his verbal rebelliousness, the Shadow is not that different from DJ Clarke. His notion of Rastafari individuality, like Clarke's two vitamin Cs, is a way of promoting an inclusive politics of belonging without explicitly addressing socioeconomic inequalities. Both men employ intricate philosophies through which they encourage locals and newcomers to see themselves as equals, because all are engaged in the money tie system. And most SXMers concurred. This begged the following question: What appeal would a disc jockey have who explicitly seeks to address socioeconomic inequality and the responsibility of the "have-mores" toward the "have-lesses"? I turn now to a disc jockey who wanted to do exactly that.

CHAPTER 6

The Hip-Hop- and Christian-Inspired Metaphysics of DJ Cimarron

It was a hot Tuesday afternoon in September, and I was on my way to SBN radio. I had an appointment with DJ Cimarron, a thin, dark-skinned man who looked a bit bookish. He would be broadcasting what was supposed to be his first intergenerational talk show, the *Talking Drums,* in which poor talented youths and influential adults would discuss issues relevant to both generational groups. As the "prodigal and radical son" of one of the most respected local families on the island, Cimarron expounded that, in dealing with the issue of educating the children of the illegal workers who keep the island's tourist industry competitive, most of the elites adhere categorically to the money tie system. According to Cimarron, their main reason for refusing to grant these children access to the same educational and social opportunities enjoyed by their own children is monetary, as it would cut into their own incomes. He believed that the human element is of less importance to them than their own surplus gains. He argued that the money tie system should be circumvented so that humanism will become the guiding principle of action on SXM.

To strengthen the self-evidential quality of his politics, Cimarron maintained that aside from the arguments that he presented to the elites, it is the ancestral spirits revered in Science who beckon them to adhere to this idea. Even while proclaiming his autonomous views on the matter, he claimed he was simply a medium through which they have made their wishes known. Cimarron wanted to further concretize his own wishes and those of the ancestral spirits through his talk show. These ancestral spirits, interceding between God and man, are popularly presented as destitute sojourners. Stories abound whereby these spirits are said to have survived because of the unconditional generosity displayed by others who have been equally disenfranchised in the region and the wider world. Cimarron highlighted these stories as the basis of his political claims that illegal youths should be awarded the same educational and social benefits as their legal counterparts and thus be treated as equals.

He wanted to use his talk show to promote social justice and the equality of all, both those with and without the appropriate French or Dutch passports. He planned to lend force to his politics of belonging by letting illegal and other disenfranchised youths present their self-penned hip-hop compositions that were critical of society. According to him, these were pieces of musical poetry inspired by the spirits. Would this Jeremiah, a man noted for preaching to his compatriots who wore earplugs, be more successful as a disc jockey? Laughing at the thought of Cimarron with a long beard, dressed in an Old Testament version of the djellaba and talking DJ talk, I arrived at SBN.

Entering the SBN radio station, I was struck by its sense of newness: fresh paint, spotless white tiles, and an impeccable interior. The millionaires Michael Soens and Han Hamaker, who was also the station manager, owned SBN, which had been on the air for four months. Born in the Dutch province of Limburg, both Soens and Hamaker were outspoken newcomers who claimed a genuine love for SXM. Through the programs of SBN, they wanted to entertain and, more important, to inform all SXMers of the interrelatedness of the world. They believed SXMers could not afford to quarrel with one another, for in the wider Caribbean, there were many impoverished peoples. Many SXMers averred that despite these noble claims, Hamaker and Soens were out to make money and widen their influence on the island.

Be that as it may, to compete with the many existing radio stations, Soens and Hamaker spared no expense when it came to SBN's recording technology. It was their dream that SBN become SXM and the northeastern Caribbean's premier news channel. Unlike the three to four hours of news reporting that most stations offered per day, SBN dedicated eight hours to local, regional, wider hemispheric, and international news broadcasting. To make their newscasting more attractive, the station was completely digitized. Through specialized software from the Silicon Valley, as Hamaker proudly asserted, the local newscasters' presentations were put into computers and synchronized with up-to-date voice bits

from CNN, BBC, and the Caribbean Broadcasting Union (CBU), lending an eyewitness feel to the SBN broadcasts and the suggestion that the
SBN anchors were reporting on the spot while conversing with their
overseas colleagues.

The management of SBN knew it would have to play attractive music
as well as broadcast interesting talk shows to maintain listeners in between the newscasting. In his search for talk show hosts, Hamaker met
Cimarron, who presented his idea for an intergenerational talk show:
musically gifted but underprivileged youths with a positive attitude
about life would present their self-penned hip-hop compositions to influential adults in society. Cimarron would lead the ensuing dialogue to
encourage possible cooperative ventures for the betterment of the island.
His agenda was not revolutionary; he did not want to legalize the undocumented youths, only to encourage improvements deemed realizable,
for instance, the organization of a clean-up week or the sponsoring of a
summer vacation camp.

No other programs on the island had a similar intergenerational format. What made Cimarron's offer even more appealing was that after
several conversations, Hamaker felt assured that Cimarron would refrain from his usual diatribes about the elites oppressing the working
classes. Cimarron was notorious for denouncing the alleged corrupt and
immoral behavior of the affluent. Instead of criticizing, he would lead the
way, showing how all SXMers could live peacefully. He also agreed to
present the talk show free of charge. I speculate that Hamaker decided
to take a gamble on Cimarron, hoping that his notoriety would induce
many SXMers to tune in and make his show successful. Once listeners
noticed that the show had a positive twist to it and continued to tune in,
advertisers could more easily be approached.

For things to go as planned, Cimarron's first show had to be a raging
success. It had to be at least as good as those of DJ Fernando Clarke and
DJ Shadow, which was a monumental task. When I arrived at SBN, ten
minutes before the recording was supposed to commence, Cimarron was
sitting in the front office waiting for me. He had contacted his three in-
terviewees to let them know that the show had been postponed for an
hour, but, since he didn't have my phone number at hand, he had been
unable to reach me. Cimarron thought that his show would be broadcast at three o'clock, but Hamaker had noted four o'clock in his orga-
nizer. It was not clear who was to blame.

After the delay, another unexpected twist presented itself. Daniel, an
outspoken intellectual and the only local of Cimarron's three guests,

seemed to be running late. Since the show was about to begin, Cimarron phoned Daniel, who apologized, saying he was caught up in meetings and could not make it. Daniel's cancellation was a blow. He was one of the persons whom Cimarron wanted to convince that awarding illegal youth equal treatment was the right thing to do. Daniel, a member of the *reformistas* (headed by the Baines brothers), was on the board of various charities and believed the SXM government should be stricter when it came to sending back illegal and other underage newcomers who engaged in petty crime. The charities he advised had their hands full with such youths. He averred that these renegade teenagers, who had little or no schooling, constituted a burden on society. They were nuisances who sooner or later would have a detrimental effect on the tourist industry.

Cimarron felt that Daniel's proposal showed little regard for these youths. Daniel condemned their practices but remained silent about the fact that very little public or private money was being spent to keep these youths on the right track. If their parents had to work long hours and the day care and after school activities were too expensive, it was not surprising that many were going astray.

But the question was how to persuade Daniel, a gifted speaker, to change his mind. Cimarron hoped that Kris and Carl, his other two guests, would act as his allies in the task of convincing Daniel that his views were inhumane. Kris was a seventeen-year-old born in Miami to a Dominican SXMer. His mother, after gaining her Dutch citizenship, illegally moved to Florida, hoping for a better life. Instead of making it in the "promised land," Kris's mother ended up in the projects, struggling to raise him while seeking to make ends meet. When his mother began to see no way out of this situation, Kris was sent to friends on SXM, at the age of sixteen, so that he could grow up in a safe environment. His mother felt that her son was exposed to a life of drugs, crime, and violence in the projects of Miami. She promised him that once she had settled into a better neighborhood, she would send for him.

Though he was a legal SXMer, Kris shared the experience of many illegal youths of having to move to a strange country and live with adults he hardly knew. In this process of mutual accommodation, Kris was struggling to hold his own. He missed the freedom he enjoyed in Miami and felt unwanted, since he was the only one sent to SXM. His younger siblings, who were the children of his mother's new boyfriend, remained in Miami. He wrote hip-hop lyrics to express his anger and grief and to help him stay on the right path. Cimarron told me that behind Kris's tough exterior and fashionable look, there was a teenager in pain. He had invited Kris on the show to give him a stage to perform his verbal art and to talk about his experiences. He told me that during the show, however, he planned to encourage Kris to discuss the harsh experiences of many illegal and other working-class youths on the island and to present his hip-hop compositions that reflected these experiences.

Carl, in contrast, was a worldly Californian with ample experience in the music business. He managed one of the island's most sophisticated recording studios. Carl hoped to make lots of money promoting Caribbean talent. For him, Caribbean music represented the next big wave in world music, and he planned to be at the forefront of this development. His main reason for consenting to be on the show was to advertise his studio and make youngsters aware that if he deemed them talented enough, he could broker their music to major record labels in the United States. In exchange, Carl would perform the role of a music connoisseur who endorsed the idea of music making as a remedy to heal the social wounds of deprived youths. Once in the studio, Cimarron thought he would be able to control the situation and keep Carl talking primarily about the healing potential of music.

Cimarron hoped that by meeting Kris and Carl, Daniel would gain a different understanding of the problem. He thought Carl could help him defend the argument that illegal youths were more than just a disaster in the making and that music-based projects catering to these and other working-class teenagers were viable ways of instilling morals and a positive purpose for life within them. Carl could also show how music was profitable, especially in the North American market. Kris would serve as an example of a youth who had been able to stay on the right track through music. If all went as planned, Cimarron would achieve three concomitant objectives that were elaborations on the wishes of the guiding spirits. First, Carl, a wealthy newcomer, would discuss the untapped potential that illegal and other working-class youths signified. Second, an influential local would be enlightened as to why he should not discriminate against these youths. Third, an underprivileged youngster would be granted the opportunity to express his emotions and confront an elite with the experiences of those he neglected.

Hamaker, who showed up a few minutes before the show commenced, decided that the program should still be aired, despite Daniel's cancellation. Two guests could surely fill an hour's show. He asked to see Cimarron's proposed format and the list of topics to address. Cimarron hesitantly admitted that he had not thought these matters through. The only thing he had done to prepare was to choose DMX's "They Don't Know

Who We Be" as the introductory tune for *Talking Drums*. He said the spirits would guide him on the air and that he would lead a lively discussion that encouraged unity. Hamaker "suggested" that instead of a live show, Cimarron should pretape the program. Only after an appropriate format had been worked out would the show be aired live. He then went behind the technicians' table and sat in on the whole broadcast.

During the first run, Cimarron interviewed both Kris and Carl simultaneously, but that did not yield the right results. Carl, who stole the show, talked about his own merits and intimidated Kris by discussing his future plans to shake up the North American music scene. Young Kris got barely any space, as Carl constantly interrupted him. Cimarron, who was supposed to lead the conversation, also seemed to be taken aback by the manner in which Carl managed to dominate the show. He was no DJ Clarke or the Shadow. He did not have their disc jockeying and people skills. Realizing that the program setup was too much for Cimarron to handle, Hamaker decided that they be interviewed apart, starting with Kris. Carl would leave the recording room so that Kris would feel comfortable.

On the spot, a workable format for *Talking Drums* came into being, one in which Cimarron interviewed talented and inspiring locals and newcomers. The original idea of an intergenerational program whereby all participants spoke and got to know one another was dropped. The new target group was to be successful SXMers who were going places. This was far removed from Cimarron's original idea, but he didn't seem to mind. But what about the spirits he claimed to be in contact with? Didn't it matter to them? I would just have to wait and see.

To get Kris and Cimarron into the right frame of mind, DMX's "They Don't Know Who We Be" was played quite loudly. It seemed to work, since they relaxed as they sang along to the tune. Following some deliberation, it was decided that, instead of jumping into the interview, Kris would start the show by giving a live performance of the *Talking Drums* rap. This powerful piece, composed by Kris and Cimarron, conveys the moments when someone's mind critically appraises society and the pains inflicted on him or her. Kris's voice, with its deep emotionality and eloquence, seemed to lend extra meaning to the words:

> When I hear the word, talking drum
> I get the vision of tons of people curious just like me
> to see or hear what is real or what is reality.
> You walk along the street
> and you see a group of old folks

laughing out loud at old jokes
that is talking drums.
When you are in school in your classroom
living in your own misery
and you're not paying attention when your teacher is talking about
     history
that is talking drums.
When you get upset because of false religions and prejudice
people and folks with crisis
and how everyday they put up gas prices
that's talking drums.
You know what
let's drop the bomb
sit back relax and let's talk some drums.

Following a short introductory talk in which he greeted the audience, welcomed Kris, and explained that *Talking Drums* was a program dedicated to highlighting positive developments on SXM, Cimarron began to ask questions. He asked Kris to talk about what brought a Miami rapper to SXM, how his experiences had been so far, and what the role of music in his life was. Kris used hip-hop tunes and artists as authoritative musical documents. For instance, he mentioned and partly defended Doctor Dré's protégé Eminem, who had a hit in which he criticized his mother for being a selfish and hard parent. The song discusses issues such as neglect, beatings, and being constantly likened to a father who had up and left. This was no doubt an allusion to Kris's feelings about his own mother. Furthermore, he likened himself to Eminem, as Kris too was channeling all his pent-up frustrations and dismay through music: "Some people say Eminem talks foul about his mother. But when you look at it differently, he's been through a lot. He is just taking all that anger inside of him and channeling that through his music. I love him. That's what it is, big time, stuff that you go through you write down, you rap about it, and you feel better."

This answer was coded, as it alluded to a public who understood this talk and knew the song: young SXMers who were into hip-hop. Since most performers of the intellectual lifestyle, the intended audience of Cimarron's show, did not listen to hip-hop and therefore were unfamiliar with its vocabulary and music, Kris's answer would seem vague. This made it unlikely as well that Kris's caretakers or other authority figures would feel offended or would reprimand him for airing his dirty laundry. The only time Kris was explicit, in fact, was when talking about music: "Music is life. Music is everything. I love it. I will never leave it."

Cimarron, knowledgeable about hip-hop and attuned to Kris's reservations about answering in straightforward terms, asked him to perform a self-penned rap about his recent experiences in life. The rap Kris performed was tellingly titled "It's OK for a Grown Ass Man to Cry":

It's OK for a grown ass man to cry
because he finally realize
that there is no other way to survive
when it comes to love and broken hearts.
Love is such a wonderful thing
but not without understanding and honesty. You can express love in so
    many ways
even if you're a grown ass man. You can express it with poetry
that's just the way I am
I am a grown ass man. Sometimes I feel trapped in a dream
and I can't wake up 'cause I am fighting emotional forces
but somehow I wake up mysteriously
fiercely and my mom hugs and tells me that she loves me
and somehow that changes everything.
My mom is like a protective shield
I think she is the only one
that I know that her love is real
that's just the way I am
I am a grown ass man.
Now you tell me why
why can't a grown ass man cry? Why does it look funny
when a grown ass man sits in his chair
passing his hand through his hair
shedding his tears?
Never keep your emotions inside
express yourself
'cause grown ass men do cry.

After this rap Kris was asked to elaborate on his love for hip-hop and his experiences performing on the island. He began by claiming that a rigid distinction between hip-hop and other music forms was inappropriate if this differentiation was based on the music underlying rap verses. Rap verses were not exclusive to the break beats or the rhythm and blues dominant in most of the North American music scene. One could rap to various beats. He had demonstrated this at bachata superstar Frank Reyes's show on the island, where he rapped to the melodies and rhythms of this Caribbean genre. Thereafter he claimed that hip-hop was a vehicle for many youths to express themselves: "Hip-hop is actually a lifesaver for a lot of young cats out there. The way I see it, songs they sing about and rap about is life. Not all young cats graduate high school. Not all know a sport that they can stick to, to make it in life. Not all of them are smart. Not all of them can be a president, judge, a lawyer, a doctor, or whatever. So they stick to hip-hop to make it. Big time." Here Kris was alluding to himself, since he was neither an ace student nor a superb athlete. Hip-hop was what he and many underprivileged youths knew best.

Cimarron took his cue from Kris and asked him if he felt that there were enough recreational activities for youths on the island. Predictably, Kris answered that there were not and that all grown-ups had a responsibility to contribute what they could to keep youths on the right path: "I bet if grown people would be more into youngsters there would be less delinquency. So more baseball and basketball courts, more music and after school programs. I know stuff is tight, but a dollar out of your check to do something for the youths, I think that would be kind of cool." Ending the session, Cimarron thanked Kris, asking him to give out his phone number so that listeners interested in booking him for a show would know how to reach him. Hamaker was pleased with the way things were going and complimented Cimarron on the outstanding job. It was time now to interview Carl.

Carl entered the recording room and began talking about the possibility of turning Kris into a star. Hamaker seemed somewhat irritated by Carl's bragging and intervened, saying that such matters should be discussed after the show, since time was money and he wasn't getting paid yet. Ignoring the irritation in Hamaker's voice, Carl asked him if he knew another Hamaker with whom he had done business in Atlanta some years ago. Hamaker then realized they had crossed paths in the past. Suddenly, time ceased to be related to money. Hamaker and Carl took about ten minutes to catch up and ponder the fact that, out of all the places in the world, they had both ended up on tiny SXM, while Cimarron and I sat patiently waiting.

Cimarron was not in control of his interview with Carl. Every question Cimarron asked led to an almost five-minute reply in which Carl advertised his studio and his plans. He was launching a glossy music magazine promoting West Indian artists in the region and abroad that would be called *Carib Beat,* like the company with which he was affiliated. He boasted that he already had distributors on various islands as well as in Canada, Great Britain, and the United States. Together with BET and others, he also planned to launch a Caribbean-wide song festival. Youths on SXM and the neighboring islands who felt they had talent could submit a demo, and if they were deemed as having "star potential," they would get free recording time in his studio. Out of all the entries, fifteen songs would be selected for recording, put on CD, and sent to major record labels and radio stations in the hemisphere. As the culmination of this stunt, a beach party held on SXM would be aired on BET, whereby the fifteen finalists would get a chance to perform their music for a potential audience of millions. The winner, judged by CEOs of major record labels, would be flown to California to meet top record executives to negotiate a possible record deal.

Even if he had wanted to, Cimarron could not touch on the importance of music for youths with social problems in this barrage of advertisement. Carl adhered to the new format of the program, which was about successful persons doing positive things on SXM. As far as the listening public was concerned, he was also addressing the young SXMers as Kris had. The only difference was that he was widening the circle, since not only rappers but also young singers of reggae, calypso, salsa, zouk, and other music forms were also invited to participate in his Carib Beat song festival. I could not help but wonder how this would appeal to intellectuals.

After Carl had filled twenty-three minutes of the show with his advertisements and self-aggrandizement, Cimarron was given the last word. He brought the show to a close by thanking his guests and listeners and then made an appointment with Hamaker to come in later that week to sit in on the mixing and editing. Since there were no other vacant slots and this was a tryout, the show would be aired Saturday at ten o'clock in the evening.

Three broadcasts later, Cimarron's *Talking Drums* was cut from the roster. There were five reasons for this. During the first broadcast, Cimarron had addressed young SXMers interested in music making. I believe he lost many of these listeners in his second broadcast, which differed significantly. In this program he had an exclusive interview with Daniel but encouraged him to avoid his polemical views about illegal youths. The show was, after all, about outstanding SXMers and not about promoting and causing divisions within the wider society. Hence, Daniel spoke solely about his achievements and about the virtues of Malcolm X, Martin Luther King, and Walter Rodney. Their ideas had been instrumental in his success, and he felt that other SXMers, especially black men, should also read their books. Daniel skillfully divorced King's and Rodney's radical civil rights and class emancipatory politics, as well as the conservative gender ideologies in their politics, from what he saw as their cultivation of a strong sense of black manhood. In true vulgar dependency theory fashion, he averred that becoming a strong black man was the only way to arm oneself against "the West" and white supremacy. This was a program that did cater to the intellectuals among the elite, the group Cimarron originally wanted to reach, in which "dictionary words" and academic theories were thrown around. It was not, however, done in a fashion that would critically interrogate their stances on illegal youths on the island.

The third program differed again. It was a show in which popular welfare workers spoke about their work with elderly persons and children with physical or mental handicaps. I would guess that the majority of those who were interested were the elderly, who formed the core of the volunteers, and persons who had relatives who were being taken care of at these types of social facilities. In short, every broadcast summoned another public. This was what the station manager wanted, but it was not feasible with the stiff competition the show faced.

The second reason why Cimarron's program was canceled was because it aired on Saturday and could not compete with the various calypso broadcasts. This was done because of a lack of available slots after it was decided that Cimarron's show should be pretaped. Because of the time and the day it was transmitted, I could find very few people who had listened to Cimarron's program. All those who did had listened had done so only briefly, for ten to fifteen minutes. Even the intellectuals were not interested in listening to such programs on a Saturday evening. Most were heading to a club, a honey, or a Spanish bar to spend time with friends and preferred to listen to calypso or other dance music that got them in the mood. As one person put it, Saturday evening was not a time "to think about politics and worry up myself." Most illegal youths I talked to had also not tuned in to Cimarron's program, since talk shows were not their thing. Even though Cimarron's program was not about politics but about positive persons, like other talk shows it still bore the stamp of straightforward societal critique.

Third, mentioning that Cimarron was the host brought a cynical smile to the faces of many of the businessmen to whom I spoke, prompting them to comment about his off-the-air politics. Admitting that he was articulate, they simultaneously referred to him as "that crazy boy," alluding to the rumor that, because of his experiences in the United States, he was dangling somewhere between sanity and insanity. They ridiculed him for claiming to be led by ancestral spirits. They saw him as insane or as a clever trickster, using the belief in spirits to get ahead. They refused to spend their money advertising their businesses on his program. The businessmen would not be so foolish as to support someone who claimed off the air that they were exploiting the illegal SXMers and neglecting their children. The station's management did not expect the advertisers to be so categorically against Cimarron. Notoriety, if it goes against the elites, is not commercially viable.

Furthermore, though many intellectuals deemed Cimarron's pleas for illegal youths noble, the idea of equal education for all youths on the island was considered unrealistic. They reckoned that the spirits would never demand such a thing from them, as they believed granting undocumented youths equal access to educational and social benefits would flood the island with poor people currently residing elsewhere. The intellectuals I spoke to mentioned that SXM already spent one-third of its budget on education and that a lot of primary and secondary schools were already being funded by the government and commercial interests. Everyone knew that many illegal children attended these. Asking SXMers to fund further education was pushing it. The locals and the wealthier newcomers felt they were doing what they could. They alluded to the United States and Western Europe, where the undocumented had it far more difficult. On SXM there were hardly ever any police raids or ID cards requested, making it possible for the parents of these kids to peacefully earn a buck and remit to love ones. Cimarron was a dangerous lunatic led by romantic ideas. The world was made up of nation-states and civil rights. If human rights to all regardless of passports had to be implemented on SXM, then the Western world had to set an example or compensate SXMers for their benevolence.

The fourth reason given by SXMers for not tuning in was that they had grown accustomed to most talk shows being interactive. They wanted to be able to participate in the conversations if they felt like doing so. Cimarron's program was pretaped and thus at odds with the format they were accustomed to. Referring to Cimarron's *Talking Drums,* an intellectual made it clear that SXMers may have accepted this form of talk show if it had been aired on cable TV but not on a local radio station.

The last issue that caused Cimarron's program to be cut was his lack of talent as a disc jockey. He was not a good talker like DJ Fernando Clarke or the Shadow. He did not have the eloquence to entice a public to tune in or the cleverness to hold their attention. With Cimarron, there were no double entendres, puns, subtle shifts in tone of voice, or unexpected questions that unsettled the guests. You were not kept on the edge of your seat, wanting to know what he would say next. His was a monotonous question-and-answer session, with his first program being the most entertaining of the three. My question was, What did Cimarron make of all of this?

Weeks later, I met Cimarron at a public meeting on parenting. After the meeting, in which he once again proclaimed that illegal youths were not being treated fairly, I spoke to him. He was somewhat disappointed that *Talking Drums* had been canceled, but he was moving on. He claimed that many people had commended him for doing a fine job. He felt he was gaining the respectability he longed for. This was why he continued the talk show, even after the format had been changed. He had hoped that in time he could use it to explicitly promote the interests of undocumented youths. As he understood it from speaking to Han Hamaker, the show had been canceled because of a lack of advertisers, who did not want to spend money in the off-season. In November, the start of the tourist season, he would try again. He made no mention of other reasons why he might have had trouble finding advertisers.

I told Cimarron that many intellectuals I spoke to were skeptical about his claim that ancestral spirits were addressing them through him. They felt that if it were so, he would not be acting as though the messages came directly from him. Cimarron's refusal to admit that he too was a performer in the money tie system was, for them, an impediment to believing in his politics. This was why they did not tune in to his program. In addition, they did not understand why the spirits would ask them to treat illegal youths the same as their legal counterparts, knowing that the island's budget could not afford such an operation.

Cimarron frowned and then yelled at me, as if these were my beliefs. He made no distinction between me as the narrator and that which was being narrated. He asked how I could claim that he was part of the system when the system had treated him so unfairly. He had lived on the streets of Washington, DC, wasn't given a chance to finish his studies, and was a product of what occurs when the money tie system is driven to its logical conclusion. People become merely means and not ends. He agreed that he equated his position with that of the spirits, but that was because in his life he had encountered the same hostility and oppression they had. He empathized with illegal youths, because their experiences compared with his in the United States. How could I claim that educating youths, even though they lacked French or Dutch passports, was not appropriate? It was a question of human rights. Those who wanted him to say that illegal youths should be treated fairly but that it was the spirits who were saying it, not he, were legitimating the system and wanted him to be part of that as well. Afterward he returned to his usual politeness and said he had to run because he had another appointment.

As he left, I sought to convince myself that, no matter how much he denied it, he too was a performer within the money tie system. Seeking to regain my composure, I reckoned that he yelled because I had touched a soft spot. For SXMers, there was no stepping outside the money tie system. Although it is not fixed and how it is enacted is in constant negotiation, no social performer can sidestep it completely. As Berger and Pullberg have argued, living in a society means entering into dialogue with others on compromised common ground: "Now the human enterprise of producing a world is not comprehensible as an individual project. Rather, it is a social process: men together engage in constructing a world, which then becomes their common dwelling" (Berger and Pullberg 1965: 201). But some men and women do not feel comfortable in this common dwelling. They contest it. However, this contestation is done using the constructs of the society that they denounce. Cimarron was no exception. He took on the identification of a local who had been victimized, therefore claiming exemption from the money tie system. By embracing this identification, he once more brought the reality of the money tie system into existence. He did this even when claiming it was the ancestral spirits who beckoned the elites to treat illegal youths justly. Had he acknowledged that he too was part of the money tie system, he probably would have been far more effective in pleading the cause of undocumented youths.

As I drove home, however, it occurred to me that the value of any explanation is grounded in experiences and desires, and my analysis was not free of these. I understood then what Michael Jackson meant when he averred that assertions are not considered truthful if they do not strike a chord in regard to the needs and experiences of those with whom one is interacting: "Our understanding of others can only proceed from within our own experience, and this experience involves our personalities and histories as much as our field research. Accordingly, our task is to find some common ground with others and explore our differences from there (Jackson 1989: 17). Experience, therefore, is not to be glossed over during fieldwork or in the process of writing ethnography. It is important for ethnographers and other scholars to question their experiences and the codified and implicit ways of experiencing these experiences. Relating to one's experiences is not a spontaneous act but one involving social registers through which one makes these intelligible. The social registers one chooses have to do with one's habits and needs at that particular time. Hence, Cimarron's refusal to claim that he was part of the money tie system was not wrong; it was I who needed to understand why he felt and reasoned the way he did. Recalling his life story led me to realize why he could not bring himself to admit that he too was part of the money tie system.

Cimarron grew up at a time when the tourist boom was beginning to lead to the growth of the civil service apparatus. The money tie system was becoming the hegemonic performative space. Children of working-class locals who had obtained some education occupied these new civil service jobs. Education became the working classes' means with which to climb the social ladder. This was one of the tangible ways through which their children could unequivocally distinguish themselves from illegal youths and children of the working-class newcomers. It led to a situation in which most locals cultivated the attitude that menial labor should be avoided and reserved for poor newcomers. Menial labor became the symbol of not having what takes to make it in society. Many of the working-class locals and their progeny were hospitable to the poor newcomers, legal or illegal , so long as the newcomers accepted their inferior social station and showed less ambition toward higher forms of education. Thus, even while interacting with the local working classes, illegal workers could not openly assert that they wanted their children to enjoy the same privileges.

From an early age, Cimarron had been taught that education was the key to being a respectable citizen. It was his right, but that right did not extend to his companions, the children of illegal immigrants. He was hardly conscious of structural discrimination back then. Some of these children went to primary school with him, but most dropped out during secondary school. Either their parents could not pay the school fees, or they were not interested in school. Others had come to live with a relative on the island in their teens and had never attended a SXM school. Cimarron's mother, a major influence in his life, paid no mind to these issues. All she cared about was that he and his elder brothers should do better than she had. Her sons had a right to be "a somebody," as he put it. Once he was educated, the elites would have nothing over him.

Cimarron internalized the value of this form of cultural capital, which was privileged by the island's middle and upper classes. As is the case elsewhere, these elites used education and the right connections to legitimate their right to make most of the major political decisions without truly consulting working-class locals and newcomers.[1] They also used their cultural and social capital (networks) to obfuscate the issue of the uneven distribution of wealth. The elites envisioned themselves as self-made and wanted the working classes to envision them this way as well. A Horatio Alger lay dormant in everyone.

It was hard to tell whether Cimarron learned to believe this lie or whether he actually regarded it as the truth from the beginning. From what I gathered, it was a combination of the two, as he remembered hearing his mother refer to the elites as crooks. He himself referred to some of his former schoolmates as children who knew that regardless of their grades, "daddy would reserve an air-conditioned job for them in government." In other words, he seemed to be aware that the educated children of the working-class locals could climb the social ladder as long as the higher posts remained in the hands of the elites. Still, a sense of being able to beat the odds won out. As a teenager he became obsessed with going abroad to earn an academic degree, which would bring a well-paying job and prestige, and, because of his intellect, would enable him to match the prominence of the elites.

Cimarron was not a cultural dupe. He was enticed to choose the intellectual lifestyle, that of the lettered SXMers who excelled in explicitly expressing their academic knowledge, a new social performance that seemed to level the playing field. I stress "seemed" because education actually blurred rather than erased differences among members of social classes who chose to perform this lifestyle.

By performing the role of intellectuals, the children of the local working classes believed they could match the monetary strength of the elites. Through strategic alliances with wealthier SXMers and entering governmental politics, they could turn their cultural capital into financial capital. Cimarron followed this trajectory and, at age eighteen, headed off to Andrew College in Georgia to study Spanish and French. Once he earned his associate's degree, he returned to the island, where he was offered a job as a primary school teacher, which he turned down. Cimarron wanted more. He wanted to be up there with what he called "the head honchos," the elites, so he applied for another scholarship to pursue his bachelor's. He felt this would enable him to obtain a high post in the education or culture department and that with such a post, his intellectual performance would be more valued. This is where his troubles began. He got a student visa immediately, but it took him two years to secure a partial scholarship.

With his partial scholarship, Cimarron enrolled at a university in Washington, DC. Since he felt he deserved more money, he sent letters and made requests to have his partial scholarship turned into a full grant.

The bureaucratic machine struck back when he was notified at the end of his second to last semester that because his student visa had expired, his scholarship would not be prolonged. He claims that something broke at that point, and he categorically refused to return to SXM. In desperation he contacted the Dutch embassy, hoping that it would intervene. It was to no avail. In the end, in accordance with the constitution of the Dutch Kingdom, it was Curaçao and SXM that decided.

Although his mother and other relatives urged him to come back to SXM, Cimarron decided he would not return without his BA. He had worked hard, been an ace student, and was determined to show those at the scholarship department that he would prevail. Feeling that his family was colluding with the scholarship department, he broke off all contact. He would prove them all wrong. The sacrifices he made to do so were quite harsh. His life took a 180-degree turn as he exchanged the campus dorms for homeless shelters, rundown basements, and even park benches. With an expired student visa and no scholarship, he became a homeless illegal on the streets of Washington, DC. As he put it, "Being out there every day was unpredictable. I lived from day to day. I moved from renting basements to staying in the shelter to sleeping on benches." In the shelter he might meet vendors for whom he would subvend flowers, T-shirts, or sweaters. He would save the little money he made, buy his own merchandise, and work for himself. During those times he rented dilapidated basements in what he euphemistically called "the not-that-affluent neighborhoods."

This situation never lasted long, however, since the municipal police would unexpectedly raid and confiscate his merchandise. Broke, he would have to return to shelters or park benches. What is surprising is that he was never asked for his ID or picked up by immigration officers, since the homeless were the domain of the municipal police, and there was no direct connection between the municipal police and the immigration department.

Cimarron claimed he was on the brink of giving in to the negative images of the homeless that abound in Washington, DC. Being broke, he was close to feeling he had lost it all until he understood wealth differently: "If you define wealth, as many do, in terms of monetary terms, then that is a small aspect of that particular word. In a country with such a tremendous amount of money, you experience a tremendous amount of spiritual and moral poverty." He said that he might have gone insane were it not for hip-hop. Cimarron and his homeless friends danced and acted out the way the working, middle, and the upper classes treated them: "We rapped about them, but they didn't have time to hear us, even when they were close enough to hear us. It was as if we were invisible. At times, some people would throw us some coins. We were cursing them, and they were giving us their small change."

Furthermore, Cimarron claimed that although, generally speaking, the competition among the homeless was enormous, some did explicitly acknowledge one another's humanity. When they could, they shared the little they had, hoping for eventual reciprocity. This coincides with the findings of scholars such as Snow and Anderson (1987), who did research among the homeless in the United States. In addition, through philosophizing about their hip-hop compositions and the bodily expressions they inspired, Cimarron and his friends reinterpreted their situation: "I learnt not to value myself on how those people perceived me. I chose to see myself not in a state of lack or deprivation. I was able to live a certain lifestyle that did not hurt anybody else or infringe on the rights of anybody else. I was very much aware of my situation, but I did not feel myself a homeless person."

After a few years, Cimarron reestablished contact with his family. In the meantime, one of his older brothers became the commissioner of tourism, and others began running successful businesses. They were now upper-middle-class locals. Like other children of working-class locals, they had united with financial and political powers and were handsomely rewarded. Cimarron asked them to lobby for him at the scholarship department or help him pay for his last semester. When they heard that he lived on the streets, they refused and suggested he return to the island.

His oldest brother visited him in Washington, and the two met at the Four Seasons Hotel. In this posh setting, Cimarron saw his "brother was living it up, looking good and everything." Cimarron told him about his desire to finish school, but his brother only wanted him to return to SXM. Cimarron decided to continue working on his BA degree on the streets. "I felt there was a purpose for me being there. I so much wanted to be in school, getting academic degrees and things like that, but in a sense I was in a whole other school. I needed to understand that situation and allow that situation to help me even understand myself better."

In 2000, when laws passed under the Clinton administration established tougher penalties for residing in the United States illegally, Cimarron allowed his family to pay his airfare so that he could return to SXM. He needed to leave the United States before the laws were enacted; otherwise, if he got caught, he would not be able to apply for a visa to return for the next ten years. Cimarron was still obsessed with getting a BA

and being respected by his fellow locals. By returning to SXM, he felt
that he would be able to obtain a new student visa and a scholarship to
finish his last semester. His plan did not work out, however, for on SXM
he was treated as a misfit and not given the recognition and help that he
had hoped for: "I did not come back as a beggar. I came back to ask for
help, but I was giving back something in return. I came with plans to establish a cultural foundation that would enrich SXM spiritually. This
was the fruit of my labor. I achieved an education on the streets. But my
brothers and cousins in government, nobody would help me."

Through his family's mediation, however, he was given a job as a government clerk. It was here that he realized illegal newcomers were socially and economically exploited in SXM's money tie system. In addition, few cared that their children enjoyed very little education and
constituted the new cheap labor force waiting to take their parents'
place. In the offices of his relatives and other influential locals, he saw
how these administrators were "the parasites and vultures of society."
While they claimed the monies already being spent on education for undocumented children were straining the government's budget, he knew
they were raping the treasury.

No longer able to stomach their hypocrisy, he quit his job and began
denouncing government officials publicly. He made it clear that as a
clerk, he had seen how these local politicians were taking bribes from the
wealthy newcomers: "All that dirty money could be put into schools instead of them buying a new Lexus." Cimarron said he gained the sympathy of many illegal workers but that they did not openly endorse his
views because they were trying to survive: "I was saying the same thing
they were while playing domino under the tree. But you see they could
not say it aloud because they couldn't afford to rock the boat. Now I had
nothing to lose. They couldn't deport me back to Santo Domingo."

Some members of the elite, however, including his relatives who
feared losing power, claimed that Cimarron's stay in the United States
had made him psychotic. They closed ranks, making it impossible for
him to find a job fitting his educational credentials. Though unemployed,
Cimarron did not resort to doing menial tasks reserved primarily for illegal workers. He felt that if he had taken such a job, he would not be
able to participate seriously at the meetings of intellectuals. Blue-collar
workers did not attend the Rotary or Toastmasters clubs, where the intellectuals met to talk politics. The price of the drinks alone was an impediment. In addition, Cimarron believed he deserved better. The irony
was that although he denounced the elites, most SXMers knew he sur-

vived on his family's financial support. He ate from the table of those he criticized. As a result, they saw his anger as stemming from his failure to enjoy the spoils to be had through bribery and other practices of the island's elites. As long as he was complaining that he had not been given an equal opportunity to enter the ranks of the elites, he appeared, to most SXMers, to be hypocritical. He longed to be where the wealthier locals and newcomers were, a fact that slowly dawned on him.

Cimarron's growing awareness of his own contradictory stance led him to begin soul searching. He critically reflected on his personal longings and on the meaning of life in general. He looked back and realized that his deceased grandfather, a known specialist in Science, had warned him that attaining worldly wealth and prestige and attempting to climb the socioeconomic ladder involved entering into a Faustian pact. It meant selling your soul to the devil: becoming like the elites who look down on the poor. The only way for him to overcome this was to remember the ancestral spirits and his social background. He needed to live differently and, through this, to let the ancestral spirits speak to him about contemporary issues. He began to understand that the future is always in the making; it is the present's hope (Hagen and Mahlendorf 1963).

Following this logic, for Cimarron, the devil was not an entity as such but a concept connoting the spiritual forces or tendencies of destruction that concretize themselves in the ills that humankind induces on itself. It was about the *thingification* of others, to use René Depestre's term, so that one could treat them as means rather than ends. God stood for the opposite: respecting people and nature as having an intrinsic worth. God stood for the equal opportunity that illegal youths should be awarded:

> For me, the concept of God and the devil are not too well defined. Perhaps in our search for some of those truths about the devil and God, we have stumbled on some of those answers. But then, perhaps we haven't come to any answers that may be approaching any measure of truth and reality. The devil and God are concepts. We are dealing here with concepts of our own making. But that does not mean that those concepts have anything to do with reality as such. And even reality—we are constantly defining reality according [to] our concepts. If we associate the devil as inspiring crime, violence, and oppression, we don't need a theology of the devil. The way things are going, the devil is becoming more real.

What about the ancestral spirits, then, were they forces as well? For Cimarron, they were the memory and spiritual forces of the deceased, closer to the pole of the creative (God) than to the pole of the destructive (the devil). Despite being loosely canonized in Science, they remain a way through which all individuals living on SXM are able to "under-stand that which is sacred, not simply dogma, bureaucracy, and institu-tionalized religion. They are that body of wisdom that you feel a certain nourishment and empowerment from." But those who nourished him were also the ones blackmailing him in his dreams.

Two recurring nightmares involving the spirits have haunted Cimar-ron since he was a teenager. In the first, Cimarron is in a mythical SXM before the tourist boom and before the hordes of newcomers. He is fac-ing a white plantation house surrounded from afar by little wooden shacks. The lush green vegetation and the blue skies camouflage the in-equalities, idyllically bringing together those who dwell in the mansion and those who live in the shacks made of two-by-fours. Then, out of the blue, a huge satellite disc appears and crashes into the plantation house, which is instantaneously reduced to rubble. As SXMers seek to repair what they can, Cimarron stands aloof, looking on. Then, suddenly, he runs to the rubble, frantically searching for the only thing that matters: a kerosene lantern. During a new moon, such lanterns provided light under which poor folks would come together to share stories. The lantern was symbolic of the overarching sense of a "we-feeling" that all local SXMers could appeal to, despite class or other subgroup differ-ences. The elites' "we-feeling" came from the obfuscation of the existing inequalities, while the working classes' came from their appeal for jus-tice and help in dire times. The lantern also signified a time before the ad-vent of electricity and modern conveniences, which Cimarron felt had led to a more egoistic lifestyle. People watched TV or went to the movies in-stead of sharing stories till the wee hours of the night.

Most locals, however, do not romanticize the past the way Cimar-ron did. They welcome the modern conveniences and do not philoso-phize about them. They claim that this uncritical acceptance of the so-ciety that came into existence as a result of electricity and running water is what makes them different from the "just come—never see people" of the poorer Antilles and the wider world. "Just come—never see people" is the phrase used for people in the Global South who are still in awe or fearful of modern conveniences. There was thus a radi-cal difference between Cimarron's idealization of the past and the opin-ions of most locals.

In Cimarron's second recurring nightmare, the spirits made their pres-ence explicitly known. In this nightmare, he tries to get out of bed to head for an air-conditioned office where he works. He never manages to leave his bed, however, because naked and faceless black phantoms stand between him and his closet full of expensive suits. He is so terrified that he freezes and is unable to confront them. At other times, he wakes up to find these phantoms hovering over his bed, staring at him. When I asked him to describe them to me, he likened them to the self-portrait of the British-Nigerian artist Seal on his 1994 self-titled CD sleeve. On this cover, Seal sits naked in front of a white backdrop. The contrast between Seal's dark brown skin and the white background gives him a jet-black metallic appearance. What makes the photograph seem mystical is that his head is bowed, concealing his facial features, and his legs are crossed to conceal his genitals. One assumes that it is Seal but cannot be sure. Cimarron probably likened this self-portrait to his tormentors because they too were naked with unidentifiable faces and genitals.

Troubled by his nightmares, seeking relief, Cimarron visited a Haitian Vodou specialist. The specialist revealed to him that the ancestral spirits, specifically those directly related to the contemporary locals, were communicating with him through these dreams. The phantoms were in fact young SXMers who had died in misery, and Cimarron's figure in the dream was a stand-in for the modern-day locals who side with the wealthy newcomers. They have forgotten that most of their grandparents were the beggars of the Caribbean, sojourners who moved from place to place, dependent on the generosity of others. Many young mouths were fed because other working-class West Indians had opened their hearts and their scarce maize sheds to them.

However, now that the locals are on top, they treat illegal youths in a demeaning fashion and do not extend to them the same unconditional hospitality. The satellite disc in his first nightmare stood for the changes brought about by the tourist industry that has led to the social and economic advancement of all locals. Cimarron was right in not striving to rebuild the plantation house, which symbolized prior inequalities. His saving of the kerosene lantern was an indication that remembering part of this past, the solidarity that it generated and the help from others that it entailed, was essential. It was not a question of a complete glorification of the past but of rescuing the egalitarian practices that it had symbolized. Cimarron's task was to awaken the consciences of the wealthy newcomers and to help the locals remember. Only by doing so would he rid himself of these nightmares and be able to sleep at night.

Cimarron believed in the Vodou specialist's interpretation of his dreams. It made good sense to him. He had known what it meant to be an illegal, a walking casualty of SXM's system of classifying people as citizens and noncitizens. Furthermore, in talking with illegal workers, he had come to see that, despite their smiles and their "sí, señors," many want their children to be given an equal chance to climb the social ladder.

This corresponded to my own experiences. Since they work long hours for meager allowances, working-class newcomers cannot afford to tutor their children, nor do they have the skills to do so. They are angry and feel their children should be permitted to develop talents that will lead to social and economic advancement. They should not have to continue living in the cycle of poverty in which their parents and grandparents lived. It is a question of applying children's rights, enshrined in the UN Declaration of Human Rights, to education, giving these children equal opportunities. Though these illegal newcomers have never read the charter, they are all for it. The working classes on SXM, as elsewhere in the Caribbean, know the ideology of liberty, fraternity, and equality by heart. It is one that most West Indians have made their own (Sanchez 2003; James 1963). This is not to say that they always implement it on SXM, but it does mean that all SXMers have to present excuses when they do not. Liberty, fraternity, and equality and their enshrinement in the notion of human rights are not considered Western imperialist notions.

Cimarron wanted to further concretize both the wishes of the working classes and those of the ancestral spirits through his talk show. He chose the format of a talk show because those whom he deemed the "legitimatizers" of the money tie system, the intellectuals, frequently listened to and participated in this form of radio. This was their stage to tell the "common man and woman," supposedly less knowledgeable than themselves, about what direction the island should take in the face of world events. They usually framed their analyses in terms of a dependency discourse: the West was strangling the rest. A similar dualistic analysis was not voiced when it came to the island's internal social makeup, which was telling. If the performers of the intellectual lifestyle were the public of talk shows, then Cimarron would become a talk show disc jockey.

Prior to turning to SBN, Cimarron had sought out other radio stations, but the executives had all refused, fearing that he would use the airwaves to further his denunciations of the well-to-do. In a way they were not far off, since most of the underprivileged youths Cimarron planned to feature in what was supposed to be his intergenerational talk show would have been undocumented. He wanted to confront the intellectuals and other elite sections of SXM society with the talent and humanity of those they consciously disregarded. The illegal youth would be given the opportunity to express themselves via hip-hop, the medium he had expressed himself in.

The choice of hip-hop may seem strange to many, since, worldwide, this form of popular culture is marketed as the contemporary jazz of ghetto America. But this is a story few young SXMers accept. Like Cimarron, they know that hip-hop is actually a Creole expression. On BET they are made aware that Fat Joe, Biggie Smalls, Wyclef Jean, Jennifer Lopez, Busta Rhymes, and many other hip-hop stars are of West Indian extraction. In fact, working-class West Indian immigrants were pivotal in the development of North American hip-hop (Patterson 1994; Gilroy 1993). So too were the Hong Kong–based kung fu movies of Bruce Lee and Hollywood gangster movies such as *The Godfather,* as evinced by groups such as the Wu-Tang Clan and N.W.A. Hip-hop was and continues to be a transcultural expression produced by the working classes, an expression that subverts the neat ethnic and racial markers that are accepted by most people. This subversive potential flickers from time to time, even though the culture industry has been rather successful in co-opting this form of immanent rebellion. Poignant critiques of class discrimination and racism can still be heard on the discs of Kanye West, Eminem, and other artists who supposedly sold their souls to Sony:

> With popular culture and the music industry it is never an either/or game. I don't want to suggest that we can counterpose some easy sense of victories won to the eternal story of our own marginalization—I am tired of those two continuous grand counternarratives. To remain within them is to become trapped in that endless either/or, either total victory or total incorporation, which almost never happens in cultural politics, but with which cultural critics always put themselves to bed. . . . It is never a zero-sum cultural game; it is always about shifting the balance of power in the relations of culture; it is always about changing the dispositions and the configurations of cultural power not getting out of it. (Hall 1998: 24)

Cimarron was interested in those expressions of hip-hop that were as far removed as possible from the culture industry. He concerned himself with the existential hip-hop of the disenfranchised. While talking about the hip-hop of artists featured on MTV and BET, he told me, "I like that hip-hop too, but that is just part of the definition. Perhaps we need to understand hip-hop as being the same as reggae or bachata. It is about the poor man's poetry. It is spiritual music. It is an expression of the talking drums. We are all spiritual drumbeats. The drums are with us, the drums are in us."

Cimarron was full of idiosyncratic terms. *Spiritual drumbeats* was one of these, and he used it interchangeably with the term *talking drums.* In his opinion, besides making us feel like dancing, drums make sounds that help us to understand that we are all spirits incarnate, regardless of our different stations in life. Further, drumming alerts us that a world of disincarnate ancestral spirits is out there, spirits with whom we are associated and whom we must obey. This was a direct borrowing from Science. Where he differed from most practitioners of Science was in his belief that only those who have experienced a personal trauma are likely to truly understand themselves as spirits. These incarnate spirits, through the intervention of the ancestral spirits, relate ideas and alternative ways of living through seemingly illogical, nonchronological, and fairly unintelligible musically based poetic expressions.

Cimarron's *talking drums* bears some resemblance to what Glissant (1999) has termed *stifled speech*. This concept refers to expressions based on alternate states of consciousness that have a counter-hegemonic potential. *Stifled speech* forms a triadic relationship with the oral and the written in Caribbean societies. For Glissant, the written in the Caribbean refers to codified laws and other official institutions. To engage with these, one must accept their codes, the prime identifications, and the reasoning they prize. This reasoning is shaped by the hegemonic politico-economic system and standardized high cultured forms of speaking and writing.

The oral, by contrast, is related to everyday norms and maxims, the life worlds wherein the working classes have a considerable say, though of course it is not solely their domain. The elites inhabit these worlds as well and are, to some extent, versed in working-class codes. Both elites and working classes in the Caribbean communicate through written and oral realms, though the elites and written realm exhort a hegemonic pressure on the working classes and the oral realm (Chevannes 2000; Austin 1983).

Stifled speech is a product of traumatic and personal experiences inadvertently created under this hegemony. It continuously disrupts the commonsense privileging of the powerful. When one is usually on the receiving end of power, ill-fitting social identifications and their repercussions are felt more severely. In the Caribbean, the frustrations of disempowerment and the subconscious desire to remedy them are expressed primarily through song and dance.[2] In his florid style, referring to West Indians as the Peoples of the Sea, Benítez-Rojo phrases the matter thus: "The Peoples of the Sea expresses the desire to sublimate social violence through referring itself to a space that can only be intuited through the poetic. . . . In this paradoxical space, in which one has the illusion of experiencing totality, there appear no repressions or contradictions; there is no desire other than that of maintaining oneself within the limits of this zone for the longest possible time, in free orbit, beyond imprisonment or liberty" (1996: 17). Nevertheless, one cannot remain in this free orbit, and the precise meanings of what one experiences in this "space" are not logically given. They have to be deciphered and then constructed into intelligent forms. In this context, they run the risk of being neutralized by the world of the written. However, because the inequality between the written and the oral leads to traumatic experiences, stifled speech is constantly replenished and cannot be fully co-opted or depleted.

Similarly, Cimarron linked subversive counter-hegemonic expressions with the experience of a traumatic event, which is more likely to occur among those who are already economically and socially deprived. He was the ultimate *talking drum,* a drum who had spoken in the idiom of hip-hop while living on the streets. His plan had been to let younger drums speak out against those who did not recognize the fundamental humanity binding legal and undocumented SXMers. But it was not to be. Cimarron seemed to me to be a modern-day Jeremiah surrounded by skeptics, a Don Quixote living in a society that did not see any reason to implement the radical changes he stood for. Few wanted to hear his stifled speech, because it was not voiced in a way that they could live with.

I could not find any SXMer who unequivocally sided with Cimarron's politics. The intellectuals did not trust him. They were skeptical about his assertion that he was simply mediating the wishes of the ancestral spirits, because he failed to perform the role of unwilling medium and actor driven by the wishes of the spirits. Cimarron always said that he *and* the spirits wanted equal rights for illegal youth. In his performance, he presented himself as an assertive individual, a notion of personhood that posits a person as an autonomous subject in full control. However widespread it may be, this notion of personhood is but one among many that humans have constructed (Mageo 2003; Carrithers, Collins, and Lukes 1985). In performing the role of the individual, Cimarron was transgressing the appropriate form of personhood when relating the wishes of the spirits. With Science, one cannot be an autonomous individual. Instead, ancestral spirits were part of one's spiritual makeup. The idea of the autonomous ego that can freely choose to agree or disagree with the spirits does not exist in a true performance of Science.

Cimarron openly refused to adhere to this performance to forward his politics of belonging. Here is where older local practitioners of Science, who were not into the intellectual lifestyle and did not tune in to talk shows, practitioners such as Miss Maria, found Cimarron disingenuous.

Even so, these locals could agree with his interpretation that the ancestral spirits who directly related to the locals had been for the most part destitute wanderers who had survived because of the mercy of others. This was one of the privileged ways the locals sought to represent themselves. They claimed descent from a meek and hospitable people whom God has rewarded. This representation should not be viewed as unique, since most nations employ noble readings of the dead to legitimize a transcendental identity for themselves, as in, "this is who we are because this is where we came from" (Harrison 2003).

However, this move is always riddled with contestations. Or, as Karl Marx put it: "The tradition of all dead generations weighs like an Alp on the brains of the living" (1987: 11). Conjuring up the dead is a social decision and therefore usually prone to contestation. Not all will agree about the set of ancestors one summons to legitimize a "we-feeling." In addition, not all will be of the same mind about the meaning ascribed to the chosen and excluded ones. Moreover, while some people agree to summon up particular ancestors and ascribe to them particular identities as the founding fathers and mothers of the collective, the nation in this case, others diverge and lay a claim to different ancestral spirits. Sometimes this divergence is built into the popular archives, the folk stories and popular rites from which these founding narratives are built.[3] This is the case with Science, which is often employed by locals.

Science, the popular archive on which many locals base their transcendental identity as a people, posits that the ancestral spirits that surround every "I" transcend the notion of biological kinship and narrow class distinctions. The ancestral spirits that locals practicing Science revere were originally natives as well as foreigners, rich as well as poor, blacks as well as whites. In short, the ancestral spirits were themselves the offspring of all the peoples who had migrated forcefully or by their own accord to the Caribbean. Even if at times the locals claim the indigenous spirits to add authenticity to their own status as natives, in daily practice they revere all when performing rites and asking for favors.

I speculated in chapter 2 that belief in Science and the ancestral spirits is a form of remembering and honoring the West Indians of old and of making past events present. Like other spiritual philosophies in the region, it functions as an alternative to official historical accounts that seek to disentangle the interrelatedness of those deemed the oppressors and the oppressed. Most spiritual philosophies throughout the Caribbean posit that Western imperialism and internal forms of oppression were horrific but not subsumable to a black and white story (Palmié 2002; Thoden van Velzen and Van Wetering 1988). Things were much messier on the ground.

Cimarron did not want to talk about this messiness. But in not doing so, he ostracized devout practitioners of Science, who wondered how it was possible that he had only destitute local spirits surrounding him. Where were those who had been filthy rich, those who had been poor but did not give a damn, and those who had never set foot on the island during their lifetime? What were they saying? And since when did the spirits communicate in hip-hop? This was young people's music, someone like Miss Maria would say. Why didn't the spirits communicate through calypso or conscious reggae, which all generations listened to? Either Cimarron was a fraud or he was exceptional. And exceptionality with regard to having a spiritual makeup that transcends class, ethnicity, and nation was not possible. How could they be sure that his quest to enlighten his fellow locals was not driven by some bid for power? All SXMers knew his story, knew about his ambitions, and did not trust him. Miss Maria once referred to Cimarron as "death" and said that she felt sorry that such an intelligent young man had stooped so low. But on the other hand, she was also critical of him because he did not work for a living. In her opinion, he was lazy and just playing crazy. Yaya also said she had no respect for a man who did not work in a country where illegal newcomers find a job two days after arriving on the island. He was one of those men who wanted a pen-and-paper job, refusing to dirty his hands with menial labor.

Cimarron's refusal to do hard work was something that illegal newcomers also pointed to, although they did recognize his claim of speaking out for them in condemning the locals' discrimination against them. In their angriest moments, they too said they often felt that they and their children were treated as outsiders. They wanted their children to receive equal rights, regardless of whether this was grounded in rational argumentation, sympathy, or the wishes of the ancestral spirits. Lamentably, this has not been the case, for on SXM, like elsewhere, only citizens are treated as full-fledged human beings with rights to proper educational and social securities. Working-class newcomers want this to change.

On the other hand, to some extent, the money tie system has also worked in newcomers' interest. If SXM were to function as France and the Netherlands do, illegal newcomers would be constantly deported. They would not enjoy freedom of movement or job opportunities. Human rights would be unattainable for them. As Gerd Baumann and others have averred, despite the UN charters for human rights and children's rights, those who fall outside the bounds of nation-states are often at the mercy of others:

> Wish as we may, and dream as we must, the superlogic of human rights remains an ideology in every way. Historically and culturally, it rests on mythical thinking, however well intentioned; legally, it remains subject to the powers of nation-state elites, however well intentioned or selfish. What human rights we may have, we can only enforce by the grace of our nation-states, and all that a government needs to renege on them is an obedient police force within, an effective immigration "service" at the borders, and a lying diplomat at the United Nations. (Baumann 1999: 6–7)

In the case of SXM, an extension of France and the Netherlands, this issue was even more problematic, since the last word on decisions of this nature is given in Paris and The Hague. The illegal workers and their offspring on SXM gravitate to a space in between unattainable civil rights and unenforceable human rights; their lots are determined by appeals to the elites' senses of guilt or altruism. Knowing the rules of the money tie system, illegal workers understand that the bottom line of most relationships on SXM revolves around money and power. They must be useful and work hard without openly complaining. Regardless of their disappointments and anger, they cannot easily leave the island because they have family members who depend on their remittances. SXM is not paradise, but it is far better than the squalor that awaits them and their offspring in their countries of origin. Moreover, many others in these countries are eager for their place, if they get too uppity and start making demands for their children to enjoy equal rights. Cimarron could not be deported, but they could. And this fact alone prevented them from openly supporting him.

I believe that Cimarron also knew this, even if it conflicted with his desires and his experiences. Cimarron, for all his open denunciation of the system, decided not to return to the United States. He knew what it meant to be homeless on the streets of Washington, DC. On SXM, his family took care of him, making sure he had a roof over his head and food on his plate. He too had to "go along to get along." How much of an exception was he, when one took this into account?

Judging by the reactions I got from most SXMers I spoke to, Cimarron seemed to be a single talking drum among nonbelievers. But was he? In analyzing my material, I realized that Cimarron's case shows us that discursive regimes (structures, institutions, and meaningful statements) that are constitutive of dominant societal identifications always "fail" to a certain extent because, as social subjects, we are never carbon copies or "one size fits all" models. Scholars such as Stuart Hall have argued that this is an issue that the social sciences will never be able to completely resolve. Scholars can merely observe how people perform and modify social identifications:

> It has never been enough—in Marx, in Althusser, in Foucault—to elaborate a theory of how individuals are summoned into place in the discursive structures. It has always also required an account of how subjects are constituted; and in this work, Foucault has gone a considerable way in showing this, in reference to historically-specific discursive practices, normative self-regulation and technologies of the self. The question which remains is whether we also require to, as it were, close the gap between the two: that is to say, a theory of what the mechanisms are by which individuals as subjects identify (or do not identify) with the "positions" to which they are summoned; as well as how they fashion, stylize, produce and "perform" these positions, and why they never do, or are in a constant, agonistic process of struggling with, resisting, negotiating and accommodating the normative or regulative rules with which they confront and regulate themselves. In short what remains is the requirement to think this relation of subject to discursive formations as an articulation. (Hall 1996: 13–14)

This modification of the performance of social roles might be even more important for people who have experienced trauma as a result of wider societal inequalities. But we all modify social roles while performing them. The inhabitants of SXM are no exception. Consequently, all SXMers are talking drums to various degrees, drums who nevertheless perform in the money tie system. Phrased differently, in their differentiated performances that constantly reenact the money tie system, alternative ideas are produced, and these are utterances of talking drums. DJ Clarke's regulating "vitamin C," Christianity, and DJ Shadow's "Rastafarian individuality" are examples hereof. In the case of Cimarron this is clearly discernible, but that might be because only radical differences catch our attention. It is hoped that Cimarron's story will cause us to listen to the talking drums.

Conclusion

This earthly totality that has now come to pass suffers from a
radical absence, the absence of our consent.

Édouard Glissant,
"The Unforeseeable Diversity of the World"

Let the salvos begin: Where are the antagonisms between the Caribbean downtrodden and the Western exploiters? Where is the neocolonial
struggle against the imperialist West? Where are the anti-Dutch and
anti-French protests? Where are the reports of corruption and misman-
agement by local government officials playing the dependency theory
card on their European overlords? Where are the struggles between
Afro-Caribbeans and Asian Caribbeans? Where are the struggles between Caribbean men and women? Where are the lighter-skinned Caribbean blacks discriminating against their darker-skinned compatriots? In short, where is the Caribbean that has become paradigmatic for
students of Caribbean studies? Or more expansively, where is the Caribbean that is part of the meta-narrative of the unholy trinity of identity politics—ethnic strife, religious fanaticism, and categorical anti-
Americanism—that we have come to know from popular and academic
reporting on the Global South? Has not your prose, and selection of
data, obfuscated the truth?

All that critical readers seek is contained in the preceding chapters.
However, it is not written in a form that essentializes or dichotomizes
identities. Perhaps therefore it confounds those accustomed to the blend-
ing of the ideal typical presentation of groups and places with life itself.
The chapters are not structured to present a story of ideal typical blacks
versus whites, browns versus blacks, locals versus newcomers, rich versus poor, or Christians versus non-Christians. The neo-reality of these

Figure 9. Celebrating multinationality during the annual Carnival parade

models, to use Jean Baudrillard's terms, is not endorsed here. The preceding chapters are written from a perspective that tries to remain faithful to the ternary of multivalued logic, common humanity, and the Us and Them dichotomy that common humanity perpetually deconstructs. I have sought to convey, not solely as lip service to the tradition of deconstructive thought, that Being is but a provisional attempt at escape within the ongoing process of Becoming. My prose tries to remain as true as possible to life itself. We live in the irreducible ternary of becoming human together, though as existential Sisyphuses, we all engage in processes of Selfing and Othering that usually fail. Extreme examples of these processes are genocide and slavery, which paradoxically show that to maintain a rigid Self versus Other distinction, to deny the ternary, one must engage in a misrecognition of our common humanity, something that occurs far more infrequently than the epistemically less violent systems of order within heterogeneity that humans usually institute (Baumann and Gingrich 2004).

Could it not be that a subtle form of misrecognition is unwittingly at play in many writings that stress discord and thereby unintentionally deny Caribbean people the common human condition of getting along far more than warring? Could it not be that to present and denounce the negative processes in these societies, many Caribbeanists have had to deny West Indians the self-reflexivity they award themselves? Could it not be that much of the writings about Caribbean people maintain the dualism of the scholar who discerns the Truth and the masses who uncritically adhere to their native common sense? Without wishing to pick a fight with any particular scholar, I deem that as a structural critique, it is undeniable that Caribbeanists have also engaged in a process of Othering those with whom, intersubjectively, they have had to engage within the field and whose thoughts spoke back to them during the process of writing. We who work in the region have yet to truly address the fact that no discursive field is fully "ours" or "theirs." As Michel-Rolph Trouillot so aptly put it: "Is native discourse a citation, an indirect quote, or a paraphrase? Whose voice is it, once it enters the discursive field dominated by the logic of the academe? Is its value referential, indexical, phatic, or poetic? The problem is compounded in the Caribbean by colonial domination whose duration and intellectual reach defy most understandings of nativeness?" (1992: 24–25).

I take Trouillot to mean that by studying the Caribbean, we may recognize the global ternary, the irreducible normative horizon, born of the bloody transmodernity intensified since colonialism and capitalism that renders the Us and Them binary highly provisional (see also Dubois 2006; Scott 2004; Dussel 2000). This does not mean that we live in one global village without opacity and miscommunications. Not at all. What it does mean is that everyone who wishes to be heard by others has to speak the universal grammar of the global village—identity, culture, nation, religion, race, private property, and so forth—even if in their usage they give these a peculiar twist.

I have tried to be true to the ternary on both the macro-theoretical level that Trouillot identifies and on the micro-theoretical level of writing about SXM. And I have recognized that doing so enables one to write sympathetically while being critical. It leads one to question the "proper" places to which one unwittingly assigns those one writes about. One questions the invisible power to assign and inhabit an Archimedean position.

It will not do to for me to represent the persons I interacted with in the field as informants who delivered the data that allow me to tease out the subtle truth that they themselves cannot see. Demystification as the art of the scholar has to be deconstructed (Rancière 2004). In doing so, I have come to the understanding that one neither writes about nor represents informants, but one presents the intersubjective encounters in the field by having these informants critically interrogate academic works. In this

spirit, I have sought to present the three disc jockeys whom I highlighted—
Fernando Clarke, the Shadow, and Cimarron—as organic philosophers
whose thinking on the issues of identity and how to construct a just politics of belonging is worth engaging without seeing these as belonging to a
plane of appearance behind which lies the *real* that I discerned.

Neither categorical anti-Americanism nor ethnic or religious particu-
larity or absolutism featured in the philosophies of Fernando Clarke, the
Shadow, or Cimarron. They sought to appeal to and simultaneously hail
a larger We that encompassed all SXMers. They did this by undoing the
exclusivity of Christianity as much as possible.

By employing Christianity as an all-inclusive metalanguage—everyone
was deemed a Christian, which meant human—Clarke, the Shadow, and
Cimarron, in their own ways, were busy encouraging SXMers to view
their society as a New Jerusalem where the peoples of the earth sought to
recognize one another. Of the three, Cimarron was unsuccessful, because
he sought to remind SXMers that in their New Jerusalem, there were
second-class humans: the illegal youths. He judged the elites, and implicitly the common folk, to be guilty of the heinous crime of allowing this
system to continue. His was a somewhat Manichaean presentation of reality based on a quixotic belief that paradise on earth is possible. He
sought to convince SXMers that by granting illegal youths equal opportunities, the island would truly be an earthly Kingdom Come.

Clarke and the Shadow employed another strategy. They knew it was
a dream, that such a kingdom was impossible in a world divided into
nation-states, a world where, to employ Étienne Balibar's terminology,
"*man is made by citizenship* and not citizenship by man" (2004: 321;
emphasis added). The best they could do was remind SXMers of what
they saw via cable TV and read in international dailies, namely, that the
costs of ethnic and religious tensions in the Global South are endemic
poverty and human carnage. In their politics, SXM was presented as a
New Jerusalem inhabited by sinners who sometimes sought to act
saintly, "Christian calypsonians," in the words of Fernando Clarke.
Through this strategy, they circumvented the issue of illegal youths and
promoted an all-inclusive politics of belonging.

This was the message that the vast majority of SXMers wanted to
hear. Most SXMers told themselves, and wanted their disc jockeys to tell
them, that God condones their fostering of hedonism. They are a people
whose job it is to behave as sinners and encourage the wealthy few of the
world to do the same. In an ideal world they would walk like Christ, but
this is not an ideal world.

Weren't these people suffering from a sense of false consciousness by having imbibed the ideology that this was the best they could do in life? I think not. Most SXMers I encountered knew very well that they were the slaves of capitalism and the geopolitical powers of the world. They were critical of the United States, the symbolic stand-in for the West, and wanted things to change, but their criticism did not incite deep sentiments of categorical anti-Americanism.

Yaya, one of my main interlocutors during my stay on the island, exemplified this criticism. She was against the economic, social, and racial discrimination that is inflicted on the masses of this world. She knew that the world is divided among the have-a-lots, the have-somes, the have-a-littles, and the masses of have-nots. Furthermore, she knew that this distinction was not based on merit but on economic exploitation and the contemporary horrors of racism. In other words, Yaya understood race and class, the fundaments of Caribbean Marxism. But she preferred not to become a full convert to this gospel.

Yaya lived life pragmatically. She could utter deep criticism of the West in the morning and entertain Western tourists in the evening without a sense of contradiction. Moreover, when it came to the issue of whether SXM should remain part of the Netherlands and France, her answer was an unequivocal "yes." The *independistas,* the fringe politicians I encountered, had not been able to convince her and most SXMers to vote for political independence. There were benefits to SXM remaining a French and Dutch dependency. If the tourist economy should fail, Yaya could easily migrate to the United States, France, the Netherlands, or another wealthy Western country without the difficulties of obtaining a visa. Since her mother's family came from the Dominican Republic, she knew about people who stood all day in the burning sun only to be informed that they could not enter Europe, the United States, or Canada. She had no illusions about the heaven that would come after political independence. Most independent nation-states in the Global South are far from heaven.

Moreover, her conscience could not act up on her, telling her that she was dependent on the handouts of the West, for she had little Veronica to feed. She would simply state, "Let the have-a-lots and the have-somes start the revolution." She had her hands full raising her daughter. Most SXMers reasoned similarly. The ideal revolution to dismantle the current capitalist system should be led by the Western middle classes, who were in a better position to influence their governments and the multinationals, and not by third world proletariats struggling to survive. I learned from her and from the other SXMers I encountered that one's principled stance against the inequalities of the world needs to be kept in check by pragmatism. In fact, it is always kept in check by pragmatism, but many of us in the West choose not to remember this. My fieldwork among SXMers answered my question, posed in the introduction, as to why class was but one of the ways of conceiving society in the Caribbean. The answer was that men and women do not live by principle alone. They also live by compromise.

Clarke and the Shadow were popular because they legitimated this truth that all SXMers had come to know by living life. They articulated the irresolvable dialectic between principle and pragmatism, between Christianity and calypso, between our attention to our personal God and our personal devil. This was the basis on which they encouraged SXMers to understand the issue of belonging. Everyone belonged—ethnic, national, and religious differences notwithstanding—because everyone inhabited this dialectic. Perhaps these small islanders had come to know one of the barest truths in our capitalist world: to assert our existence, we are all socialized to seek economic and status gains. This is what binds all the peoples of the globe. This is the truth they termed the *money tie system,* and no interaction is free of this truth. No society is outside the sphere of capitalism. Or as Trevor put it, "All man is sinners, and this here is Babylon land too. A thing that all over. The money tie system all over." In other words, we are all slaves to the logic of capitalism.

These experiences on SXM led me to reimagine the system of capitalism as a machine on automatic pilot. This system was created by humans but now has gathered such momentum that most simply adhere to it out of fear, creed, greed, self-interest, or a sense of nihilism. Capitalism exists because we enact its existence on a daily basis. The sum of all the reasons why SXMers of various classes adhere to capitalism is what keeps the system working on the island. These reasons are combined with the reasons of individuals all over the globe who contribute to the continued existence of capitalism. Inequalities and power differences qualify rather than demolish this social fact. Capitalism is based on this shifting tapestry of reasons that tie all social classes to one another. This machine on automatic pilot is thus also a sewing machine, constantly stitching societies together.

This is just taking the Gramscian idea of hegemony, rule by consent, to its ultimate consequence in a world dominated by a complexly interrelated service sector where there is no world state. In such a world, where capitalism is reconfigured, class ceases to be a self-evident category of identification. The necessary articulations, which lead to class awareness on a national and translocal level, are not voiced in the dominant media. Nor are there organic intellectuals with a strong enough following who are able to convincingly convey this new imagining of capitalism. The older forms of socialist critique, those in which we insinuated that there were innocent and guilty and that leftist intellectuals did not need to take their positions in the capitalist order into consideration, are ill-suited to this imagining. Interestingly, Baudrillard comes to a similar conclusion when he writes:

> In ancient society, there was the master and the slave. Later came the lord and the serf. Later still, the capitalist wage-labourer. There is a servitude particular to each of these stages: you know who is the master, who is the slave. It is all different now. The master has disappeared. Only the serfs and servility remain. Now what is a slave without a master? A person who has devoured his master and internalized him, to the point of becoming his own master. He has not killed him in order to become master (that is Revolution); he has absorbed him while remaining a slave—indeed more slavish than a slave, more servile than a serf: his own serf. . . . Our service-based society is a serf-based society, a society of individuals rendered servile for their own use, slaves to their own functions and performance—perfectly emancipated, perfectly servile. (2001: 55–56)

What this way of understanding capitalism begs for, and what we have yet to provide, is a new way of critiquing it. This imagining of capitalism, however, does not cancel out other imaginings. I am well aware that the precise workings of global capitalism remain opaque. Thus, in my opinion, whether one perceives a shady group in a dark room pushing buttons, multinational conspiracies, honorary gentlemen's agreements among the Western thieves-exploiters voted into office, the willing dependency of the Global South elites, the false consciousness of the proletariat, some invisible hand or force running the market, or a machine on automatic pilot, all are intelligent deductions as to how global capitalism works.

It is not the truthfulness of one of these deductions that matters; it is how they correspond to one's knowledge gained through inductive processes such as doing fieldwork. On SXM it made sense to see capitalism as a machine on automatic pilot, for all the classes were against anyone who dared to be harshly critical of their dependence on Western tourism. Such critiques, they felt, were usually uttered by people "who have it good," to use Yaya's words. It was their contention that the money tie system bound them, just as it binds everyone else in the world. We are all tied to one another because our shifting tapestry of reasons forms the basis of capitalism. An unwillingness to see this shifting tapestry, or the *unheimlich* sensation this world without Others conveys, is perhaps an important driving force behind the continuing appeal of racism, class prejudice, religious intolerance, ethnic strife, and even the self-righteous critiques of many well-meaning activists. By claiming that this is an important factor, I am not reducing these phenomena to the machinations of capitalism. What I am arguing is that one has to take capitalism seriously in one's analysis of these congruent forms of intolerance. The inverse is necessarily also the case (Gilroy 2006, 2000; Geschiere 1997).

Taking capitalism seriously from a perspective that consistently blurs the Self versus Other distinction leads us to the recognition that we all want to be little gods. And to be gods, others need to be our devils, our subordinates, or a people needing to be schooled. The major difference between SXM and other societies in the Global South, where violent forms of identity politics are rampant, may be that when gods realize and accept this truth, they are, paradoxically, better able to acknowledge the Other. The Other ceases to be that different.

If one takes what I have argued as a plausible truth—a convincing perspective of the world—this raises the question as to how people living on an island of just thirty-seven square miles have come to this understanding. In what follows, I will seek to answer this inquiry by returning to my findings and addressing the theoretical issues raised throughout the preceding chapters.

While the politics of autochthony is a major theme in the work of Africanists and Asianists, this is not the case for most Caribbeanists. An important reason that Caribbeanists such as Mintz (1996), Lamming (2001), and Glissant (2002, 2000, 1999) put forward is that ethnicity and nationalism have never been able to completely alienate Caribbean people from one another. This is because West Indians have been moving around and visiting one another's islands since the earliest days of colonialism. Moreover, the autochthons of the region have descended from Africans, Asians, and Europeans who migrated to the islands by force or by their own accord. They know they are newcomers of a slightly earlier time. In the faces of newer immigrants, they recognize their own ancestors. The myth of having possessed these islands since time immemorial is something they cannot believe.

My stay on the island led me to realize that these arguments hold true for SXM. The Shadow phrased it brilliantly when he stated, "We don't have to travel to really know Africa, Europe, or Asia because they are here. We born from them." The rest of the Americas also have a similar Creole genesis. Nonetheless, although they were born from Africans, Asians, and Europeans in the Americas, neither the Shadow nor most of the other West Indian locals I encountered have lost themselves in a facile pan-Africanism, pan-Asianism, or blind adherence to Europe. It is a matter of degree. For instance, they acknowledged that being black means facing discrimination similar to that of Africans or Indians, that solidarity is sometimes necessary, but this does not make West Indians the same as Africans or Indians. Five hundred years of historical difference—black Atlantic and other kinds of overlaps notwithstanding—of habitation on other continents, lie between them. West Indian locals are not Africans, Asians, or Europeans. They are not carbon copies, despite the racist logic that still clouds the minds of many and that they sometimes employ for their benefit. They are a different people, who bear creolized traces of the Old World.

West Indian locals on SXM did not incessantly accentuate difference when discussing the nationality and ethnicity of themselves and of newer immigrants to the region. This was a new insight my study offered, for few authors address the fact that many West Indian islands remain centers of immigration. The creolization of the West Indies continues, with the local West Indians continuing to meet both one another and newcomers from the rest of the world. On SXM I was offered a unique opportunity to see how this has transpired and to gain insight into what role the local media have played in this.

The wealthy newcomers on the island hail primarily from Western countries and Asian superpowers such as India, Pakistan, and China. The working classes, on the contrary, are for the most part West Indian locals, Asians, and Latin Americans. While most persons introduced in this study are West Indian locals, my experiences on the island have taught me that all SXMers find ways to bridge their differences, and the relationship between West Indian locals and newcomers is a topic for another book. As an aside: so too would be the manner in which the West Indian locals from the various administrative units and subdivisions therein deconstruct and reconstruct new racial logics where, for instance, *Negro* in Kreyol, Spaniol, and English carries different connotations; and we may ask further how the category of *Negro* is being reconfigured as a result of the influence of BET and other black cable stations. Similarly, a Trinidadian of East Indian descent will have to present her Indianness in a different manner on an island where she encounters first-generation East Indians from Delhi. These issues deserve to be studied.

What became clear to me on SXM was that the often-repeated truth that national identity is a super-ethnic category through which performance becomes part of who people think they are, the thesis made famous by Benedict Anderson, has its critical contrast on this island, where everyday life leads SXMers to a multiethnic and multinational sense of self. On this island, where almost everyone comes from elsewhere and everyone's livelihood depends on tourism, bridges of communality have to be continuously built. If SXMers fight among one another, Western tourists will choose another island with sun, sea, and sand. The sixty thousand SXMers composing eighty nationalities have to get along. They have to be creative and inventive regarding national identity and cannot believe too religiously in the exclusiveness of it.

Miss Maria, who speaks throughout this book and whose insights kept me sharp, was exemplary of this social fact. Depending on who she was interacting with, Miss Maria performed her localness, Curaçaoness, Anguillanness, Dutchness, Britishness, Caribbeanness, and pan-Africanness. She, like so many other SXMers I encountered, was a walking "family of islands" who exemplified *relation identity,* to use George Lamming's and Éduoard Glissant's term. While her national and transnational identities were dear to her, as they symbolized her personal and wider family history, I never experienced her being engulfed by uncontrollable sentiments while performing one of these. In fact, she was quite peevish when I asked her whether being a local was the most important national identity for her. She replied, "All of them are important to me; they have a reason. Now stop minding my business."

Like most locals, Miss Maria's love for and commitment to the island was conditional. SXMers of all ilks remain on the island because it is one of the few places in the Global South where they can make a decent living and where the rule of law to a large extent still holds sway. It is not nationalism that keeps them on the island but economic benefits and a relatively easy life. Abject poverty and war on the streets are things SXMers read about in the international dailies or see via cable TV. And if they do not get the message, popular radio disc jockeys say it loud and clear: "Thou shall not destroy the good thing we have going on here, for this is one of the closest things to paradise in the Global South." DJ Shadow articulated the pragmatism of most SXMers regarding nationalism when he stated that he had "a nationalism for the good times." If SXM's tourist economy were to enter into an irremediable recession, he would be one of the first ones to leave.

While most SXMers had no qualms about expressing similar views in public, there was a small but vocal minority of fringe politicians who did. These were the upper-middle-class locals headed by the Baines and

Larosso brothers. The Baineses, the leaders of the *reformista* group, the social reformers, championed the enactment of special laws that would privilege locals. These laws would guarantee that in the granting of business licenses, tenders, and government jobs, locals would be given preference. Theirs was a direct attack on all newcomers, newer West Indians as well as second- and third-generation SXMers.

Whereas the Baineses wanted to reform the existing laws while remaining within the Dutch Kingdom, the Larossos, the faces of the *independista* group, were for complete political independence. They employed an anti-colonial rhetoric whereby French and Dutch government officials were presented as oppressive neocolonialists in cahoots with Western multinationals. In the Larossos' politics, SXM was presented as a territory exploited by Western powers. They claimed that the only way for SXM to regain its lost dignity is for it to be ruled by its own people.

The difficulty the Larossos ran into was assigning which of the varied ethnic groups should rule SXM after it became independent. Should it be the wealthy newcomers, who represented many of the Western powers the Larossos criticized, or the locals, who already had a monopoly in the current political arrangements? And what about the working-class newcomers? What if they chose a representative of their group? While the Larossos did not explicitly address this issue, in their writings and speeches it became clear that they implicitly privileged the locals and those who sided with them. They would be the political vanguards of an independent SXM, tolerating the participation of newcomers. An independent SXM without locals in the most prominent positions was unthinkable for the *independistas*.

As I mentioned before, the *reformistas* and *independistas* had a very small following on the island. Most SXMers interpreted their politics as just another decoy within the money tie system. The *reformistas* were seen as a group of sly businessmen who wanted to increase their wealth by having government work solely for their benefit. What they wanted was that all tenders should go to their companies first, regardless of whether this was best for SXM. The foremost motivation of the *independistas* was their quest for historical recognition. They wanted to go down in history as the group that led SXM to independence.

The Baineses and the Larossos could also not entice popular radio disc jockeys to endorse their politics. Ethnic- or religious-based discrimination was prohibited by the management of all radio stations, because radio stations were dependent on wealthy newcomers for their sponsorship and on working-class immigrants for their public. Whatever the managers or DJs might feel personally, they could not broadcast programs that would incite ethnic or religious discord. The Baineses and the Larossos lacked substantial media support. These proponents of essential identity, *root identity,* as Glissant would put it, were surrounded by a multitude performing *relation identity,* which expresses a plurality of roots and routes.

While most disc jockeys, including Clarke, simply ignored the *independistas* and *reformistas,* DJ Shadow did not. Although his upper-class family had connections to political parties, he was known for his general anti-politician stance. It was a stylistic trope that worked well, with the Shadow being the anti-politician's politician. Clothed in his Rastafari-inspired rhetoric, this spiritual philosophy, being an acceptable mode of Christianity on the island, was his political advice to his public. The articulation he made between Rastafari and anti-nationalism was acceptable, since this spiritual philosophy had a universal bent to it. In his programs, which I described in chapter 5, he labeled the *independistas* and *reformistas* "politricksians" and advised SXMers not to put their faith in them. He was especially cross with these two groups because he felt they were selfish. In his opinion, they were willing to sacrifice the welfare of all SXMers for their personal economic and status gains.

The Shadow reasoned that SXM was too small and too dependent on tourism to become an independent country. In addition, he was against all forms of deep belief in nationalism. Performing a national identity should be about gaining legitimacy to be able to act and secure one's livelihood, not about nurturing what he termed *tribal sentiments* that blind one from seeing the humanity in the Other. Over and above nationality, the Shadow claimed that every human being consists of a somewhat autonomous self and a personal God and devil that he or she has to reckon with. He termed this mode of understanding the human condition *Rastafari individuality.* Those who promote exclusive nationalism were said to be under the spell of their personal devils. The Shadow had come to the Freudian truism that nationalism is but the narcissism of small differences (Gilroy 2006, 2000; Kristeva 1991). But he went further by universalizing the precepts of Christianity outside the narrow confines of the creed.

The Shadow's Rastafari philosophy resonated with the general way of life of the vast majority of SXMers. Despite their pragmatic adherence to national identity, their constant building of bridges of commonality among one another, they too had come to the implicit understanding that nationalism cannot be totally disconnected from exclusive ideas of territoriality and ethnicity. The category has a history; it bears traces of bio-cultural and territorial exclusiveness that are inerasable. Moreover, there was no general national identity that could encompass all SXMers. To create an all-inclusive category of belonging, SXMers turned to Christianity.

This turn to Christianity is not surprising given that Christian discourse is used to create inclusivity in the Caribbean and is therefore SXM's public religion. Christian-derived discourses were prominent in the economic, political, and social fields that constitute SXM society. I did not have to go to church to hear the word of God, for even behind the blackjack table, dealers would quote scripture while relating an unjust practice of one of their superiors. Politicians were also quick to employ biblical phrases during their public speeches. Devout Christians and those who believed that Christianity should be the island's only religion were a minority on the island.

Christianity was the metalanguage that enveloped all discussions about ethnic and religious tolerance. For instance, Terry Gumbs, the popular social worker who helped me understand the social importance of public Christianity, was quite explicit on the issue of religious tolerance when she declared that, for her, Christianity was about tolerating different faiths and recognizing that we all serve the same God. Most Christians on SXM were quite liberal in their view of other religions, which has to do with three interrelated factors. First, the Christianity employed as a metalanguage is creolized. Within it one can discern tenets of Science, a spiritual philosophy bearing a strong resemblance to other pan-Caribbean spiritual complexes such as Santeria and Vodou. Because of this creolization, many SXM Christians believe that they are surrounded by personal spirits who make up their existential identity. These spirits are direct ancestors as well as symbols of the diverse people who have populated the region. The spirits revered through Science do not respect ethnic, gender, or class boundaries. They actually transcend these. Yaya, for instance, had a white male spirit whom she had to appease. During his lifetime, this spirit belonged to the upper classes of Caribbean society. Through Science, many SXM Christians are once more implicitly brought to the realization that the Other is within oneself and that the world is not black and white. The world is ternary.

Besides fusing Science with Christianity, SXM Christians also borrow across other religious divides. For instance, they frequently visit non-Christian houses of worship. Some, such as Ida Boyard, who was one of the first persons to systematically explain to me that most Christians love mixing religions, had no qualms about attending a Buddhist service while claiming to be a devout Pentecostal. Pastor Vlaun was so inventive within the Christian tradition that he preached that Judgment Day had already come to pass, that the New Testament was in fact an old book. These experiences led me to conjecture that many Christians unwittingly overcome orthodox Christianity within the Christian tradition. They are giving birth to new forms of Christianity that only slightly resemble older versions and, in potential, are tolerant toward other religions and embrace the worldly.

I do not think that the flexibility with which SXMers perform and reinterpret Christianity is an isolated phenomenon. While interviewing Clarke it became clear that on the island of Aruba, where he grew up, Christianity was also being transformed because of the processes of creolization. I am also strengthened in my conjecture by scholars' arguments that the wide-scale adoption of Pentecostal styles outside the confines of the churches may be signaling the birth of new forms of post-Pentecostalism in Africa (see Meyer 2004). Though active church members and high-profile preachers continue to stress the need to be born again and speak the language of war against non-Christians, one of the points stressed in Meyer's oeuvre is that, among nominal believers, a less predatory Pentecostal religiosity exists and may be growing. Media play an important role in this process. No dominant center controls the dissemination of the Pentecostal style. I believe that only when one conducts research on Christianity inside and, more important, outside churches can one begin to discern the contours of these newer forms of Christianity. Further research on SXM public Christianity, comparing it with developments elsewhere and investigating their links with the established churches, should be conducted.

It would be more revolutionary to recognize with David Chidester (2005) that because we confine the study of religion to a proper place—shrines, temples, mosques, and churches—we are blinded to its prominent role in various forms of popular culture, the culture industry, civil society, and multinational marketing, which cannot be reduced to derivatives of the strict theologies and practices of traditional houses of worship. Perhaps this shift may help us recognize that although fundamentalist Pentecostalism and Islam have returned and are conquering the masses, this is but a minor chord in the overall symphony of Man's pragmatic religiosity.

On SXM the newer and more flexible forms of Christianity, far removed from fundamentalism, are sanctioned by the political and economic elite. This brings me to my second reason why Christianity on SXM is tolerant toward religious differences. Its tourist industry is based on selling the island as a hedonistic paradise. Besides the pearl white beaches and lush green vegetation, the island is famous for its casinos, nightclubs, expensive restaurants, and boutiques. Tourists come to SXM to live intemperately. Even the most devout born-again Christians there earn their livings encouraging the hedonism of Westerners. They cannot point their fingers at others when they too earn a living by condoning the worship of mammon. Moreover, if they wish to remain employed, they are "advised" to keep their beliefs to themselves during working hours.

The Christianity that is expressed in the public realm is one divorced from proselytizing and exclusive expressions of being a Christian. It is thus a Christianity that devout Christians cannot, and most likely would not, claim as solely their own. This resonates with the works of Caribbeanists such as Catherine Hall (2002), Stuart Hall (1999, 1995), and Barry Chevannes (1995, 1994), who have argued that the established churches have not been able to monopolize the signifier of Christianity. However, whereas these authors interpreted this phenomenon as resistance by the masses, on SXM the political and economic establishment have a stake in maintaining this public expression of Christianity. It is a mode of Christianity that is compatible with the tourist industry and the multiethnic and multireligious situation on the island.

Employing a Durkheimian framework, sensitized to Caribbean realities, and using an interpretation of Derek Walcott's classic essay "The Muse of History" (to be found in the collection of essays *What the Twilight Says,* 1999), I argued in chapter 3 that Christianity is the way in which the various groups on SXM have sought to create a transcendental sense of their society. We may recall that for Émile Durkheim, less cryptically, religion in its most transcendental and inclusive form is society. This form of religion should not be confused with the specific forms of exclusive worship one encounters. Durkheim predicted that through processes of interaction—in Caribbean studies we would say transculturation or creolization—human societies would progressively shed their particularities, eventually leading to the recognition of elemental humanity:

> If society is something universal in relation to the individual, it is none the less an individuality itself, which has its own physiognomy and its idiosyncrasies; it is a particular subject and consequently particularises whatever it thinks of. Therefore collective representations also contain subjective elements, and these must be progressively weeded out, if we are to approach

reality more closely. . . . If logical thought tends to rid itself more and more of the subjective and personal elements which it still retains from its origin, it is not because extra-social factors intervened; it is much rather because a social life of a new sort is developing. (1954: 444)

Durkheim had no conception of power, nor did he sufficiently recognize the bloody transmodernity ushered in by colonialism and the global expansion of capitalism. While it is true that today we all recognize a human face regardless of skin color, phenotype, or sex, it is also true that sufficient conceptual maps remain that cause us to misrecognize and brutalize each other. For Durkheim's predictions to come to fruition, we must come to terms on a global level with our bloody transmodernity (Gilroy 2006; Dussel 2000).

Derek Walcott, like Durkheim, also theorizes that a transcendental religion without religion will lead us to recognize elemental humanity. Yet he is aware of the enduring scars of the cultural encounters of the last five hundred years. It is within these that a creolized Christianity has emerged that is uniquely Caribbean and ternary. This public Christianity, not tied to any Caribbean nation-state, contains African and Asian traces without being African or Asian.

Walcott argues that most West Indians instinctively understand that their ancestors were not converted but actually converted themselves by being transformed and simultaneously making use of the conceptual and institutional conditions that emerged as a result of the processes of transmodernity. And in so doing, they created and nurtured a creolized Christianity that survived outside the established churches. Contemporary West Indians are the bearers of the historical legacy of seeking to make Christianity a truly humanistic religion. Therefore, even non-Christians are able to tolerate this public Christianity, for it is about fundamentally acknowledging the humanity of all human beings, regardless of their creed. This creolized Christianity, the collective myth for many West Indians, indirectly privileges plural religious roots and transnationality. It opens up to the Other.

I recognized Derek Walcott's poetic intuitions about a public Christianity on SXM. For while most of my cases involved Christians, many non-Christians such as Shamiran, my main Muslim interlocutor, also participated in this process. Shamiran was quite laconic when I asked her if as a Muslim she felt uncomfortable teaching biblical verses to children. Her response was that it was a job, and employing a Christian meta-idiom was just the way that she and other social workers taught children mores. Looking back, however, I conjecture that one can interpret what

Shamiran and other non-Christians were doing was ensuring that Christianity as a public religion remained divorced from the Christianity of exclusive-minded Christians. She told me that if any of her Christian colleagues employed Christianity to criticize her religion, they would be reprimanded or dismissed.

Besides Shamiran's teaching the Bible to Christians and non-Christians alike, another of the things that intrigued me was that many of the sponsors of Clarke and the Shadow were wealthy Muslim and Hindu merchants. They bought many advertisement slots. I often wondered why they had not sought to have their own religious radio programs. Were they employing a tactic similar to Shamiran's? Did they think that promoting more than one public religion and thus contesting the Christian metalanguage could create social tensions? Further research into how non-Christians contributed to maintaining Christianity as a metalanguage divorced from Christian churches and devout Christians could prove whether my conjecture is correct.

Third, because of their overall dependence on tourism, SXM Christians have developed a generation-specific practice of Christianity. Young children and the elderly go to church on a regular basis. They are the backbone of church life. The vast majority of the middle generation attends church sporadically if at all, yet in good SXM fashion considers themselves Christians. When I asked what the reasons were behind this, I was told that after six days of hard work, most adults were too tired to attend church. For instance, Yaya never visited church on Sundays. She did, however, send her daughter with her parents.

It was quite a sight to see hordes of young children walking behind the elderly who took them to church. I was told that since these two generation groups do not have to work in the tourist industry, they are free to dedicate their lives to God. The elderly, who usually perform the role of Sunday school teachers, instruct the young in the ways of the Lord without condemning the practices of their parents.

Popular priests and pastors whom I encountered also did not criticize the tourist industry or the practices of the majority of the working population. Neither were they explicitly critical of other religious groups. Churches on SXM are too small to be independent from government subsidies and sponsorship by the business community. These monies come earmarked, which leads to compromise regarding Christian teachings. For instance, the political establishment supports only the churches that promote a Christian-inflected ecumenical understanding of SXM society and a pro-tourism stance. To be subsidized, churches must express tolerance toward members of other faiths and condone the hedonism of tourism. As if this government pressure were not enough, many non-Christian and nominally Christian business owners sponsor church buildings. Religious leaders cannot be wholeheartedly critical of those who have paid for the pews.

Christianity is SXM's metalanguage, because everyone enacts it as a way of constructing an all-inclusive category of belonging. It is the category that everyone, Christians and non-Christians, locals and newcomers, politicians and their constituencies, disc jockeys and their publics, can employ equally. It is the assigned position of inclusiveness that reminds SXMers that to maintain their standard of living, solidarity and tolerance of one another's differences are necessary. It is the brighter side of the inescapable social fact that no one is outside the money tie system, not even the churches. And most SXMers want it to remain that way.

Clarke verbalized the connection between the money tie system and Christianity brilliantly when he called them "the two vitamin Cs for successful living." According to him, calypso—the money tie system—signifies the continuous need to perform various seemingly incompatible identities to earn a living. It also symbolizes the unscrupulousness that was part of these performances. Christianity's role, on the contrary, is to constantly counterbalance the hedonism occurring in the money tie system.

Clarke endeavored in his radio program, discussed in chapter 4, to temper the anti-newcomer sentiment among local women, who felt that many of these newcomers were stealing their men. In a humorous manner, Clarke played calypso music that addressed infidelity, combining these songs with his creolized readings of the Bible to remind all SXMers that none is exempt from sin. Locals and newcomers, men and women, were equally lured to commit infidelity. Clarke reminded SXMers that they should see themselves as inevitable sinners who nevertheless have to believe in the universal Christian principles of brotherly and sisterly love.

This realization strengthens my prior argument that from the perspective of SXM, capitalism can be conceived of as a machine on automatic pilot. Within the constantly shifting play of identity and the selfishness-inducing money tie system, Christianity as a public religion offers the semblance of unity. Through a Christian metalanguage, SXM's high priests, who are in fact its radio disc jockeys, encourage SXMers to believe in one another and in a force greater than themselves, despite their sinful lifestyle. This is the only way to keep the island prosperous. This is just another way of saying that the pragmatism that reigns in everyday life needs to be kept in check by principle.

Was this dialectic, whereby pragmatism had an edge over principle, irresolvable? Cimarron felt that it was not. He wanted a society where principle rules, where illegal immigrants have the same opportunities as citizens. He wanted the laws to change immediately. Most SXMers disagreed. They felt they were doing the best they could under the global circumstances. Only when the world of nation-states ceases to be the organizing principle will Cimarron's option be plausible.

There is a third option that does not go far enough for Cimarron but that does go further than the philosophies of many other societies of the world. This option is a deepening of the senses of communion that Clarke and the Shadow promote by combining their creolized Christian wordings with the equally creolized Caribbean music. This communion can come to signify a Creole utopianism, a planetary humanism to come, a hope than one day people will understand all identities as always in a process of becoming. There are no pure identities and thus no pure Self or Other.

While endorsing capitalism, Clarke and the Shadow unwittingly promote a truth that Martin Luther King Jr. identified: "All men are caught in an inescapable network of mutuality, tied in a single garment of destiny" (quoted in Raboteau 1988: 95). Speaking from outside the exclusively constructed boundaries of politics, citizenship rights, ethnicity, and religion, these disc jockeys are seeking to remind SXMers that the Other is both within and a human like oneself. Clarke, the Shadow, and even Cimarron are Walcottians and radical Durkheimians chanting down the New Jerusalem. Whether this will ever lead to a post-capitalistic world is something only time will tell.

Notes

INTRODUCTION

Epigraph: Paul Gilroy, *Postcolonial Melancholia,* Wellek Library Lectures (New York: Columbia University Press, 2006), 8.

1. SO MANY MEN, SO MANY HISTORIES

1. See Beckford 2000 and Trouillot 1998 on the enduring presence of the plantation model.
2. Quoted in Paula 1993: 11.
3. For a study on the pre-Columbian presence on SXM, see Halley 1995.
4. See both Gilroy 2005 and Cooper 2004 (179–206) for critiques of this sanitized version of Bob Marley.

2. PERFORMING IDENTITIES ON SAINT MARTIN
AND SINT MAARTEN

1. Anguilla is not the only British Overseas Territory in the Caribbean. There are also Bermuda, Montserrat, the Turks and Caicos Islands, and the British Virgin Islands. Since 2002, all citizens carry British passports.
2. Though it would have been interesting to pursue this dark side of globalization, it would have exceeded the scope of this study.
3. The Dutch Antillean guilder is a fairly strong and stable currency. It trades at 1.70 to the US dollar. With the further integration of Dutch SXM into the EU, the euro will become the official currency on both sides of the island.

4. There is of course no denying that in a time when the UN promotes the rights of indigenous peoples, "minorities" in the Global South are presenting essentialized versions of themselves in the hope of achieving equal rights. The work of Gilroy (2000, 1993) and Baumann (1999, 1996) demonstrates that this is also the case for ethnic minorities facing unequal opportunities in Western societies.

5. There is thus a difference between this study and those of Carolyn Cooper (2004) and Norman C. Stolzoff (2000), both on popular culture in Jamaica. These scholars, in the wake of their fieldwork experiences and their theoretical frameworks, had to engage gender directly because it mattered to their informants.

6. See Bayart 1991, which makes this point.

7. See Sheller 2005 for a discussion of the relationship between patriarchy and black struggles against infra-humanity. See Austin-Broos 1997 for a rich ethnographic and historical study of how black women contested this.

8. See Römer (1999), who writes about the anti-Lodge sentiment among Catholic priests in the Dutch Leeward Islands.

9. See also Gilroy 2000, 1993.

10. The Dutch Leeward Islands consist of Aruba, Curaçao, and Bonaire.

11. Like their counterparts on the Dutch side of the island, the people of French SXM do not wish to become independent. They do wish to change their status within the French Republic, however. It has been decided in the French parliament that together with Saint Barthélemy, French SXM will be awarded the status of a *collectivité d'outre-mer,* an overseas collectivity (a *département d'outre-mer,* a French overseas department) with fewer administrative responsibilities). Changes are also underway for the Dutch side of the island, to help cope with the further integration of the Netherlands into the EU. The statute will amplify the Kingdom parliament to include separate representation by Aruba, the Netherlands, Sint Maarten, and Curaçao. The smaller islands, Saba, Saint Eustatius, and Bonaire, will then fall under the responsibility of the Dutch ministry of internal affairs. It is widely believed that Dutch SXM will become a full-fledged member of the EU.

3. CHRISTIANITY AS A METALANGUAGE OF INCLUSIVENESS

1. Maranatha was a collaboration of Baptist, Seventh-Day Adventists, Salvation Army, and Pentecostal churches.

2. These books along with others such as *The Keys of Solomon* are said to contain the names of all the angels and demons and to "teach" one how to communicate with them and tap into the invisible forces of the universe. Interestingly, the *Sixth and Seventh Books of Moses* forward the idea that white and black magic, good and evil, are two sides of the same coin.

3. See, for example, www.st-martin.org/us/discovery/art_and_culture.php, which bills itself as the "Official Tourism website of the Island of Saint Martin."

4. See also Lemert 1999 and Baumann 1992. Baumann has argued that Durkheim was well aware that society is made up of several competing groups, and thus his ideal typical argument on religion was more of an ideal and a theoretical abstraction.

4. CLARKE'S TWO VITAMIN Cs FOR SUCCESSFUL LIVING

1. This particular disc jockey had vehemently criticized several leaders of the ruling party. Unlike other disc jockeys, he did not envelope his criticism in humor or double entendre. After complaints by the public and the affronted politicians, he was forced to resign. I was informed by fellow disc jockeys that he had broken the most important rule, since radio personalities had to appear to be above party politics.

2. I employ the term *soul* to describe a person's sense of his or her individuality. It has been the pursuit of anthropologists to investigate how people construct categories of the person and existential theories based on this sense of self (Mageo 2003; Carrithers, Collins, and Lukes 1985). *Soul* remains the popular term for this individuality on SXM and in the wider Americas.

3. For a study of Claude Wathey, see Badejo 1989.

5. DJ SHADOW'S PRESCRIPTION FOR RASTAFARI INDIVIDUALITY

1. See my online article "Healing of the Transnation," in which I present the views of Rastafari youths on SXM: www.diasporainternational.org/pdf/healing _of.pdf.

2. See Moyer 2005 for a similar take on Rastafari in her work on street youths in Tanzania.

3. I am quite aware that the nation-state is also gendered, but such a discussion does not tie into the points made by DJ Shadow. It is an important omission but one that, if elaborated on, would exceed the scope of this chapter.

4. Nationalism's bad track record has led some to argue that this social construct has to be transcended. Derrida states: "Like those of blood, nationalisms of the native soil not only sow hatred, not only commit crimes, they have no future, they promise nothing even if, like stupidity or the unconscious, they hold fast to life" (1994: 169). Others have argued that in a world where a further expansion of global capitalism in the guise of WTO recommendations, which advocate that all trade tariffs should be lifted, it is unwise to promote a wholesale deconstruction of nationalism and nation-states. Doing this would exacerbate the poverty of millions already adversely affected by capitalism. For an ethnographic study that forwards this point, see Glick Schiller and Fouron 2001.

5. Bob Marley even sang at the independence celebration of Zimbabwe.

6. For a detailed overview on the development of center and peripheral colonies in the Dutch Antilles, with Curaçao as the dominant territory, see Oostindie and Klinkers 2003.

6. THE HIP-HOP- AND CHRISTIAN-INSPIRED METAPHYSICS OF DJ CIMARRON

1. See Rancière 2004 for a structural critique of the transculturality of this phenomenon.

2. See Gilroy 1993, which shows that this expression is a wider black Atlantic phenomenon. See Mageo 2003 for a contrasting view from the Pacific,

whereby the stifled speech primarily finds expression in dreams. Mageo employs the Derridean concept of *différance* together with Freudian and Jungian analytics. For a theoretical discussion that seeks to ground the existence and expressions of stifled speech and alternate states of expressions in cognitive psychology and psychoanalytics, see Stephen 2003.

3. See Glissant 2000. He argues that within many of the founding myths of peoples and nations, one encounters the contradictions that deconstruct their chosen-people status.

CONCLUSION

Epigraph: Éduoard Glissant, "The Unforeseeable Diversity of the World," trans. Haun Saussy, in *Beyond Dichotomies: Histories, Identities, Cultures, and the Challenge of Globalization*, ed. Elisabeth Mudimbe-Boyi (Albany: State University of New York Press, 2002), 287.

References

Anderson, Benedict.
> 1991. Imagined Communities: Reflections on the Origin and Spread of Nationalism. London: Verso.

Asad, Talal.
> 1993. *Genealogies of Religion: Discipline and Reasons of Power in Christianity and Islam.* Baltimore: Johns Hopkins University.

Austin, Diane J.
> 1998. Falling through the Savage Slot: Postcolonial Critique and the Ethnographic Task. *Australian Journal of Anthropology* 9 (3): 295–309.

> 1983. Culture and Ideology in the English-Speaking Caribbean: A View from Jamaica. *American Ethnologist* 10 (2): 223–240.

Austin-Broos, Diane J.
> 1997. *Jamaica Genesis: Religion and the Politics of Moral Order.* Chicago: University of Chicago Press.

Badejo, Fabian.
> 1990. Sint Maarten: The Dutch Half in Future Perspective. In *The Dutch Caribbean Prospects for Democracy,* edited by Betty Sedoc Dahlberg, 119–150. New York: Gordon and Breach.

> 1989. *Claude: A Portrait of Power.* Sint Maarten: International Publishing House.

Baker, Houston A., Jr.
> 1995. Critical Memory and the Black Public Sphere. In *The Black Public Sphere: A Public Culture Book,* edited by the Black Public Sphere Collective, 5–38. Chicago: University of Chicago Press.

Baldwin, James.
    1977. *The Fire Next Time.* New York: Dial Press.

Balibar, Étienne.
    2004. Is a Philosophy of Human Civic Rights Possible? New Reflections on
    Equaliberty. *South Atlantic Quarterly* 103: 311–323.

Barber, Karin.
    1997. Preliminary Notes on Audiences in Africa. Special issue, *Africa* 67 (3):
    347–362.

Baudrillard, Jean.
    2001. *Impossible Exchange.* Translated by Chris Turner. London: Verso.

    1983. *Simulations.* Translated by Paul Foos, Paul Patton, and Philip Beitch-
    man. New York: Semiotext(e).

Baumann, Gerd.
    1999. *The Multicultural Riddle: Rethinking National, Ethnic, and Religious
    Identities.* London: Routledge.

    1996. *Contesting Culture: Discourses of Identity in Multi-ethnic London.*
    Cambridge: Cambridge University Press.

    1995. Music and Dance: The Royal Road to Affective Culture? *World of
    Music: Journal of the International Institute for Traditional Music* 37 (2):
    31–42.

    1992. Ritual Implicates "Others": Rereading Durkheim in a Plural Society.
    In *Understanding Rituals,* edited by Daniel de Coppet, 96–115. London:
    Routledge.

Baumann, Gerd, and Andre Gingrich, eds.
    2004. *Grammars of Identity/Alterity: A Structural Approach.* Oxford, UK:
    Berghahn Books.

Bayart, Jean-François.
    1991. Finishing with the Idea of the Third World: The Concept of the Politi-
    cal Trajectory. In *Rethinking Third World Politics,* edited by James
    Manor, 51–71. New York: Longman Inc.

Beckford, George L.
    2000. *The George Beckford Papers.* Selected and Introduced by Kari Levitt.
    Kingston, Jamaica: Canoe Press.

Bellah, Robert N.
    1967. Civil Religion in America. *Daedulus* 96 (1): 1–21.

Benítez-Rojo, Antonio.
    1996. *The Repeating Island: The Caribbean and the Postmodern Perspective.*
    2nd ed. Translated by James E. Maraniss. Durham, NC: Duke University
    Press.

Berger, Peter, and Stanley Pullberg.
    1965. Reification and the Sociological Critique of Consciousness. *History and
    Theory* 4 (2): 196–211.

Berrian, Brenda F.
  2000. *Awakening Spaces: French Caribbean Popular Songs, Music, and Culture*. Chicago: University of Chicago Press.

Besson, Jean.
  2002. *Martha Brae's Two Histories: European Expansion and Caribbean Culture-Building in Jamaica*. Chapel Hill: University of North Carolina Press.

Blacking, John.
  1990. *A Commonsense View of All Music: Reflections on Percy Grainger's Contribution to Ethnomusicology and Music Education*. Cambridge: Cambridge University Press.

  1969. The Value of Music in Human Experience. *Yearbook of the International Folk Music Council* 1: 33–71.

Blacking, John, and Joann W. Keali' Inohomuke.
  1979. *The Performing Arts: Music and Dance*. The Hague: Motion Publishers.

Bourdieu, Pierre.
  1997. Forms of Capital. In *Education: Culture, Economy, Society*, edited by A. H. Halsey et al., 46–58. Oxford, UK: Oxford University Press.

Brennan, Denise.
  2000. Tourism in Transnational Places: Dominican Sex Workers and German Sex Tourists Imagine One Another. *Identities* 7 (4): 621–663.

Brenneis, Donald.
  1987. Talk and Transformation. *Man, New Series* 22 (3): 499–510.

Brown, David.
  2000. *Contemporary Nationalism: Civic, Ethnocultural and Multicultural Politics*. London: Routledge.

Brown, Karen McCarthy.
  1991. *Mama Lola: A Vodou Priestess in Brooklyn*. Berkeley: University of California Press.

Bryan, Patrick E.
  2003. Aiding Imperialism: White Baptists in Nineteenth-Century Jamaica. *Small Axe* 7 (2): 137–149.

Carrithers, Michael, Steven Collins, and Steven Lukes, eds.
  1985. *The Category of the Person: Anthropology, Philosophy, History*. Cambridge: Cambridge University Press.

Cassidy, Frederick G.
  1961. *Jamaica Talk: Three Hundred Years of the English Language in Jamaica*. London: Macmillan Education.

Césaire, Aimé.
  1972. *Discourse on Colonialism*. New York: Monthly Review Press.

Chamoiseau, Patrick, et al.
  1997. Creolite Bites. *Transition* 74: 124–161.

Chevannes, Barry.

2000. Those Two Jamaicas: The Problem of Social Integration. In *Contending with Destiny: The Caribbean in the 21st Century,* edited by Kenneth O. Hall and Denis Benn, 179–184. Kingston, Jamaica: Ian Randle Publishers.

———, ed. 1995. *Rastafari and Other African-Caribbean Worldviews.* London: Macmillan.

———, ed. 1994. *Rastafari: Roots and Ideology.* New York: Syracuse University Press.

Chidester, David.

2005. *Authentic Fakes: Religion and American Popular Culture.* Berkeley: University of California Press.

1996. *Savage Systems: Colonialism and Comparative Religion in Southern Africa.* Charlottesville: University of Virginia Press.

Cladis, Mark S.

1992. Durkheim's Individual in Society: A Sacred Marriage? *Journal of History of Ideas* 53 (1): 71–90.

Cohen, R.

1989. Human Rights and Cultural Relativism: The Need for a New Approach (in Commentaries). *American Anthropologist,* n.s., 91 (4): 1014–1017.

Conde, Maryse.

2001. *Tales from the Heart: True Stories from my Childhood.* Translated by Richard Philcox. New York: Soho.

2000. Order, Disorder, Freedom, and the West Indian Writer. *Yale French Studies* 97: 151–165.

Conway, Fredrick J.

1980. Pentecostalism in Haiti: Healing and Hierarchy. In *Perspectives on Pentecostalism: Case Studies from the Caribbean and Latin America,* edited by Stephen D. Glazier, 7–21. Washington, DC: University of America Press.

Cooper, Carolyn.

2004. *Sound Clash: Jamaican Dancehall Culture at Large.* New York: Palgrave Macmillan.

Cooper, Frederick.

2005. *Colonialism in Question: Theory, Knowledge, History.* Berkeley: University of California Press.

Crowley, Daniel J.

1957. Plural and Differential Acculturation in Trinidad. *American Anthropologist* 59 (5): 817–824.

Da Costa Lima, Vivaldo.

1977. *A Familia-De-Santo Nos Candombles Jeje Nagôs da Bahia: Um Estudo de Relações Intra-Grupais.* Salvador: UFBA.

Dawson, Michael C.

1995. A Black Counterpublic?: Economic Earthquakes, Racial Agenda(s), and Black Politics. In *The Black Public Sphere: A Public Culture Book,* edited by the Black Public Sphere Collective, 199–228. Chicago: University of Chicago Press.

De Boer, Sean.
2001. *Census Atlas 2001: Sint Maarten, Netherlands Antilles.* Willemstad, Curaçao: CBS.

Derrida, Jacques.
2002. *Negotiations: Interventions and Interviews, 1971–2001.* Translated by Elizabeth Rottenberg. Stanford, CA: Stanford University Press.

2001. *On Cosmopolitanism and Forgiveness.* Translated by Mark Dooley and Michael Hughes. London: Routledge.

1994. *Specters of Marx: The State of the Debt, the Work of Mourning, and the New International.* Translated by Peggy Kamuf. New York: Routledge.

Dubois, Laurent.
2006. An Enslaved Enlightenment: Re-thinking the Intellectual History of the French Atlantic. *Social History* 31 (1): 1–14.

Durkheim, Émile.
(1893/1933) 1984. *The Division of Labour in Society.* Translated by W. D. Halls. London: Macmillan Education.

(1911/1912) 1983. *Pragmatism and Sociology.* Cambridge: Cambridge University Press.

(1915) 1954. *Elementary Forms of Religious Life.* Translated by Joseph Ward Swain. New York: Free Press.

Dussel, Enrique.
2000. Europe, Modernity, and Eurocentrism. *Nepantla* 1 (3): 465–478.

Flax, Jane.
1992. The End of Innocence. In *Feminists Theorize the Political,* edited by Judith Butler and Joan Wallach Scott, 445–463. New York: Routledge.

Ford, John.
2004. Representations of Deference and Defiance in the Novels of Caryl Phillips. In *Beyond the Blood, the Beach and the Banana: New Perspectives in Caribbean Studies,* edited by Sandra Courtman, 373–386. Kingston, Jamaica: Ian Randle Publishers.

Fortes, Meyer, and Robin Horton.
1959. *Oedipus and Job in West African Religion.* Cambridge: Cambridge University Press.

Frankenberg, Ruth.
1993. *White Women, Race Matters: The Social Construction of Whiteness.* London: Routledge.

Geschiere, Peter.
1997. The Modernity of Witchcraft: Politics and the Occult in Postcolonial Africa. Charlottesville: University Press of Virginia.

Geschiere, Peter, and Francis Nyamnjoh.
  2000. Capitalism and Autochthony: The Seesaw of Mobility and Belonging. *Public Culture* 12 (2): 423–452.

Gilroy, Paul.
  2006. *Postcolonial Melancholia*. Wellek Library Lectures. New York: Columbia University Press.

  2005. Could You Be Loved? Bob Marley, Anti-politics and Universal Sufferation. *Critical Quarterly* 47 (1–2): 226–245.

  2000. *Between Camps: Nations, Cultures, and the Allure of Race*. London: Penguin Press.

  1993. *The Black Atlantic: Modernity and Double Consciousness*. London: Verso.

Glasscock, Jean.
  1985. *The Making of an Island: Sint Maarten and Saint Martin*. New York: Wellesley.

Glazier, Stephen D.
  1983. *Marchin' the Pilgrims Home: Leadership and Decision-Making in an Afro-Caribbean Faith*. Westport, CT: Greenwood Press.

Glick Schiller, Nina, and Fouron Georges.
  2001. *Georges Woke Up Laughing: Long-Distance Nationalism and the Search for Home*. Durham, NC: Duke University Press.

Glissant, Édouard.
  2002. The Unforeseeable Diversity of the World, translated by Haun Saussy. In *Beyond Dichotomies: Histories, Identities, Cultures, and the Challenge of Globalization,* edited by Elisabeth Mudimbe-Boyi, 287–296. Albany: State University of New York Press.

  2000. *The Poetics of Relation*. Translated by Betsy Wing. Ann Arbor: University of Michigan Press.

  1999. *Caribbean Discourse: Selected Essays*. Translated by Michael J. Dash. Charlottesville: University of Virginia Press.

Goffman, Ervin.
  1967. *Interaction Ritual: Essays on Face-to-Face Behaviour*. New York: Anchor Books.

Gorelick, Sherry.
  1991. Contradictions of Feminist Methodology. *Gender and Society* 5 (4): 459–475.

Guadeloupe, Francio.
  2006. Carmelita's In-possible Dance: Another Style of Christianity in the Capitalist Ridden Caribbean. *Journal for the Study of Religion* 19 (1): 5–22.

Gwaltney, John L.
  1980. *Drylongso: A Self-Portrait of Black America*. New York: Vintage Books.

Hagen, Fred, and Ursula Mahlendorf.

1963. Commitment, Concern, and Memory in Goethe's Faust. *Journal of Aesthetics and Art Criticism* 21 (4): 473–484.

Hagenaars, Charlotte.

2006. How to Define St. Maarten Culture. In *St. Martin Studies 2006: A Publication for Caribbean, Human and Social Studies,* edited by Silvio Sergio et al., 201–203. Phillipsburg: University of St. Martin Press.

Hall, Catherine.

2002. *Civilising Subjects: Metropole and Colony in the English Imagination, 1830–1867.* Cambridge, UK: Polity Press.

1992. Missionary Stories: Gender and Ethnicity in England in the 1830s and 1840s. In *White, Male, and Middle Class,* edited by Catherine Hall, 205–254. Cambridge: Polity Press.

Hall, Stuart.

1999. Thinking the Diaspora: Home-Thoughts from Abroad. *Small Axe* 3 (6): 1–18.

1998. What Is This "Black" in Black Popular Culture. In *Black Popular Culture,* edited by Gina Dent, 21–33. New York: New Press.

1997. The Spectacle of the "Other." In *Representation and Signifying Practices,* edited by Stuart Hall, 223–291. London: Sage Publications.

1996. Introduction: Who Needs Identity. In *Questions of Cultural Identity,* edited by Stuart Hall and Paul du Gay, 3–17. London: Sage Publications.

1995. Negotiating Caribbean Identities. *New Left Review* 209 (January–February): 3–14.

1992. Cultural Identity and Cinematic Representation. In *Ex-iles: Essays on Caribbean Cinema,* edited by Mbye. B. Cham, 220–236. Trenton, NJ: Africa World Press.

1991. *Het Minimale Zelf en andere Opstellen.* Translated from the original English by Ien Ang et al. Amsterdam: SUA.

1988. *The Hard Road to Renewal: Thatcherism and the Crisis of the Left.* London: Verso.

Hall, Stuart, and Paul du Gay, eds.

1996. *Questions of Cultural Identity.* London: Sage Publications.

Halley, Yvette J. C.

1995. De oorspronkelijke bewoners van Sint Maarten. Master's thesis, University of Leiden.

Hallward, Peter.

2004. *Haitian Inspiration: On the Bicenentary of Haiti's Independence. Radical Philosophy* 123 (January): 2–7.

Harding, Susan.

2000. *The Book of Jerry Falwell: Fundamentalist Language and Politics.* Princeton: Princeton University Press.

Harris, Wilson.
    1998. Creoleness: The Crossroads of a Civilization. In *Caribbean Creoliza-tion: Reflections on the Cultural Dynamics of Language, Literature, and Identity,* edited by Kathleen M Balutansky and Marie-Agnès Sourieau, 23–35. Tallahassee: University Press of Florida.

    1970. *History, Fable and Myth in the Caribbean and the Guianas: The Edgar Mittelholzer Lecture.* Kingston, Jamaica: University of the West Indies.

Harrison, Robert P.
    2003. *The Dominion of the Dead.* Chicago: University of Chicago Press.

Hartog, Jan.
    1981. *History of Sint Maarten and Saint Martin.* Sint Maarten, Netherlands Antilles: Sint Maarten Jaycees.

Higginbotham, Evelyn B.
    1996. African-American Women History and the Metalanguage of Race. In *Feminism and History,* edited by Joan Wallach Scott, 183–208. New York: Oxford University Press.

Ho, Christine G. T.
    1999. Caribbean Transnationalism as a Gendered Process. *Latin American Perspectives* 26 (5): 34–54.

Hoefte, Rosemarijn.
    2005. Different Modes of Resistance by British Indian and Javanese Contract Labourers in Suriname. In *Contesting Freedom: Control and Resistance in the Post-emancipation Caribbean,* edited by Gad Heuman and David V. Trotman, 142–155. Oxford, UK: Macmillan Caribbean.

Hoetink, Harmannus.
    1967. *The Two Variants in Caribbean Race Relations: A Contribution to the Sociology of Segmented Societies.* Translated by Eva Maria Hooykaas. London: Oxford University Press.

Hogg, Donald.
    1964. Jamaican Religions: A Study of Variations. PhD diss., University of Michigan, Ann Arbor.

Horton, Robin.
    1960. A Definition of Religion and Its Uses. *Journal of the Royal Anthropo-logical Institute of Great Britain and Ireland* 90 (2): 201–226.

Jackson, Michael, ed.
    1996. *Things as They Are: New Directions in Phenomenological Anthropol-ogy.* Bloomington: Indiana University Press.

    1989. *Paths toward a Clearing: Radical Empiricism and Ethnographic In-quiry.* Bloomington: Indiana University Press.

James, C. L. R.
    (1964) 1969. *Beyond the Boundary.* Tiptree, Essex, UK: Anchor Press.

    (1938) 1963. *The Black Jacobins: Toussaint L'Ouverture and the San Domingo Revolution.* New York: Vintage.

Jones, Robert A.
    1986. Durkheim, Frazer, and Smith: The Role of Exemplars in the Develop-
    ment of Durkheim's Sociology of Religion. *American Journal of Sociology*
    92 (3): 596–627.

Keil, Charles, and Steven Feld.
    1994. *Music Grooves: Essays and Dialogues*. Chicago: University of Chicago
    Press.

Kelley, Robin D. G.
    1997. *Yo Mama's Disfunktional: Fighting the Cultural Wars in Urban Amer-
    ica*. Boston: Beacon Press.

Kersell, John E.
    1991. French-Dutch Integration in St. Martin. In *Forging Identities and Patterns
    of Development in Latin America and the Caribbean*, edited by Joanna A.
    Rummens and P. D. M. Taylor, 59–68. Toronto: Canadian Scholars Press.

Klomp, Anke.
    2000. Saint Martin: Communal Identities on a Divided Caribbean Island.
    Ethnologia Europaea 30 (2): 73–86.

Kristeva, Julia.
    1991. *Strangers to Ourselves*. Translated by Leon S. Roudiez. New York: Co-
    lumbia University Press.

Laclau, Ernesto.
    1990. *New Reflections on the Revolution of Our Time*. London: Verso.

    1977. *Politics and Ideology in Marxist Theory: Capitalism—Fascism—
    Populism*. London: New Left Books.

Lamming, George.
    2001. Caribbean Labor, Culture, and Identity. In *Caribbean Cultural Identi-
    ties*, edited by Glyne Griffith, 17–32. Lewisburg, PA: Bucknell University
    Press.

Lemert, Charles.
    1999. The Might Have Been and Could Be of Religion in Social Theory. *So-
    ciological Theory* 17 (3): 240–263.

Levine, Daniel H.
    1992. *Popular Voices within Latin American Catholicism*. Princeton: Prince-
    ton University Press.

Luhrmann, Tanya M.
    1989. *Persuasions of the Witch's Craft: Ritual Magic in Contemporary En-
    gland*. Cambridge, MA: Harvard University Press.

MacDonald-Smythe, Antonia.
    2005. The Privilege of Being Born in . . . a Backward Society: Derek Walcott's
    Prodigal Provincialism. *Callaloo* 28 (1): 88–101.

Mageo, Jeanette M., ed.
    2003. *Dreaming and the Self: New Perspectives on Subjectivity, Identity, and
    Emotion*. Albany: State University of New York Press.

Mahabir, Joy A.
  2002. Rhythm and Class Struggle: The Calypsoes of David Rudder. *Jouvert* 6 (3): 1–22.

Mahabir, Noor, and Ashram Maharaj.
  1996. Hindu Elements in the Shango/Orisha Cult of Trinidad. In *Across the Dark Waters,* edited by David Dabydeen and Brinsley Samaroo, 90–107. London: Macmillan Caribbean.

Manning, Frank E.
  1990. Calypso as a Medium of Political Communication. In *Mass Media and the Caribbean,* edited by Stuart H. Surlin and Walter C. Soderland, 415–428. New York: Gordon and Breach.

Mansingh, Ajai, and Laxmi Mansingh.
  1985. The Impact of East Indians on Jamaican Religious Thoughts and Expressions. *Caribbean Journal of Religious Studies* 10 (1): 36–52.

Manuel, Peter, Kenneth Bilby, and Michael Largey.
  1995. *Caribbean Currents: Caribbean Music from Rhumba to Reggae.* Philadelphia: Temple University Press.

Martin, David.
  1990. *Tongues of Fire: The Explosion of Protestantism in America.* Oxford, UK: Basil Blackwell.

Marx, Karl.
  1987. *The Eighteenth Brumaire of Louis Bonaparte.* Translated by Daniel de Leon. Chicago: C. H. Kerr.

Messer, Ellen.
  1993. Anthropology and Human Rights. *Annual Review of Anthropology* 22: 221–249.

Meyer, Birgit.
  2004. Praise the Lord: Popular Cinema and the Pentecostalite Style in Ghana's New Public Sphere. *American Ethnologist* 31 (1): 92–110.

  2003. Visions of Blood, Sex, and Money: Fantasy Spaces in Popular Ghanaian Cinema. *Visual Anthropology* 16 (1): 15–41.

Meyer, Birgit, and Peter Geschiere, eds.
  1999. *Globalization and Identity: Dialectics of Flows and Closures.* Oxford, UK: Blackwell Publishers.

Miller, Daniel.
  1994. *Modernity, an Ethnographic Approach: Dualism and Mass Consumption in Trinidad.* Oxford, UK: Berg Publishers.

Mintz, Sidney W.
  1996. Enduring Substances, Trying Theories: The Caribbean Region as Oikoumene. *Journal of the Royal Anthropological Institute* 2 (2): 297–298.

Mintz, Sidney W., and Richard Price.
  1976. *The Birth of African-American Culture: An Anthropological Perspective.* Boston: Beacon Press.

Monnier, Yves.
1983. *L'immuable et le changeant: Etude de la partie Française de l'île de Saint-Martin*. Paris: Centre Études de Géographie Tropicale.

Moyer, Eileen.
2005. Street-Corner Justice in the Name of Jah: Imperatives for Peace among Dar es Salaam Street Youth. *Africa Today* 51 (3): 31–58.

Mulhren, Francis.
2002. The End of Politics: Culture, Nation, and Other Fundamentalisms. *Radical Philosophy* 112 (May–April): 25–30.

Nettleford, Rex.
2001. Draw Wisdom and Listen: How to Eat and Remain Human. In *The Caribbean Community: Beyond Survival*, edited by Kenneth O. Hall, 182–189. Kingston, Jamaica: Ian Randle Publishers.

Oostindie, Gert.
2006. Dependence and Autonomy in Subnational Island Jurisdictions: The Case of the Kingdom of the Netherlands. *Round Table* 95 (386): 609–626.

2005. *Paradise Overseas. The Dutch Caribbean: Colonialism and Its Transatlantic Legacies*. London: Macmillan Caribbean.

1999. *Het Verleden onder Ogen: Herdenking van de Slavernij*. Amsterdam: Arena.

1995. Slavery and Slaves in Suriname and Curaçao. In *Fifty Years Later: Antislavery, Capitalism and Modernity in the Dutch Orbit*, edited by Gert Oostindie, 143–178. Leiden, the Netherlands: KITLV Press.

Oostindie, Gert, and Inge Klinkers.
2003. *Decolonising the Caribbean: Dutch Policies in a Comparative Perspective*. Amsterdam: Amsterdam University Press

Oostindie, Gert, and Peter Verton.
1998. *Ki Sorto di Reino: Visies en verwachtingen van Antillianen en Arubanen omtrent het koninkrijk*. The Hague: Sdu Uitgevers.

Ortiz, Fernando.
(1940) 1995. *Cuban Counterpoint: Tobacco and Sugar*. Durham, NC: Duke University Press.

Palmié, Stephan.
2002. *Wizards and Scientists: Explorations in Afro-Cuban Modernity and Tradition*. Durham, NC: Duke University Press.

Patterson, Orlando.
1994. Ecumenical America: Global Culture and the American Cosmos. *World Policy Journal* 11 (2): 103–118.

Paula, Alejandro Felipe.
1993. *Vrije Slaven: Een Sociaal-historische Studie over Dualistische Slavenemancipatie op Nederlands Sint Maarten*. Zutphen, the Netherlands: Walburg Press.

Phillips, Caryl.

    2002. *A New World Order: Selected Essays*. New York: Vintage.

    1994. *Crossing the River*. London: Picador.

Price, Richard.

    1998. *The Convict and the Colonel*. Boston: Beacon Press.

Raboteau, Albert J.

    1988. A Hidden Wholeness: Thomas Merton and Martin Luther King, Jr. *Spirituality Today* 40 (Winter Supplement): 80–95.

Rancière, Jacques.

    2004. *The Philosopher and His Poor*. Edited and with an introduction by Andrew Parker. Translated by John Drury, Corinne Oster, and Andrew Parker. Durham, NC: Duke University Press.

Rock, David.

    1987. Intellectual Precursors of Conservative Nationalism in Argentina, 1900–1927. *Hispanic American Historical Review* 67 (2): 271–300.

Rohlehr, Gordon.

    2001. The Calypsonian as Artist: Freedom and Responsibility. *Small Axe* 5 (1): 1–26.

Römer, Rene.

    1999. Katholicisme en Vrijmetselarij: Naar verandering in de oude verhoudingen. In *Veranderd Curaçao: Colectie Essays Opgedrage aan Lionel Caprilles ter aangelegenheid van zijn 45-jarige Jubileum bij Maduro en Curiel's Bank N.V.*, edited by Henny E. Coomans, Maritza Coomans-Eustatia, and Johan van't Leven, 351–359. Bloemendaal, the Netherlands: Stichting Libri Antilliani.

Rony, Fatimah T.

    1996. *The Third Eye: Race, Cinema, and the Ethnographic Spectacle*. Durham, NC: Duke University Press.

Rose, Anne C.

    2004. "Race" Speech—"Culture" Speech—"Soul" Speech: The Brief Career of Social-Science Language in American Religion during the Fascist Era. *Religion and American Culture: A Journal of Interpretation* 14 (1): 83–108.

Rose, Tricia, et al.

    1995. Race and Racism: A Symposium. *Social Text* 42 (Spring): 1–52.

Rummens, Joanna A.

    1991. Identity and Perception: The Politicization of Identity in Saint Martin. In *Forging Identities and Patterns of Development in Latin America and the Caribbean*, edited by J. W. A. Rummens and P. D. M. Taylor, 265–278. Toronto: Canadian Scholars Press.

Sanchez, Rafael.

    2003. The Dancing Jacobins: A Genealogy of Latin American Populism (Venezuela). PhD diss., University of Amsterdam, Amsterdam.

Sankeralli, Burton, ed.
  1995. *At the Crossroads: African Caribbean Religion and Christianity.* Port of Spain, Trinidad and Tobago: Caribbean Conference Churches.

Schueller, Malini J.
  1999. Performing Whiteness, Performing Blackness: Dorr's Cultural Capital and the Critique of Slavery. *Criticism: A Quarterly for Literature and Art* 41 (2): 234–258.

Scott, David.
  2004. *Conscripts of Modernity: The Tragedy of Colonial Enlightenment.* Durham, NC: Duke University Press.

  2000. The Re-enchantment of Humanism: An Interview with Sylvia Wynter. *Small Axe* 8 (September): 119–207.

Scott, Joan W.
  1992. Experience. In *Feminists Theorize the Political,* edited by Judith Butler and Joan Wallach Scott, 22–40. New York: Routledge.

Sekou, Lasana M., ed.
  1996. National Symbols of St. Martin: A Primer. Sint Maarten: House of Nehesi Publishers.

Sheller, Mimi
  2003. *Consuming the Caribbean: From Arawaks to Zombies.* London: Routledge.

Selvon, Sam.
  1993. *An Island Is a World.* Toronto: TSAR Publications.

  2005. Acting as Free Men: Subaltern Masculinities and Citizenship in Post Slavery Jamaica. In *Gender and Slave Emancipation in the Atlantic World,* edited by Pamela Scully and Dana Paton, 79–98. Durham, NC: Duke University Press.

Simpson, George E.
  1978. *Black Religions in the New World.* New York: Columbia University Press.

Skurski, J.
  1994. The Ambiguities of Authenticity in Latin America: Dona Barbara and the Construction of National Identity. *Poetics Today* 15 (4): 605–642.

Smith, Michael Garfield.
  1991. *Pluralism, Politics and Ideology in the Creole Caribbean.* New York: Research Institute for the Study of Man.

Smith, R. T.
  1996. *The Matrifocal Family: Power, Pluralism, and Politics.* New York: Routledge.

Snow, David A., and Leon Anderson.
  1987. Identity among the Homeless: The Verbal Construction and Avowal of Personal Identity. *American Journal of Sociology* 92 (6): 1136–1371.

Spitulnik, Deborah.
  2000. Documenting Radio Culture as Lived Experience: Reception Studies and the Mobile Machine in Zambia. In *African Broadcast Cultures,* edited

by Richard Fardon and Graham Furniss, 144–164. Oxford, UK: James Currey.

Stephen, Michele.
2003. Memory, Emotion, and the Imaginal Mind. In *Dreaming and the Self: New Perspectives on Subjectivity, Identity, and Emotion*, edited by Jeannette Marie Mageo, 97–129. Albany: State University of New York Press.

Stewart, Kathleen.
1996. *A Space on the Side of the Road: Cultural Poetics in an "Other" America*. Princeton: Princeton University Press.

Stoll, David.
1990. *Is Latin America Turning Protestant? The Politics of Evangelical Growth*. Berkeley: University of California Press.

Stolzoff, Norman C.
2000. *Wake the Town and Tell the People: Dancehall Culture in Jamaica*. Durham, NC: Duke University Press.

Sypkens Smit, M. P.
2005. *Beyond the Tourist Trap: A Study of St. Maarten Culture*. Amsterdam: Natuurwetenschappelijke Studiekring voor het Caraïbisch Gebied.

Taylor, Patrick.
2001. Sheba's Song: The Bible, the Kebra Nagast, and the Rastafari. In *Nation Dance: Religion, Identity, and Cultural Difference in the Caribbean*, edited by Patrick Taylor, 65–78. Bloomington: Indiana University Press.

Telfair Sharpe, Tanya.
2000. The Identity Christian Movement: Ideology of Domestic Terrorism. *Journal of Black Studies* 30 (4): 604–623.

Thoden van Velzen, H. E. U, and Wilhelmina Van Wetering.
1988. *Great Father and the Danger*. Dordrecht, the Netherlands: Foris.

Thomas-Judson, Jacinth P.
1995. *Religious Language: Its Role in Nativizing Caribbean English*. Ann Arbor, MI: University Microfilm International.

Travers, Andrew.
1992. How Interactants Are Other Than They Are. *British Journal of Sociology* 43 (4): 601–637.

Trouillot, Michel-Rolph.
2003. *Global Transformations: Anthropology and the Modern World*. New York: Palgrave Macmillan.

2002. The Perspective of the World: Globalization Then and Now. In *Beyond Dichotomies: Histories, Identities, Cultures, and Challenge of Globalization*, edited by Elisabeth Mudimbe-Boyi, 3–20. Albany: State University of New York Press.

1998. Culture on the Edges: Creolization in the Plantation Context. *Plantation Societies in the Americas* 5 (1): 8–28.

1995. *Silencing the Past: Power and the Production of History*. Boston: Beacon Press.

1992. The Caribbean Region: An Open Frontier in Anthropological Theory. *Annual Review of Anthropology* 21 (October): 19–42.

1990. *Haiti: State against Nation: The Origins and Legacy of Duvalierism*. New York: Monthly Review Press.

Van der Pijl, Yvonne.
2003. Room to Roam: Afro-Surinamese Identifications and the Creole Multiple Self. *Focaal* 42: 105–114.

Vergés, Françoise.
2001. Vertigo and Emancipation: Creole Cosmopolitanism and Cultural Politics. *Theory, Culture, and Society* 19 (2–3): 169–183.

Walcott, Derek.
1999. *What the Twilight Says: Selected Essays*. New York: Farrar, Straus and Giroux.

1974. The Caribbean: Culture or Mimicry? *Journal of Interamerican Studies and World Affairs* 16 (1): 3–13.

Warner, Michael.
2002. *Publics and Counterpublics*. New York: Zone Books.

West, Cornel.
2004. *Democracy Matters: Winning the Fight against Imperialism*. New York: Penguin Press.

1993. *Race Matters*. Boston: Beacon Press.

1988. *Prophetic Fragments: Illuminations of the Crisis of American Religion and Culture*. Grand Rapids, MI: Wm. B. Eerdmans Publishing Co.

Wharton, Amy S.
1991. Structure and Agency in Socialist-Feminist Theory. *Gender and Society* 5 (3): 373–389.

White, Hayden.
1990. *The Content of Form: Narrative Discourse and Historical Representation*. Baltimore: Johns Hopkins University Press.

Williams, Brackette F.
1991. *Stains on My Name, War in My Veins: Guyana and the Politics of Cultural Struggle*. Durham, NC: Duke University Press.

Wilson, Gladstone.
1990. Reggae as a Medium of Political Communication. In *Mass Media and the Caribbean*, edited by Stuart H. Surlin and Walter C. Soderland, 429–449. New York: Gordon and Breach.

Wilson, Peter.
1969. Reputation and Respectability: A Suggestion for Caribbean Ethnology. *Man* 4 (1): 70–84.

Wynter, Sylvia.

1992. Rethinking Aesthetics. In *Ex-iles: Essays on Caribbean Cinema,* edited by Mbye B. Cham, 238–279. Trenton, NJ: Africa World Press.

1984. A Ceremony Must Be Found: After Humanism. *Boundary* 2 12 (3): 19–70.

Yelvington, Kevin A.

2001. The Anthropology of Afro-Latin America and the Caribbean: Diasporic Dimensions. *Annual Review of Anthropology* 30 (October): 227–260.

ONLINE SOURCES

http://worldatlas.com
http://www.diasporainternational.org/pdf/healing_of.pdf
http://www.insee.fr/fr/insee_regions/guadeloupe/home/home_page.asp
http://www.internationalspecialreports.com/archives/00/stmaarten/7.html
http://www.st-martin.org/us/discovery/art_and_culture.php

Index

Text:	10/13 Sabon
Display:	Sabon
Compositor:	Binghamton Valley Composition
Indexer:	Thérèse Shere
Cartographer:	Bill Nelson
Printer and binder:	Maple-Vail Book Manufacturing Group